POLICY, POLITICS & GENDER

Kumarian Press

Selected Titles

Gender Analysis in Development Planning: A Case Book
Aruna Rao, Mary B. Anderson, Catherine Overholt, editors

*Tools for the Field: Methodologies Handbook for Gender Analysis
in Agriculture*
Hilary Sims Feldstein and Janice Jiggins, editors

All Her Paths Are Peace: Women Pioneers in Peacemaking
Michael Henderson

*A Commitment to the World's Women: Perspectives on Development
for Beijing and Beyond*
Noeleen Heyzer with Skushma Kapoor and Joanne Sandler
(UNIFEM)

POLICY, POLITICS & GENDER
Women Gaining Ground

Kathleen Staudt

Kumarian Press

Policy, Politics & Gender: Women Gaining Ground.

Published 1998 in the United States of America by Kumarian Press, Inc.,
14 Oakwood Avenue, West Hartford, Connecticut 06119-2127 USA.

Production supervised by Jenna Dixon
Copyedited by Linda Lotz   Typeset by CompuDesign
Text design by Jenna Dixon   Proofread by Beth Richards
Index by Kathleen Staudt
The text of this book is set in 10/13 Adobe Sabon.
The display type is Agfa Bodega Sans.

Printed in Canada on acid-free paper by Transcontinental Printing and
Graphics. Text printed with vegetable oil-based ink.

∞ The paper used in this publication meets the minimum requirements of the
American National Standard for Information Sciences—Permanence of
Paper for Printed Library Materials, ANSI Z39.48-1984.

Library of Congress Cataloging-in-Publication Data
Staudt, Kathleen A.
  Policy, politics & gender : women gaining ground / Kathleen Staudt.
       p.   cm.
  Includes bibliographical references and index.
  ISBN 1-56549-080-0 (cloth : alk. paper). — ISBN 1-56549-079-7 (pbk. : alk. paper)
  1. Women in development. 2. Economic development—Political aspects. I. Title.
HQ1240.S68   1998
305.42—dc21
                                                                98-5309

07 06 05 04 03 02 01 00 99 98   10 9 8 7 6 5 4 3 2 1   1st Printing 1998

Contents

Illustrations

Tables

Figures

Introduction: Crossing Boundaries and Acknowledging Support

Research and action on international women, I am convinced, are more interdisciplinary and collective enterprises than other intellectual, teaching, service, and action passions of a lifetime. A constant synergy among the ideas and the people, fueled with labors of love, multiplies the insights and supports.

Background for This Book

Several others have written comprehensive texts on women and international development. I salute them and acknowledge their energy and commitment to the field. Several are friends and colleagues whose books have been adopted in my courses, including Sue Ellen Charlton, V. Spike Peterson and Anne Runyan, and Lynne Brydon and Sylvia Chant.[1] Many others have edited collections of enormous usefulness in the field.

Despite this rich work, a great need exists for an up-to-date, comprehensive analysis of women and gender in international development—including countries both rich and poor, from the North and the South. The book needs to be readable and insightful—interesting for both students and faculty, researchers and practitioners. This book is designed to fit those needs. It will work well in upper-division and graduate courses in many fields—from international development and politics to geography, sociology, and anthropology—for it both reflects and provides testimony to disciplinary boundary crossing.

In 1990, I wrote a book with some of the above characteristics. It emphasized cultural and political contexts, and its chapters contained real and hypothetical exercises, role plays, and problems around which classroom groups could organize to discuss and pose solutions, with all their ethical dilemmas. The book supplied technical tools in "transitions" between chapters on program substance and levels of political and policy action.

Managing Development was and continues to be useful in its fourth printing, working well in upper-division and graduate courses.[2] Knowing the common tendency in mainstream courses to dismiss books and articles with "women" or "gender" in the title, I deliberately omitted those words,

1

yet threaded the themes throughout, hoping to transform the way students and faculty understood development administration. Sure enough, the book was reviewed well in mainstream journals and probably reached a different and wider audience than was possible, at the time, with women and gender texts.

Contentions and Contributions

Time has passed, however. It is important not only to bring some of the material from *Managing Development* up-to-date but also to make women and gender central. Unlike *Managing Development*, with its emphasis on the state and project proposals, this book focuses on political activism and strategies to change state and international policies. The 1990s has been a decade in which participants at world conferences have dialogued and built consensus on connecting mainstream policies to women and gender. Similarly, women, gender, and population conferences have made more connections than ever to mainstream policies. It seems high time, then, that I write a book that builds on the strength of *Managing Development*, makes similar connections, and puts women and gender squarely in the title and the content. Will mainstream courses and journals marginalize it, even as we approach the new millennium? Maybe so, but perhaps not.

Several themes make this book special. First and foremost, it covers institutions of many types, from nongovernmental organizations (NGOs) to governments and international agencies. More specifically, it focuses on the people and their political processes within, between, and outside those institutions. The book puts bureaucracies on the analytic table, including their policies (both enforced and unenforced) and their staff. Whereas some analysts trace all social change from the top of bureaucracies, or from global economic forces, others stay on the ground, as if larger forces matter little. This book tries to balance those perspectives, examining realities from all perspectives. As Remedios Rikken once said, in connection with her work at the Philippine Commission on the Status of Women, their tasks are somewhat like traditional Filipino cake baking: heat from the top, heat from the bottom, and heat from all sides.[3] Institutions, however, remain an important focus for analysis, for they mediate and channel macro-level forces and people's lives.[4]

A key premise of this book is that all institutions, within and outside government, are sources and sites of struggle. To dismiss the opportunity to struggle is to perpetuate institutional injustices. Although I certainly understand the global and national hegemonic forces that aim to engulf our lives—including those that connect with seemingly democratic government and operate with seeming consent—my hope is that people refuse to succumb to those forces. Change is made through people's resistance to and negotiation with such forces. To give up hope and action for change is to succumb to those forces.

Second, this book aims at breadth, in both global and interdisciplinary terms. Rather than sacrifice depth for breadth, though, it periodically integrates cases in the text or in appendixes. And institutions are covered in some depth. Usually the cases pose ethical dilemmas with which readers and players must grapple. Most solutions and action (or inaction) plans have flaws when viewed comprehensively and from multiple vantage points. This is the real world. Other case studies might complement this in courses on development, gender, and policy.[5]

Whenever this book is used in courses, I encourage participants to research, act, and collaborate with activists in their own communities for changes in policies and programs.[6] Global forces are present in virtually all local communities. "Bringing development home" is an idea that is built into the book with realistic situations that transcend or are adaptable across national boundaries. Earlier chapters that problematize international assistance institutions are bridges to chapters that dissect the more or less progressive bilateral institutions (progressive in the sense of having transformative agendas on women and gender, human development priorities, and structural inequalities, as discussed later). For those readers who are frustrated with the enormous scope or pace of global progress in enhancing people's capabilities, the book might problematize their own governments' actions. I am convinced that service learning, or learning based on applications that make that learning meaningful, is vital. Other research backs me up on this: studies that track students over a decade or two find that education-inspired involvement and political activism are associated with later community activism, political engagement, and public service.[7]

Finally, the book joins approaches that focus on women with those that focus on gender. Of late, "gender" has become the terminology of choice for many who are active in development, whether researchers, activists, or policymakers. Gender analysis puts social structures—institutional and cultural—on the agenda. Women are made, as much as born, in different institutional and cultural settings. Otherwise, we would see little variation around the world or throughout history. Gender also puts men on the agenda, both problematizing their practices and seeking their support in coalition-building strategies for change. Yet women in all of their diversity continue to have a place in analysis and strategies for change. Sometimes people overstate differences between the women in development (WID) and the gender and development (GAD) approaches. I seek to build bridges in the practical realities of political change.

Most early WID analysts did not deal with women as biological as opposed to social beings; they recognized structure. Moreover, many dealt with institutional and political-economic change rather than small-scale women's activities. Their work occurred at a time when the word "gender" had not yet been rescued from the bowels of academic jargon in linguistics and sociology. Once rescued, "gender" was meant to be differentiated from "sex," that is, social versus biological approaches, rather than to render women invisible. Most importantly, though, I share the concerns of many scholar-activists who are troubled with a process that seems to replace women and redistributive political struggles with technical discourse that works best in the English language, a mostly Northern-driven language. The word "women" translates into all languages, but the word "gender" does not—particularly the nuanced meanings discussed above. We will revisit these issues in the text. In the meantime, my own position involves identification as an early WID analyst who used many of those gender nuances then and continues to use them now in writing and in action.

Readers of this book will take from it the following. First, readers will appreciate that there is more to policy analysis than rational decision making in the hands of trained technicians. All too often, development "experts" (even the audaciously labeled gender, feminist, and/or women "experts") search for the one best way, or the right recipe, to transform institutions and to end gender hierarchy and subordination. Although Deborah Stone is located at the margins of core approaches to policy analysis in the United States, she criticizes "the rationality project," which tries to turn policymaking into a production model that uses market metaphors for the whole of society.[8] We cannot dismiss politics, ideologies (including gendered variants), and their practical arts in "communities," a word better connected to societies than to markets.

Second, readers will acquire insight on some practical political arts, tools, and skills. Chapters highlight contrasting political strategies, proposal-writing skills, and evaluation research designs.

Third, readers will be introduced to sources and voices to which they can turn for further analysis. My hope is to internationalize those sources and voices, yet choose references that are accessible so that readers can follow up if they desire. We now live in a world of information overload for those with Internet access. Books like this one help sort through the mass of material and make some sense of it all. Nothing is quite so daunting as doing Web-site searches wherein keyword crosstabs "limit" findings to 69,000 sources or to list servers that bring in scores of messages daily. Appended to this introduction, I have included favorite Web sites that readers might consider visiting, based on tips from subscribers to the femisa listserv, who number more than a thousand.

Finally, readers will acquire substantive knowledge on several key policy areas. In two of these—education and work, each covered by a chapter—my aim is to make gender central to mainstream policies. In another two—reproductive health and sexual violence—my aim is to take policies more typically viewed as "women's issues" and make them central to the mainstream of population and safety. Environmental concerns are not addressed in a separate chapter but are embedded throughout the others. In each policy chapter, I address local, global, and in-between levels and arenas in which change occurs. Each chapter also focuses heavily on institutional and political issues.

Vantage Points

My own background involves lots of boundary crossing. Although trained as a political scientist—my first academic love, because of its attention to power and structure—I have long operated at the boundaries of the discipline. This stance was virtually mandated when I first began to write two decades ago, for the discipline was hostile to studies of women and gender.[9] I crossed academic boundaries to anthropology (my second academic love) and to sociology and geography for insights and intellectual rejuvenation. I continually cross methodological boundaries; although trained as a positivist, I am at home and compatible with interpretivist and ethnographic immersion. Mostly, though, I am a great believer in multiple methods for comprehensive understanding. Thus, readers will find chapters that include numbers on the one hand and literary references on the other.

Throughout my working life, I have also crossed the boundaries of academic, governmental, and nongovernmental organizations. Most of my time is devoted to teaching and research at the University of Texas at El Paso, but I have been on "loan" to a large bilateral development agency, consulted for several United Nations agencies and NGOs, and served in binational community organizations.[10] Three decades ago, ancient history for some of my students, I was a Peace Corps volunteer in the Philippines. Building bridges between these institutions is challenging, as well as frustrating. But those locations give me experience in multiple vantage points and discourses, and I hope that my understandings and my ability to convey those understandings are improved as a result.

My biggest but most important bridge is between professor and mom. My children, Mosi and Asha, have taught me much about vantage points, nurturing, and boundary crossing, with its opportunities and threats. My husband, Robert Dane'el, has stood by me through stress and satisfaction. My colleagues have always supported my interdisciplinary activities ("We know you're a political scientist at heart," some have said), and the university has encouraged academic boundary crossing. The University of Texas at El Paso just happens to be situated on an international boundary itself, with a majority of students of Mexican heritage—daily border crossers for the purposes of education, commerce, and kinship connections.

Trained as an Africanist, I made the decision (given my location at the boundaries of the Americas) to begin focusing more on Mexico and Latin America. By the 1990s, I directed a large study on informal economies on both sides of the U.S.-Mexico border, just as official "free trade" under the North American Free Trade Agreement was about to go into effect. Years of immersion in the life and study of the border gave me some new vantage points from which to gaze at the movement of people and of capital at national borders.[11] Always, we consider ways to connect the research with action in classes.

All this background informs this book. Many people contributed to the effort, and my spatial location strengthened the whole project. Thanks to people, spaces, and institutions alike.

Notes

1. Sue Ellen Charlton, *Women in Third World Development* (Boulder, Colo.: Westview Press, 1984). Charlton is a political scientist and one of the first in a field of sociologists and anthropologists to put women's political disadvantage on the agenda in development analysis. V. Spike Peterson and Anne Runyan, *Global Gender Issues* (Boulder, Colo.: Westview Press, 1993). Peterson and Runyan are political scientists who specialize in international relations. They emphasize global political economy but are perhaps more wary than I am of working with existing institutions. Lynne Brydon and Sylvia Chant, *Women in the Third World: Gender Issues in Rural and Urban Areas* (New Brunswick, N.J.: Rutgers University Press, 1989). In sociology and geography, with connections to Latin American studies, Brydon and Chant take a more spatially oriented approach. In a slim, descriptive volume, *Women and Development in the Third World* (London: Routledge, 1991), Janet Momsen introduces students to women's productive and reproductive work. Kate Young also wrote a short volume, *Planning Development with Women: Making a World of Difference* (London: Macmillan, 1993). In these geographic volumes, planning is addressed, but not in the fuller fashion possible in political science.
2. Kathleen Staudt, *Managing Development: State, Society and International Contexts* (Newbury Park, Calif.: Sage, 1991).
3. She is quoted in Aruna Rao, Hilary Feldstein, Kathleen Cloud, and Kathleen

Staudt, *Gender Training and Development Planning: Learning from Experience* (Bergen, Norway, and New York: Chr. Michelsen Institute and Population Council, 1991), p. 40.

4. Louise Lamphere, "Introduction: The Shaping of Diversity," in *Structuring Diversity: Ethnographic Perspectives on the New Immigration*, edited by Louise Lamphere (Chicago: University of Chicago Press, 1991), p. 4.
5. See, especially, Ann Leonard, ed., *Seeds: Supporting Women's Work in the Third World* (New York: Feminist Press, 1989), and the second edition, called *Seeds 2: Supporting Women's Work around the World* (New York: Feminist Press, 1995). I have afterwords in each, "Planting Seeds in the Classroom," which complement the longer work by Kathleen Staudt, Irene Tinker, and Kathleen Cloud, *Teaching Women in Development Courses* (New York: U.S. Council for INSTRAW, 1988), distributed through the Association for Women in Development. See also Catherine Overholt et al., *Gender Roles in Development Projects: A Case Book* (West Hartford, Conn.: Kumarian Press, 1985), the Kumarian-sponsored monograph series edited by Ingrid Palmer; and Kathleen Staudt, ed., *Women, International Development and Politics: The Bureaucratic Mire*, 2d ed. (Philadelphia: Temple University Press, 1997).
6. This is broadly called "service learning." Global-local connections come in more or less obvious forms. For example, El Paso's vaccination rate for two-year-olds bottomed out (along with Newark, New Jersey's) in the fall of 1997, according to media headlines, at rates lower than those in so-called developing countries. Thanks to the Federación Mexicana de Asociaciones Privadas (FEMAP), I work with a transborder group, Seeds Across the Border, that provides South-to-North technical assistance and ideas.
7. See the special issue of *American Behavioral Scientist* (1997) for documentation.
8. Deborah Stone, *Policy Paradox: The Art of Political Decision Making, 2d ed.* (New York: W. W. Norton, 1997).
9. On the discipline, see Kathleen Staudt and William Weaver, *Political Science and Feminisms: Integration or Transformation?* (New York: Twayne/Macmillan, 1997). On the women-gender differentiations, see the classic by Eva Rathgeber, "WID, WAD, GAD: Trends in Research and Practice," *Journal of Developing Areas* 24 (1990): 489–502.
10. I thank those organizations, but especially the United Nations Research Institute for Social Development, which gave me access to interviews conducted with over a score of bilateral and multilateral technical assistance agencies. Some of that material is analyzed in later chapters.
11. See Kathleen Staudt, *Free Trade? Informal Economies at the U.S.-Mexico Border* (Philadelphia: Temple University Press, 1998), and David Spener and Kathleen Staudt, eds., *The U.S.-Mexico Border: Transcending Divisions, Contesting Identities* (Boulder, Colo.: Lynne Rienner, 1998).

Appendix: Femisa's Favorite Web Sites

From Laura Guymer   www.publishaust.net.au/~spinifex
(international feminist books, with a title drawing on the native Australian desert grass [spinifex], which is drought resistant and holds the earth together)

From Patience Agyare-Kwabi   www.aviva.org
(listings of women's groups and events worldwide)

From Jutta Zalud   www.ifs.uni-linz.ac.at/female/
(feminist publication listings in German)

From Lara Stancich   www.igc.apc.org/neww/
(network of East-West women, drawing on central and eastern European and former Soviet areas)

From Laura Parisi*   www.igc.org/gfw/
(Global Fund for Women, with links to many other networks)

From Joan Korenman†   www.umbc.edu/wmst/links.html
(a directory of women's studies and women's issues resource sites)

From Kathleen Staudt   www.un.org/womenwatch
(United Nations Internet gateway on the advancement and empowerment of women)

---

* Parisi's paper "Using the Internet to Teach about Gender and Politics" was presented at the International Studies Association, March 1998. She has a database of good Web sites by categories.

† Korenman's electronic book, *Internet Resources on Women: Using Electronic Media in Curriculum Transformation*, is a useful source, especially scrolled down to pages 85–86, with Political Science/International Relations Sites (http://www.umbc.edu/wmst/pagenum.html). Also see her listserv, WMST-L. To subscribe, send the usual message (subscribe WMST-L Your Name) to listserv@umdd.umd.edu.

Thanks also to others who responded but whose references could not be accessed: Gregory Kelson, Stacy Harwood, Diane Glass, and Barbara Welling Hall.

Femisa's listserv address is femisa@csf.colorado.edu.

Part I
Understanding Contextual Settings

1 Beginning Reflections on Language, Power, and Ethics

> The Master's Tools Will Never
> Dismantle the Master's House.
> —Audre Lorde

This book is about people, processes, and things international. It is about women and men who claim, or have imposed on them, different identities in national and cultural terms. It is also a book about different economies, wherein—and between which—resources and opportunities are distributed at wide-ranging and obscenely different levels. A basic assumption in this book is that political decisions drive those differences. And political decisions are rarely, if ever, made in the context of power balance. Hierarchy pervades political decision making, not the least of which is a male-female hierarchy.

So far, so good. I have used words that are relatively uncontested. (My assumption, of course, would be hotly contested by mainstream economists.) But from here on, much of the analysis involves contested words, many of them developed in the master's house, to draw on Lorde's eloquent warnings.[1] But women and other nonmasters want to develop their own words in their own houses. We do so from the margins—the periphery, the ends, or perhaps the front lines of our institutions and disciplines. And multiple houses mean that we often contest among ourselves the meanings, agendas, and implications of these words.

In this chapter, I discuss some basic discourse of women, men, and international development: by discourse, I mean the words, the putting together of words, and the categories of use. Already I have let the loaded term "development" slip in, but I will get to that almost immediately in the section on mainstream words (many of them derived from the masters?), just after I examine the ethical dilemmas associated with challenge from the margins. I conclude with the new words we develop at the margins, in our own homes. We don't all agree about the meaning of these words, much less about whether they should be used at all. But we need to know them and how to find out more about them, for many of us seek to shift the margins, to mainstream the margins, to recenter the entire development enterprise.

(And an *enterprise* it often is, in commercial agendas and in advocacy language.) I hope that readers will dialogue and debate the contested language but tolerate the ambiguity of withholding their tentative judgments on the language until well into the book or near its closure.

Ethics

Women at the margins are "on the line," or at the boundary of many distinctions. One boundary distinction is disciplinary, that is, fields of knowledge or categories that control knowledge (often excluding the study of women and of relations between men and women). Another distinction is institutional; women are outside of the bureaucratic spaces or excluded from the decision-making positions in which policy and implementation are determined. Yet another distinction is ethical, for disciplinary and institutional work can involve compromises, accommodations, or even co-optation—all of which occur in the interests of engagement and sustained dialogue. Should bridges be built, or should the lines be strengthened and reinforced? Like Lorde, we should worry about the master's house and his language.

At four key United Nations women's conferences, government and non-governmental leaders from all parts of the globe developed near-consensus agendas about policies, programs, and principles initially associated with the broad issues of development, equality, and peace. These conferences took place in Mexico City in 1975, Copenhagen in 1980, Nairobi in 1985, and Beijing and Hairou in 1995. The agendas used much of the master's language but merged it with language from the margins. Activists also built bridges with other world conferences using that merged language, among them conferences on the environment (1992), human rights (1993), population (1994), social development (1995), and the habitat (1996). With hindsight, we might wonder and worry about whether that language was effectively used or abused, toward change or co-optation. "Co-optation," a term implying capture, is at the heart of ethical dilemmas of engaging with or distancing from the arenas of power and decision making from local to global settings.

Probably no analysis grapples with ethical questions quite like that of Carol Cohn.[2] Academics are perhaps freer than many other workers in retaining a purist and autonomous stance, even though they too should consider the ethical dilemmas of the master's higher educational institutions or their disciplinary founding fathers. Women's studies offers the opportunity to break from those disciplinary boxes in the masters' houses with cues from founding mothers that can be pursued, it is hoped, in an egalitarian and nonhierarchical climate of intellectual growth.

Cohn had the opportunity to participate in a seminar with "defense intellectuals" who spoke a language and operated with a set of assumptions far different from her own. She listened to and learned new terminology about death and massive destruction—a terminology that not only made light of it all but also sexualized and feminized the weapons, targets, and consequences. Cohn faced the dilemma of learning the language for engagement and dialogue without being swept up into it. Surely such dilemmas face activists, civil servants, and readers every day. I, for one, celebrate Cohn's decision to engage and ultimately to expose defense intellectuals through analysis.

With a larger philosophical and ethical agenda, Kathy Ferguson makes *The Feminist Case against Bureaucracy.*[3] (We will grapple with the plural meanings of feminisms soon.) Ferguson argues that the technicality, control, and hierarchy of bureaucracy make it incompatible with women's everyday experiences. To integrate women or their visions in bureaucracy is to perpetuate the bureaucratic domination that increasingly governs our lives. Two women have written powerful critiques on related ethical matters. The first is Maria Mies, who focuses her critique as much on accumulation and global capitalism as on the hierarchical domination they spawn. The second is Vandana Shiva, labeled an ecofeminist by some, who positions women with life and nature rather than with the destructive forces that all too often characterize "development."[4]

Some would question the ways in which women's everyday experiences become universalized in these accounts. Can we generalize about women or about feminism for that matter? Writing from the margins of the United States, it is all too obvious that women are diverse—as diverse as men—and that they prioritize different interests and identities, depending on their region, class, age, political ideology, occupation, party affiliation, religion, immigration status, and ethnicity, among other categories. And the United States is just 5 percent of the world's population. Just how much more diverse are women in the world, once we add national identity and Southern and Northern vantage points?

South and North are 1990s geographic catchwords for what was once known as the third world versus the first and second worlds. Readers should memorize the maps that nationalizing men have made and into which women have been fit. Diverse women's experiences in national boundaries are based in part on the political economies therein.

Chandra Mohanty has rightly criticized the tendencies of some writers to make global generalizations about women.[5] Early advocacy writing also

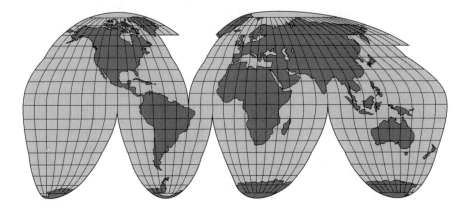

misrepresented women as universal victims—acted upon, but lacking agency of their own. Not only is the victimization of all women inaccurate, but it does no group any favor to portray it as essentially pathetic.

Analysts and activists have increasingly considered the way that society *constructs* social categories. In so doing, they use the word "gender," rather than the biological term "sex" or the eternal feminine "woman." In this book, I alternate between the words "gender" and "women" (and "men"), but the categories are generally understood as *social* ones that change over time and across national and cultural boundaries. A gendered policy analysis would focus on the ways that all policies—from tax, land, and labor to safety and health—differently serve and/or burden diverse men and women, including women who head households.

Yet that diverse group called women shares some overlapping ground with policy implications and common agendas. This book, therefore, uses the word "women" but does not put quotation marks around it with each use.[6] DAWN (Development Alternatives with Women for a New Era), an organization of the South, puts women's diversity squarely in the center of its analysis. DAWN identifies a common ground in gender hierarchy that privileges men. DAWN envisions a world without hierarchy and domination.[7]

To what extent, then, should people work within the hierarchy in order to achieve outcomes that would undermine that hierarchy? Are these means and ends fundamentally incompatible? Will reformers and transformers become tainted along the way? Such are the ethical issues that confront people with the option of working in government, international agencies, universities, and even some nongovernmental organizations (NGOs) large enough for a hierarchy to have emerged.

In the minds of some, international and national institutions cannot be written off. They have an enormous capability to influence people's lives, and they control significant resources, much of it generated from the public. Can we absolve those institutions from the responsibility to serve men and women?

Rarely is a single answer necessary in response to these quandaries. Work is necessary both on the inside and on the outside. And pressure needs to come from all directions. Recall Remedios Rikken's reflections on her work in the national women's commission of the Philippines, likened to traditional Filipino cake baking: heat from the bottom, the top, and the sides. Scattered throughout this book, readers will find additional material ripe with ethical dilemmas in research, policy analysis, and political action, within and outside of bureaucracies.

From the margins, we take our ethical dilemmas to the mainstream. To engage, dialogue, and change the mainstream, we probably need to learn, though not necessarily accept, the language and its underlying assumptions.

The Mainstream

Several words are commonplace in our foraging through the mainstream. In chapter 2, I examine the changing political and economic landscape after World War II, including its changing buzzword "development," in the changing containers known as nation-states. Chapter 3 examines institutions within those nation-states. But now, let us whet the appetite with some of the value-laden terminology of the mainstream.

In the commercial landscapes of Northern countries, the word "developers" is a code for real estate agents and housing and infrastructure contractors. It is business. In the international community, development has taken on a broader meaning, usually reified as a positive and benevolent movement from a rural subsistence society to a "modern" urban and industrial society. Historically, the word "development" was invented in the aftermath of the chaos and disorder wrought by the industrial revolution in early-nineteenth-century Europe.[8]

In its *Human Development Report*, the United Nations Development Programme (UNDP) continually reminds readers that development is more than economic growth, commerce, business, money in circulation, and the commodification of labor.

> [Economic growth] is a means to an end—enlarging people's choices. So, it should be evaluated for its impact on people. How many people have their income expand? Is the income disparity among groups of people narrowing? What does growth mean for the poor?[9]

The UNDP always attaches the adjective human to the noun development, lest it be forgotten. Its executive director states over and over in public speeches that development is pro-people, pro-poor, pro-women, and pro-environment.[10] In so doing, he overturns the usual way the word development gets used and measured.

Development policies encompass many different sectors. In many governments, work is subdivided into ministries and departments, the policies and programs of which are ostensibly coordinated by the chief executive, national planning agencies, and, ultimately, the budget or treasury ministry. In national budgets, one finds implicit priorities among development policies, ranging from education, housing, and health to public works (roads, bridges), safety (anticrime and violence), commerce, and transportation.

In the international community, different development policies are supported in both single- and multipurpose agencies. The agencies can also be differentiated on other bases: *bilateral* agencies transfer funds and technical services from one government to another country, whereas *multilateral* agencies transfer funds and technical services from multiple sources to multiple countries, filtered through the professional staff. The multilateral World Bank lends money for a wide variety of development projects: road and dam construction, education, and urban infrastructure (sewers, potable water), among others. The World Health Organization has a more focused mission. Bilateral agencies, sometimes maligned as the "foreign aid" agencies, usually have multiple development missions covering numerous policy and program areas (not the least of which are their own national commercial and foreign policy agendas; see the next chapter).

Beginning with the pioneering work of Danish economist Ester Boserup in 1970, researchers began to document the uneven distribution of development benefits to men and women.[11] Agencies and governments responded with token efforts, initially called women in development offices, women's desks (literally a desk moved into a room), and even ministries of women's affairs. These efforts were meant to be more than the data collection and periodic reporting of, for example, the Women's Bureau in the U.S. Department of Labor. With an office, women could be "integrated" into the multiple development policies, singular missions, or even the whole of government. The implication was that women would gain a piece of the budgetary action with women's projects or with separate components for women in other projects. Few questions were raised about the overall operations, missions, and agendas of development agencies. Yet those overall operations are where most of the action and spending took place.

Integration carried some steam for a decade or so, but by the 1985 United Nations women's conference in Nairobi, mainstreaming became the goal. By mainstreaming, people meant that attention and accountability to women ought to be infused in all program operations. Rounaq Jahan distinguishes between two mainstreaming strategies. One involves integrating women into existing strategies and priorities, and the other involves setting new agendas.[12] Chapter 3 develops this more fully.

Most current development strategies are not pro-environment, pro-women, and pro-poor. Instead, economic growth plunders on, with nary a thought given to people or workers displaced and environments destroyed. The institutions in which such thought might occur, but does not necessarily occur, are those associated with democratic governance. In democracies, people or their representatives speak and act for such interests, using what was once considered the binding authority of nationally sovereign states, whose leaders and institutions govern territory. Speech and action occur within the context of rule by law, respect for human rights, and periodic changes for leaders who are accountable to the public. Men monopolize most government decision-making positions, and policy agendas rarely incorporate gendered understandings of policy and implementation. Are there any democracies of, with, and for women?

In the last decade, a groundswell of voices has proclaimed the need for democracy and good governance. Those who study politics give those words different meanings from those who study economics. When the World Bank's *World Development Report* of 1983 focused on the state, its economists emphasized swollen and inefficient government, whose officials delayed structural adjustment, to liberate resources for markets and international free trade. The World Bank refers to "institutions of governance (firms, markets, mechanisms) . . . [and] the governance of contract, investment and private ordering through the lens of economising on transaction costs."[13]

Small-d democrats must beware of language that is co-opted by the masters. Governance is not the only such term, for antipoverty, empowerment, cooperatives, and workers are part of the rhetorical menu. Diane Elson warns that "democratic politics is at the heart of a transformatory approach to structural adjustment."[14] The same could be said for transformative approaches to gender mainstreaming. The problem of multilateral agencies, as Jahan has outlined, is that they are not embedded in contexts of political or democratic accountability. Bilateral agencies, in contrast, might be so embedded that democratic majorities exercise voice in those nation-states.[15]

I use the words "state" and "nation-state" in this book. Most international data are organized around comparisons of such units. This is problematic for two reasons. First, in our global economy, the centers of capital in global cities may exercise as much authority as seemingly sovereign political elites.[16] Second, women had little or no voice in the construction of nation or the discourses of nationalism. Writer Virginia Woolf made a poignant comment nearly a century ago, which was emblazoned on a tent at the 1985 United Nations women's conference in Nairobi: "As a woman, I have no country. As a woman I want no country. As a woman my country is the whole world."[17] Does this speak to situatedness at country margins or at the center of the world?

The Margins

However diverse, women often operate at the margins of political and economic power. Those who make and enforce policy decisions rarely act in ways that reflect understanding of women's diverse vantage points. All too often, officials operate in ways that perpetuate men's privileges in matters of material interests and authority. In this book, we aim to "see the world through women's eyes." This phrase, too, was emblazoned on tents and poster boards at the United Nations women's conference in 1995 in Beijing and Hairou.

Those who design and implement public policies do so with rationales, principles, and justifications that have consequences and implications for subsequent actions. Advocates for marginal women, in strategic (or marginal) positions of organizations, straddle discourses when they adopt or align with justifications. Mayra Buvinić and Caroline Moser have each outlined the major principles that bring women into policy and program actions: efficiency, empowerment, equality, poverty alleviation, and welfare (in alphabetical order).[18]

The words themselves appeal to different audiences. Economists use and respond to efficiency principles; redistributional advocates use and respond to the language of poverty alleviation; feminists of different sorts use and respond to the language of equality and empowerment. But the principles are often mixed together, and their meanings used and abused. Terms such as "equality," seemingly fixed for equal consequences, are muddled in the practice of different treatment for the same situation or different consequences for people in different situations. Some of the muddle is a result of time frames of long or short duration.

Consider the now common distinction of practical and strategic gender interests, invented in Maxine Molyneux's analysis of Nicaragua and elevated for global use in Moser's analyses.[19] To address strategic interests is to challenge the underlying structures of gender domination and subordination. To address practical interests is to address everyday needs in household and neighborhood contexts. When and where do those interests overlap?

And what is the optimal sequence for reformist and structural struggles? Part of the art of politics (or of co-optation?) involves assessments of resistance, backlash, and prospects for success. Along with this art, activists use styles that range from confrontational to gentle dialogue.

Hindsight aids in the quest for possible answers. An insightful analysis of postrevolutionary Soviet strategy in central Asian republics shows the setbacks of confrontational *zhenotdal* (women's bureau) strategies to address gender subordination through legal and public action. The strategies did not work.[20] Practical efforts can, over long periods, alleviate poverty but not necessarily challenge gender subordination.

One of the real messages of such hindsight is the inspiration and source for change. Soviet strategies in central Asia were top-down strategies rather than instigated from within, percolating from those who would experience the consequences of that change. It is easy enough to recognize the flaws of 1920s-style Leninism, but policy directives of the 1990s share some of the same flaws. For reasons like these, we need to listen to voices of those with stakes in change, whose authority is preeminent. Collections such as Amrita Basu's *The Challenge of Local Feminisms* or Barbara Nelson and Najma Chowdhury's *Women and Politics Worldwide* are a good place to begin.[21]

Most chapters in these collections are organized on national bases, and they give voice to diversity within and across nations. At some point, it is useful to simplify the complexity and outline feminist frameworks in which to organize the diverse conceptualizations of female subordination, solutions, and critiques. In these frameworks falls a "decentralized feminism," which, according to Charlotte Bunch, is a salient concept happening all around the world. As women grapple with gender/women/feminist questions, they build their theories out of daily practice.[22] To broad frameworks we now turn.

The "F" Word

Early studies of women (later gender) and development seemed to avoid use of the words "feminist" and "feminism." Back then, in the early 1970s, perhaps writers and activists worried that they carried too much baggage, clouding or complicating issues for audiences with stereotyped interpretations of feminism. These audiences often fell within the groupings of mainstream academics and national and international government officials. Perhaps writers and activists should revisit the terminology—in its multiple meanings—using it for gendering the mainstream of politics and policies.

In its singular form, the word "feminism" was perceived as Western in philosophical terms or Northern in spatial terms. Feminism made technical reform efforts seem political, thus denying development rationales for including women in programs or transforming institutions with gendered understandings. Resistance was ample; advocates worried about adding backlash on top of that. Opponents of gender justice and equality attacked feminism as cultural imperialism.[23] Moreover, postcolonial studies criticized the way a singular feminism seemed to universalize women and their diverse experiences.[24] Worse yet, the way some Northern feminists wrote about women of the South seemed to transform women into victims, without embracing the real agency and vantage points of diverse women. The important work of Chandra Mohanty was cited earlier, followed up with critics who positioned themselves as postmodern and postcolonial.

DAWN's analysis represented a turning point in distancing strategies toward feminist language. DAWN talked about multiple feminisms and legitimized their usage among diverse women of South and North. For DAWN there is, however, common ground.

> There is and must be a diversity of feminisms, responsive to the different needs and concerns of different women, and *defined by them for themselves*. This diversity builds on a *common opposition to gender oppression and hierarchy* which, however, is only the first step in articulating and acting upon a political agenda.[25]

Moreover, after the United Nations Women's Conference in Nairobi, women from around the world began to use the terminology with its diverse and multiple meanings. Collections gave voice to the multiple meanings of feminism, born and nurtured in various countries and cultures.

Given the centrality of politics and policy reform to this book, we must engage the discourses of feminisms. Feminisms provide frameworks within which to define problems, their causes, visions for change, and the strategies and solutions toward transformation. As Rani Jethmalani states: "Women cannot be shy of the fact that feminism is politics—because it intends to change and transform power structures which have made women invisible, oppressed, and subservient."[26]

Yet there is a lot more to movements toward gender justice and equality than feminist movements. Not all women (or progressive men) identify with feminisms. Nor do all feminists identify with all of women's struggles. Feminist *encuentros* (encounters), drawing women from the Americas, began as meetings among feminists; they later embraced women organizing over practical issues such as improving neighborhoods with water, sewers, and roads; and occasionally they burst into contentious debates over priorities,

Table 1.1   Latin American Feminist Encounters

Year	Location	Number of Participants	
1981	Bogotá, Colombia	230	(F,P)
1983	Lima, Peru	650	(F,P,N)
1985	Bertioga, Brazil	1,000	(F,P,Sh,I,B)
1987	Taxco, Mexico	1,500	(F,P,Sh,I,B,G,C)
1990	San Bernardo, Argentina	3,000	(F,P,Sh,I,B,G,CC,E,L,U)
1993	Costa del Sol, El Salvador*	1,300	(F,P,Sh,I,B,G,CC,E,L,U)

Source: Adapted from Inter-American Development Bank, *Women in the Americas: Bridging the Gender Gap* (Washington, D.C.: IDB, 1995), p. 114.

Key: F = feminists   P = party activists   N = NGO representatives
Sh = shantytown/neighborhood activists   I = indigenous leaders
B = black leaders   G = government leaders   C = Catholic activists
CC = Catholic and Christian activists   E = ecologists
L = lesbian activists   U = union activists

*Almost moved, due to death threats and security risks.

divisions of labor, and strategies in women's political struggles. The sequence is instructive (see Table 1.1). The larger and more diverse the encounters, the greater the tensions and divisions, especially in the middle 1980s. However, the issues and policy agendas also widened, creating actual and potential spinoffs in subsequent network building.[27]

Molyneux's naming of the different interests around which women cohered—*practical* and *strategic*—led to claiming by various parts of women's movements. For addressing strategic interests that institutionalize subordination, feminists claimed responsibility, as in the *encuentros*. Other kinds of women's groups claimed practical interests in their realm, addressing everyday problems amenable to collective action or public service provision, such as urban services and communal kitchens. In the end, though, the very process of organization, says Alejandra Massolo, creates a sense of citizenship with prospects to redistribute household power relations.[28] Thus, the separation of these practical and strategic interests is perhaps more an intellectual than an action project.

Many kinds of feminism exist. To clarify differences among several, I examine six versions that women commonly give voice to worldwide: liberal feminism, socialist feminism, state feminism, radical feminism, maternal feminism, and group-affirming feminism. These six have bodies of theories and action, around which writing and action have cohered. Theories should illuminate, not straitjacket understanding; the diverse approaches "free us from the authoritarian trap of 'having to know it all,'" says Rosemarie Tong.[29]

Liberal Feminism. Perhaps the oldest of feminisms, liberal feminism was born amid ferment in Europe over individual rights in a limited state, with lines clearly drawn between private lives and public action, including market activity. Public-private lines, drawn differently throughout the world and in various world religions, spread with the extension of the modern state during the colonial era. Part of the early ferment involved the impulse to apply rational thought and action on the part of both citizen and state. Liberal feminists, male and female alike, sought legal changes to educate women, to enfranchise them with political rights, and to create equal entitlements and playing fields on which to compete for opportunities and resources. It is a big question, however, whether such fields can ever be equal, given women's considerable unpaid responsibilities for child rearing and household maintenance.

By relegating much "private" activity outside the realm of government, early liberal feminism bypassed the opportunity to address central dilemmas for women and gender justice. For many women, considerable time, labor, and energy are invested in so-called private activities such as child care and household labor, including the arduous hauling of water and firewood that is part of household labor in many rural areas of the South. Moreover, health and safety issues threaten women in this "private" sphere, including domestic violence and coerced sex. Until the last decade or two, these private and personal issues were not considered political and were not part of public policy agendas in many countries. In fact, other versions of feminism helped politicize patterns that heretofore seemed personal, even to an early liberal feminist.

Liberal feminists generally work for reform within existing political and economic systems, rather than for revolution or transformations. Men have monopolized decision-making positions in the past and present existing political systems. Those states have privileged men as actors in and beneficiaries of state patronage. Indeed, anarchist and libertarian feminists (the latter advocating an extreme form of liberal feminism) are highly suspicious of the state, so much so that they identify the state as the source of women's subordination to men.

For many liberal feminists, a key target for change is the law and its enforcement. To the extent laws are enforced (always a big question), a change in law has the potential to affect large numbers of people, reinforced with government authority or even coercion. Of course, feminist legal victories may become threaded with government, for better or for worse. For better, those victories institutionalize government actions, entitlements, and resource allocations. Feminists who struggle with self-help efforts, meagerly funded through their own fund-raising, volunteerism, and user fees, can look forward to publicly funded programs and support, to the extent that their political clout raises these priorities in political action. For worse, feminist legal victories become tainted with otherwise corrupt and nondemocratic government. If law enforcement is sporadic and weak, the very "victory" deludes people into believing that justice mechanisms are in place, but it exhibits symbolic rather than real action and follow up.

Yet many states are weak, embedded in societies in which custom, religion, and force operate to sustain female subordination.[30] Again, this has its better and worse dimensions. On the one hand, those local forces may offer better recourse to women than the modern state, about which people have understandable suspicions. Many countries have histories of authoritarian rule or have the trappings of democracy for a small middle class and a tiny elite. For the poor majority, especially those in rural areas, distant from capital city or regional state power concentrations, the state has often represented an unresponsive machine that extracts more than it delivers by way of taxes and forced conscription. States have often ruled in arbitrary ways rather than through rules of law consistently and fairly applied to all citizens. In such circumstances, family, extended household, and village leadership are lines of defense around which residents—including women—withdraw, resist, or occasionally engage with rulers, their agents, or representatives. In these circumstances, individuals who seek their rights operate under great constraints or even delusions about the possibilities of real reform.

On the other hand, the long arm of the state may not reach far beyond the capital city. Legal pluralism may prevail, with women able only to win or lose under customary law, unless they have the resources or visibility to purchase legal counsel and navigate through the mystical court systems with their trappings of justice, rituals, and new or unknown sets of players.

Once women reach those courts, whom do they encounter? In Tanzania-based conversations between Marjorie Mbilinyi and Rebecca Kalindile, the latter named her experiences in striking terminology: "male colonization, female slavery." After she spoke of physical violence, Mbilinyi queried about using the court. Kalindile replied, "Is the court a woman? Will you accuse him to his fellow male?" Mbilinyi concludes, "she had no illusions about the gender and class characteristics of the court system."[31]

Liberal feminism is often dismissed as individualistic, thereby aligned with Western thought or Northern countries. At worst, it exemplifies "legal fetishism," or the belief that domination and subordination can be addressed through legal tools. (See Chapter 6 and Charlesworth in note 8 of that chapter.) Since 1979, much energy has been spent on ratification of the Convention on the Elimination of All Forms of Discrimination against

Women (CEDAW) (reprinted in the appendix at the end of this book). Now, most countries of the world (154 countries, as of 1997) have signed on to this comprehensive document, even those countries with the worst human rights abuses against women and without consistent rule of law.

CEDAW ratification in and of itself does little to liberate women. However, women and courts have used ratification as political leverage to press for real change or to enforce laws. As detailed in a later chapter, the Tanzanian High Court decided in favor of women's land ownership, partly due to the national position on CEDAW. In another example, Japan ratified CEDAW with some trepidation, for it would commit the government to changing at least 150 laws. This spurred women's groups to act in three priority areas relating to equal employment and educational opportunities.[32]

In various countries, women's individual rights in personal violence or body matters are conditioned by law. If women can seek contraception without their husbands' approval, or if husbands are punished for domestic violence, the charge of "fetishism" seems misplaced. Other feminist critics might be asked, to paraphrase an old union song, which side are you on?

Activists in many countries of the South take human rights conventions quite seriously. It becomes an ethical basis for feminism, a language

> to counter cultural religious right language: When the religious right says family values, we say human rights. . . . If they say family values and you say feminism, you are dead in the water. But when they say family values and you say, "We are defending women's human rights," you are on a different level of discourse.

For Charlotte Bunch, director of the Center for Global Leadership, this approach is something women of the North can learn from women elsewhere.[33]

Nevertheless, the absence of democracy, rule of law, and checks on virulent accumulation and corruption in many countries leads some feminists to argue for systemic change in the entire political economy. To such comprehensive approaches we now turn.

Socialist Feminism. Perhaps second in feminist birth order is Marxist feminism, later elaborated and expanded as socialist feminism. In spatial terms, this version also comes out of Europe, with the writings of eighteenth-century theorists Karl Marx and Friedrich Engels, but these ideas have spread widely, with many homegrown adaptations during and after revolutions in Russia (1917), China (1949), Cuba (1959), Vietnam, Nicaragua, and other national settings (not to mention many leftist opposition groups in a wide variety of other places).

In the context of multiparty politics, those parties that espouse ideologies *left* of center are often the first to acknowledge and support the programs and leaders that loosely fall within feminists' agendas. The relationship between the male Left and feminists has a synergy. Thanks to feminists, socialists widened the narrow productive focus of nineteenth-century theorists to include reproductive concerns. And reproduction was conceived not merely in physical terms but also in terms of sustaining and supporting household labor and child rearing, usually on unpaid terms. A provocatively titled campaign about "Wages for Housework," never a realistic legal or program prospect, spread awareness about the value of women's unpaid work and its connection to the paid workforce.[34]

Socialist feminists give priority to economic factors. Women's economic dependency on men gives them little leverage in social contexts, from household to national and international. Women's work, unpaid and paid, is generally undervalued, deriving benefits to employers, husbands, and government, which relegates responsibility for child rearing and volunteerism onto women's shoulders. Once in the paid labor force, women are used as temporary, cheap labor. Women's unpaid labor in the home enables men to be productive and sustains family life.

Socialist feminists work to integrate women in the labor force, to support their collective organization in struggles to gain more value for their labor, and to acquire political voice for public policies that would redistribute wealth and opportunity. Ultimately, though, socialist feminists would seek to transform "savage capitalism"[35] into democratic socialism, wherein the wider public controls and benefits from once private, profit-making property. Among those gendered benefits are widespread child care, public health, poverty alleviation, and social programs for those unable to support themselves. Given women's overrepresentation among the poor and the growing prevalence of female-headed households, socialism is expected to redistribute resources to women.

The twentieth-century track record of *authoritarian* socialism is not a model about which socialist feminists would boast. It controlled and planned economies, but it enfeebled them and authorized few political mechanisms for political accountability. Authoritarian socialist states often extracted labor and revenue from their citizens in arbitrary fashion, despite the rhetorical public agenda on the collective good. Moreover, authoritarian socialist regimes seemed to reproduce tendencies within capitalism to use women as cheap labor. Everyday commerce was burdensome for women shopping for household needs, tasks that fell on female shoulders.

Still, socialist regimes expanded the public agenda to embrace considerable support for widespread child care and health care. Most but not all socialist regimes expanded women's reproductive rights from contraception to abortion. In centrally planned economies, however, little priority was accorded to the manufacture or import of various contraceptive options.

The record during and after the so-called transitions to democratic market economies calls into question the effectiveness of authoritarian socialist strategies to transmit and infuse their egalitarian rhetoric into people's mind-sets. Among countries affiliated with the former Soviet Union, women's participation in politics has shrunk, their unemployment rates have risen higher than men's, and their ability to use legal leverage against discrimination has diminished.[36]

Socialists still prioritize wage labor participation, but the meaning of female participation in the late-twentieth-century global economy has changed (see Chapter 5 on work.) Profit makers' search for cheaper labor dovetails with female labor force participation. Simultaneously, the real value of men's wages has been shrinking in many places. Thus, multiple adults in households pursue multiple wage-earning strategies, but often in contexts wherein women continue their responsibilities for unpaid domestic labor, resulting in a double work burden.

Democratic socialism continues to inspire idealists who believe that government has a role in responding to the human condition. But if capitalism has "triumphed," to use Robert Heilbroner's term, idealists are challenged to democratize the rules and contexts that govern capitalism.[37]

State Feminism (A Misnomer?). In 90 percent of governments, some form of "women's machinery" (to use United Nations terminology) exists to promote and defend women's interests. They come in many sizes and shapes, from women's desks to women's bureaus and whole ministries of women. In this machinery, political appointees and civil servants might work with women's organizations to establish policy agendas, priorities, and outcomes that make government more accountable and responsive to women.

In China, the All China Women's Federation is perhaps the largest of such machineries. Established in 1949 after the socialist revolution, it aimed to mobilize and represent women with authority and resources from the state. According to Naihua Zhang, in "1994, it had over ninety-eight thousand full-time cadres on the state payroll [and] . . . its functions rely heavily on hundreds of thousands of grassroots activists through the five-tier system from the village to the center."[38]

China relaxed its controls over the economy in the 1980s, but it continues to exercise authority over the press. Magazines and newspapers contain cues that semiofficially legitimize new attitudes and behaviors.[39] Below are headlines and titles of stories and letters that have been translated from the state-managed press. Are they feminist in some form or another?

- Why Such a Wide Gap in the Proportions of Boys and Girls Entering the Upper Grades?

- It Is Not Permissible to Defame Woman's Image

- I Mistakenly Blamed Her (husband repents after abusing wife who gave birth to a girl)

- Is It Right to Refuse Someone a Job Just Because She Is Female?

- To Discriminate against Women Is to Discriminate against Your Own Mother

In many other countries, political appointments can work for or against the resolution of practical and strategic gender interests. Much depends on the political climate and support for such change. Under President Corazon Aquino, the Filipino Commission on the Status of Women developed a parallel plan for women to guide the work of government departments. The commission took advice from a board consisting of leaders from various women's organizations. Commission staff worked with "focal points" in each government department to monitor and follow up progress toward the plan.[40]

In women's machinery, appointees with connections to women and women's movements can open up space within government for new voices and wider policy agendas. Much, however, also depends on the staff and resources available in such machinery. All too often, budgets are minimal, as later chapters discuss.

Given men's monopolization of politics, it is invariably men who make these appointments. Appointments are made for many reasons, among them rewarding campaign supporters and placating or controlling constituencies. In state feminism, ethical concerns about co-optation are heightened. The very survival of women's machinery depends on prevailing political winds. Despite the successes of the Brazilian Commissions on the Status of Women, their budgets were undermined, and the commissions themselves were outlawed in subsequent governments.[41]

Radical Feminism. Radical feminisms form a catchall category that refers to several kinds of feminists. What ties radicals together are the problems, issues, and public policies that seem to fall through the cracks of liberal, state, and socialist agendas. Among the most important of these agendas are "body" issues, including violence against women (battering, rape), reproductive health, and sexuality. Radical feminists also take on cultural traditions that symbolize and sustain female subordination to men. By definition, these cultural traditions are numerous. Liberals and socialists often disdain political programs that provoke cultural backlash.

Zimbabwe's minister for women, an appointee whose nom de guerre during the nationalist struggle meant "spill blood," said that bureaucratic infighting was worse than the war. She and her staff found it difficult to challenge *lobola*, or bridewealth exchange, without being accused of "western cultural imperialism."[42] Insiders operate under great constraints (sometimes self-imposed, in the interest of political survival). Outsiders can broaden agendas with independence and autonomy, but will they seek engagement with the state?

Radical feminists have often kept a distance from the state. They prefer instead the purity and autonomy of responding to women's concerns, untainted with the inevitable compromises and mentalities that prevail in the male political machineries in all their national, homegrown versions. Radical self-help measures, such as battered women's shelters, typically starve for resources and consequently serve smaller populations than government programs might serve. These outsiders, however, offer model programs and opportunities for differentiation with other insider feminists (whether liberals or socialists working inside compatible political parties).

Radical feminists also use nonconventional political strategies that underline their unease about establishment politics. They resist and ignore state action, both individually and collectively. They use the streets, fields, and homes rather than the hallowed institutional halls of men's political machinery. They refuse to use the language of contemporary and conventional political discourse. In countries with no respect for human rights, radicals are subject to jail and even torture, making this form of feminism highly risky.

Even though radical feminists consciously distance themselves from engagement in politics with a corrupted state, their political work has far-reaching effects. They serve at the front lines of political change, using discourse and taking action in ways that offer contrasts to more mainstream feminists who use more moderate voices to broaden the agenda. Witness the ways that liberal feminists have made violence against women a priority, pursuing even legalistic strategies with potentially far-reaching effects.

Maternal Feminism. Maternal feminists believe that women differ from men and that the difference should be valued—even celebrated—in the norms, models, and behaviors that societies encourage. Maternal feminists disagree over whether that difference is the result of biology, socialization, or life experience, but whatever the source, maternal feminists praise qualities such as nurturing, caregiving, relationality, and nonviolence. Some ecological feminists, such as Vandana Shiva, conceivably fit within this framework, focusing on women's essential connectedness with environmentally sustainable activities.

Do maternal feminists shy away from challenging power imbalance and the structures of gender hierarchy? Some African feminists envision female-male complementarity, while others invoke past structures of gender power balance. Perhaps maternal feminists pursue gentler and longer-term strategies to nudge away at dominance and subordination. They ask that society revisit its valuation of male and female capabilities and characteristics.[43] In so doing, however, they come close to making enormous generalizations about male and female capability and behavior, using biology as the lowest common denominator rather than recognizing the social constructions that make the world (and nations within it) a place of enormous diversity and variation.

Carol Gilligan's research on moral decision making has inspired maternal feminism. Unlike researchers who focused on boys and men as they developed models of moral decision making (in which females got relatively undeveloped ratings), Gilligan focused on girls and women to come up with an alternative model. She begins with a hypothetical moral dilemma: Suppose Heinz needed expensive medicine for his dying wife. Should he steal it? Of course, that life prevails over theft is one morally developed response. Girls and women asked other questions: Can't Heinz talk to the pharmacist? Could friends give him loans? Gilligan found that women's moral decisions occurred in relational webs, a probable product of girlhood socialization.[44]

As inspiring as her research is, Gilligan's informants are from the mainstream United States, not even representing that 5 percent of the world's population. Dare we Gilliganize the world? Other studies aimed at replicating the original (male) model found relational models, even among men, in other parts of the world.[45]

The choice of the word "maternal" is contentious, for not all women are mothers, aspire to motherhood, or behave similarly as mothers. In her now classic critique of modernization, Jane Jaquette used "female sphere" in ways similar to maternal feminism.[46] Alice Walker uses the term "womanist" in making some of the same references.[47] Still others view maternal feminism as conservative in its political implications. After all, male political machinery of the past used male-female difference as the rationale for segregation and subordination.

In many Latin American countries under past dictatorships, mothers' movements served to criticize regimes with a moral mantle that gave them some protection from the brutalities that other opponents suffered. In Argentina, the mothers of disappeared children, many of them student activists, did daily walks around the Plaza de Mayo in Buenos Aires with pictures of their children hanging around their necks. During Argentina's dirty war against its own population, an estimated 30,000 people disappeared. Mothers occupied the preciously limited political and moral space to raise questions about these regimes. Although some were jailed, tortured, or disappeared, others were visible reminders of the immoral regimes, and military men dared not touch most of them because of the sanctity of and respect for the idea of motherhood. Similar mothers' movements occurred in Chile and Central American countries. Maternal feminists sometimes drew parallels between authoritarian governments and authoritarian homes. A Chilean rallying cry that spread to all its feminisms was "democracy in the country and in the home."[48]

Group-affirming Feminism. Other feminisms affirm a cultural group in reaction to exploitation, racism, and segregation of dominant groups, men and women alike. To embrace the variants of this perspective, my referent is group-affirming feminists. These groups adopt specific identities. Perhaps the best known is Black feminism. Homegrown versions of Black feminism occur in many continents, following the African diaspora.[49] What unites Black feminists is agreement about the priority to combat racism, including racism in mainstream feminist groups.

The group affirmation may also be based on a cultural, national, or regional group that positions itself as different from others for a variety of reasons. The African Association of Women for Research and Development, based in Dakar, Senegal, sought a voice for Africans in the analysis and interpretation of women in countries of that region.

What makes group-affirming feminism complicated is its simultaneous commitment not only to confront sexism but also to defend attacks on men of their cultural, national, or regional group. However men are beleaguered under racism, relations of gender subordination coexist within groups.

Coalescing Feminisms? Taken together, feminisms share some common ground on which real and fictive coalitions might be built. At the bottom line, they recognize power and value imbalance between men and women. They look toward active women to foster more balance.

Feminisms differ, however, in the issues to which they give priority and the strategies they use to address those issues. On the surface, they pursue multiple political strategies—in and outside the establishment, macro and micro, legal and cultural. Taken together, these strategies complement one another in multiple fronts. As in other politics, feminists also compete with one another.

Different feminists have the potential to build coalitions around the common ground they share, ground that may change from one policy issue to another. In so doing, that potential can translate into shifts in power relations, resulting in empowerment. Empowerment is a term that was born in critiques of unequal power relations. However the term matures, it should be aligned with politics and its root, power.

Feminisms differ from one part of the world to another. Most importantly, multiple feminisms also differ *within* countries. In the lively and provocative feminist presses of Mexico, three tendencies can be traced among radical feminists alone. One analysis compares the way *fem*, *Debate Feminista*, and *La Correa Feminista* define issues and pose solutions, contrasting those that focus on women with those that align gender with other inequalities.[50] Feminists like these operate with neighborhood women (and their practical interests), party women of different ideological stripes, and women's studies academicians.

In the end, is there common ground? And does the common ground mean more than opposition to gender hierarchy? Readers might review the Platform for Action of the Beijing Fourth World Conference on Women, summarized and appended, for an answer.

We have examined the master's tools in this chapter, tools that claim comprehension of development and associated institutions. From the margins, other claims and frameworks coexist, including those associated with feminisms and women's strategic and practical interests. To engage in politics and policymaking, we must consider using those tools to change the political house, its machinery, and its outcomes for men and women. In doing so, treacherous ethical dilemmas continually emerge. These dilemmas are analyzed in subsequent chapters to bring out the threat and opportunity inherent in transitional times like these.

For Further Reflection

Following is a summary of the *Platform for Action* adopted by 184 countries at the Fourth World Conference on Women, Beijing, China, in September 1995.

Poverty Among the more than 1 billion people living in extreme poverty, "the overwhelming majority of them are women." The number of women "living in poverty has increased disproportionately to the number of men," and their "risk for falling into poverty is higher."

- "Review, adopt, and maintain macroeconomic policies and development strategies that address the needs and efforts of women in poverty."
- Revise laws and administrative practices.
- Provide women with access to credit.
- Develop gender-based methodologies to address feminized poverty.

Education and Training Education, a human right and a tool, is provided to girls and women in discriminatory ways.

- Ensure equal access (with goals and timetables).
- Eradicate female illiteracy (goals and timetables).
- Develop nondiscriminatory education/training.
- Allocate resources for reform.

Health Women's health involves emotional, social, and physical well-being, based on human rights without violence and coercion.

- Increase access to quality health care.
- Reduce maternal mortality (goals and timetables).
- Encourage women and men to take responsibility for sexual and reproductive behavior.
- Undertake gender-sensitive initiatives, with resources.

Violence Women and girls are subject to physical, sexual, and psychological abuse in both public and private life and during war. Inattention to preventive and protective law and its enforcement perpetuates violence.

- Adopt and implement laws to end violence against women and to punish and rehabilitate abusers.
- Dismantle networks that traffic in women.

Armed Conflict Women rarely take part in decisions that lead to armed conflict, but they preserve order and contribute to conflict resolution. They are victims of rape, a criminal and genocidal act.

- Increase women's participation in conflict resolution.
- Reduce military expenditures and control armaments.
- Protect women during conflict, displacement, and refuge.

Economy Women contribute to economic life but are excluded from economic decision making and discriminated against in education, wages, and counting terms.

- Promote economic rights and control over resources.
- Provide training.
- Eliminate occupational segregation.
- Promote harmonized work-family responsibilities.

Decision Making "Women's equal participation in decision-making is not only a demand for simple social justice or democracy. It is essential for achieving transparent and accountable government."

- Ensure women's equal access to and full participation in power structures and decision making in government bodies and public administration entities.
- Increase women's capacity to participate.

Institutional Mechanisms Women's machineries lack clear mandates, adequate resources, and political support. "Gender based policy analysis [is] applied sporadically or not at all."

- Strengthen machineries, vested in the highest government levels.
- Integrate gender perspectives in policies, programs, and laws.
- "Generate and disseminate gender-disaggregated data and information for planning and evaluation."
- Measure unremunerated work outside national accounts.

Human Rights Human rights are universal, to be enjoyed by women and girls.

- Implement CEDAW.
- Achieve legal literacy.

Media Gender-biased programming projects negative and degrading images of women (especially pornography) that do not reflect their diverse lives.

- Increase women's participation in media decision making.
- Promote balanced, nonstereotyped portrayals of women.

Environment Women use and manage natural resources as consumers and producers but are absent from decision making.

- Involve women in decision making.
- Integrate gender perspectives into policies and programming.

The Girl-child Girls face discrimination from the earliest life stages due to customary practices, prejudice, and sexual and other exploitation. "Fifteen million girls aged 15 to 19 each year give birth and face pregnancy-related complications."

- Eliminate discrimination, exploitation, and negative cultural attitudes against girl-children.

Institutional and Financial Arrangements Immediate action and accountability are necessary to meet goals. Governments are primarily responsible, but public and private regional and international institutions also require authority and resources.

Source: UN Department of Public Information, 1995.

Notes

1. Audre Lorde, "The Master's Tools Will Never Dismantle the Master's House," in *Sister Outsider* (Freedom, Calif.: Crossing Press, 1984), pp. 110–113. She

alludes to that horrific and lengthy period of U.S. history when slavery was legal—initiating a racialized inequality—and when the master's (plantation) house was its symbol.

2. Carol Cohn, "Sex and Death in the Rational World of Defense Intellectuals," *Signs: Journal of Women in Culture and Society* 12, no. 4 (1987): 687–718.

3. Kathy Ferguson, *The Feminist Case against Bureaucracy* (Philadelphia: Temple University Press, 1984).

4. Maria Mies, *Patriarchy and Accumulation on a World Scale: Women in the International Division of Labour* (London: Zed, 1986); Vandana Shiva, *Staying Alive: Women, Ecology and Development* (London and New Delhi: Zed, Kali for Women, 1988).

5. Chandra Mohanty, Ann Russo, and Lourdes Torres, eds., *Third World Women and the Politics of Feminism*, 2d ed. (Bloomington: Indiana University Press, 1991).

6. Although Christine Sylvester makes the point well about the construction of "women," her use of the word in quotes throughout an entire book is daunting (*Feminist Theory and International Relations in a Postmodern Era* [Cambridge: Cambridge University Press, 1994]). At a talk Sylvester gave at the University of Texas at El Paso in May 1995, she described following up Zimbabwean respondents' presentations of themselves as "women" with the query, "How do you know?" After consultation with others, they responded with justifications related to kinship. Readers might query audiences in the United States to understand their rationales.

7. Gita Sen and Caren Grown, *Development, Crises, and Alternative Visions: Third World Women's Perspectives* (New York: Monthly Review Press, 1987). DAWN networks activists, researchers, and policymakers, largely from Southern countries.

8. M. P. Cowen and R. W. Shenton, in *Doctrines of Development* (London: Routledge, 1996), historicize the concept well, but do so in ways that view agency as Western and male driven. See my review in *Journal of Developing Areas* 31, no. 3 (1997): 422–23.

9. UNDP, *Human Development Report* (New York: Oxford University Press, 1996), p. 11. Amartya Sen's notion of human development as capacitation underlies much of this thinking, although the UNDP writers use the discourse of choice. See Chapter 4.

10. James Speth, the current UNDP director, is frequently quoted in forewords and speeches.

11. Ester Boserup, *Woman's Role in Economic Development* (New York: St. Martin's Press, 1970); also see Irene Tinker's early, influential work, "The Adverse Impact of Development Policies on Women," in *Women and World Development*, edited by Irene Tinker and Michele Bo Bramsen (Washington, D.C.: Overseas Development Council; New York: Praeger, 1976).

12. Rounaq Jahan, *The Elusive Agenda: Mainstreaming Women in Development* (London: Zed, 1995).

13. The World Bank comments are found in its quarterly *Policy Research Bulletin* (1994).

14. Diane Elson, "From Survival Strategies to Transformation Strategies: Women's Needs and Structural Adjustment," in *Unequal Burden: Economic Crises, Persistent Poverty, and Women's Work*, edited by Lourdes Benería and Shelley Feldman (Boulder, Colo.: Westview Press, 1992), p. 39.

15. Jahan, *The Elusive Agenda*.

16. Saskia Sassen does the definitive work on global cities. See *Cities in a World Economy* (Thousand Oaks, Calif.: Pine Forge Press of Sage, 1995).

17. Virginia Woolf's words are prominent in graphics from the International Women's Tribune Center, 777 United Nations Plaza, New York, NY 10017. Also see Jan

Jindy Pettman, *Worlding Women: A Feminist International Politics* (London: Routledge, 1996); Lois West, ed., *Feminist Nationalism* (London: Routledge, 1997).

18. Mayra Buvinić, *Women and Poverty in the Third World* (Baltimore: Johns Hopkins University Press, 1983); Caroline O. N. Moser, *Gender Planning and Development: Theory, Practice and Training* (London: Routledge, 1993).

19. Maxine Molyneux, "Mobilization without Emancipation? Women's Interests, the State, and Revolution in Nicaragua," *Feminist Studies* 11, no. 2 (1985): 377–89.

20. Gregory Massell, *The Surrogate Proletariat: Moslem Women and Revolutionary Strategies in Soviet Central Asia, 1919–1929* (Princeton, N.J.: Princeton University Press, 1974). As the title makes clear, Soviet strategy had no intrinsic interest in liberation or equality, but only in using gender as a substitute conflict to provoke change in preindustrial class society.

21. Amrita Basu, ed., *The Challenge of Local Feminisms* (Boulder, Colo.: Westview Press, 1995); Barbara Nelson and Najma Chowdhury, eds., *Women and Politics Worldwide* (New Haven, Conn.: Yale University Press, 1994).

22. Charlotte Bunch, in Heidi Hartmann, et al., "Bringing Together Feminist Theory and Practice: A Collective Interview," *Signs: Journal of Women in Culture and Society* 21, no. 4 (1996): 942–43.

23. This is discussed in my "Gender Politics in Bureaucracy: Theoretical Issues in Comparative Perspective," In *Women, International Development and Politics: The Bureaucratic Mire*, 2d ed. (Philadelphia: Temple University Press, 1997), p. 21.

24. Marianne H. Marchand and Jane L. Parpart, eds., *Feminism/Postmodernism/Development* (London: Routledge, 1995).

25. Sen and Grown, *Development, Crises, and Alternative Visions*, p. 19; emphasis in original.

26. Rani Jethmalani, "India," in *Empowerment and the Law: Strategies of Third World Women*, edited by Margaret Schuler (Washington, D.C.: Overseas Education Fund, 1986), p. 63.

27. IDB, "Interamerican Development in Comparative Perspective," in *Women in the Americas: Bridging the Gender Gap* (Washington, D.C.: IDB, 1995), p. 114.

28. Alejandra Massolo is cited in Vivienne Bennett, "Gender, Class, and Water: Women and the Politics of Water Service in Monterrey, Mexico," *Latin American Perspectives* 22, no. 2 (1995): 76–99.

29. Rosemarie Tong, *Feminist Thought: A Comprehensive Introduction* (Boulder, Colo.: Westview Press, 1989), p. 8. Among comparative feminism texts, Tong's is quite extensive.

30. On statist literature, see Jane Parpart and Kathleen Staudt, eds., *Women and the State in Africa* (Boulder, Colo.: Lynne Rienner, 1989); Sue Ellen Charlton, et al., eds., *Women, the State and Development* (Albany, N.Y.: SUNY Albany Press, 1989); and Joel Midgal, Atul Kohli, and Vivienne Shue, eds., *State Power and Social Forces: Domination and Transformation in the Third World* (New York: Cambridge University Press, 1994). Feminists who focus on the law include Schuler, *Empowerment and the Law*; also see the useful newsletter published by the IWRAW (International Women's Rights Action Watch), University of Minnesota, 301 19th Ave. South, Minneapolis, MN 55455.

31. The research is cited in Kathleen Staudt, *Managing Development: State, Society and International Contexts* (Newbury Park, Calif.: Sage, 1991), p. 23.

32. Nuita Yoko et al., "The U.N. Convention on Eliminating Discrimination against Women and the Status of Women in Japan," in Nelson and Chowdhury, *Women and Politics Worldwide*, pp. 403–4.

33. Bunch, in Hartmann et al., "Bringing Together Feminist Theory," p. 944.

34. Among those associated with widening the historical socialist agenda are Juliet Mitchell and Kate Young.
35. Robert Bellah et al. cite this French characterization in *The Good Society* (New York: Vintage, 1991), p. 91.
36. Barbara Einhorn, *Cinderella Goes to Market: Citizenship, Gender, and Women's Movements in East and Central Europe* (London: Verso, 1993). Also see Sharon Wolchick, "Women and the State in Eastern Europe and the Soviet Union," in Charlton et al., *Women, the State and Development*, pp. 44–65.
37. Robert Heilbroner, "Reflections: The Triumph of Capitalism," *The New Yorker*, January 23, 1989, pp. 98–109.
38. Naihua Zhang with Wu Xu, "Discovering the Positive within the Negative: The Women's Movement in a Changing China," in Basu, *The Challenge of Local Feminisms*, p. 30.
39. Emily Honig and Gail Hershatter offer translations of the popular press in *Personal Voices: Chinese Women in the 1980s* (Stanford, Calif.: Stanford University Press, 1988).
40. Remedios Rikken outlined these strategies at the gender training conference, summarized in Aruna Rao et al., *Gender Training and Development Planning: Learning from Experience* (Bergen, Norway, and New York: Chr. Michelsen Institute and Population Council, 1991), p. 40.
41. Sonia Alvarez, "Contradictions of a 'Women's Space' in a Male-Dominant State: The Political Role of the Commissions on the Status of Women in Postauthoritarian Brazil," in Staudt, *Women, International Development and Politics*, pp. 37–78.
42. In Staudt, *Women, International Development and Politics*, p. 21.
43. Rosalyn Terborg-Penn et al., eds., *Women in Africa and the African Diaspora* (Washington, D.C.: Howard University Press, 1987). Some posit a "complementary" relationship with men that includes dual-sex political authority. Kamene Okonjo evokes and revives this indigenous authority in calling for contemporary gender political balance in "The Dual Sex Political System in Operation: Igbo Women and Community Politics in Midwestern Nigeria," in *Women in Africa: Studies in Social and Economic Change*, edited by Nancy Hafkin and Edna Bay (Stanford, Calif.: Stanford University Press, 1976).
44. Carol Gilligan, *In a Different Voice* (Boston: Harvard University Press, 1981). Naihua Zhang, "Discovering the Positive," also compares "women's rights-ism" (Western, legalistic) with "female-ism" (nationalist, essentialist) (pp. 37, 39).
45. Staudt, *Women, International Development and Politics*, pp. 31–32, n. 44.
46. Jane Jaquette, "Women and Modernization Theory: A Decade of Feminist Criticism," *World Politics* 34, no. 2 (1982): 267–84.
47. Alice Walker, *In Search of Our Mothers' Gardens: Womanist Prose* (San Diego: Harcourt, Brace, Jovanovich, 1983).
48. Alicia Frohmann and Teresa Veldés, "Democracy in the Country and in the Home: The Women's Movement in Chile," in Basu, *The Challenge of Local Feminisms*, pp. 276–301; Patricia Chuchryk, "Subversive Mothers: The Women's Opposition to the Military Regime in Chile," in Charlton et al., *Women, the State and Development*, pp. 130–51. Also see examples of Latin American feminist writing in Jane Jaquette, ed., *The Women's Movement in Latin America* (Boulder, Colo.: Westview Press, 1994).
49. See, for example, Patricia Collins, "The Social Construction of Black Feminist Thought," *Signs* 14, no. 4 (1989): 745–73, and Stanlie James and Abena Busia, *Theorizing Black Feminisms* (London: Routledge, 1993).
50. Rebecca Biron, "Feminist Periodicals and Political Crisis in Mexico: *fem, Debate Feminista*, and *La Correa Feminista* in the 1990s," *Feminist Studies* 22, no. 1 (1996): 151–69.

2 Postwar Development
International Institutions Marginalize Women

Making a difference in people's lives.
—World Bank

Fifty years is enough!
—1994 NGO coalition

International and national institutions operate within a global political-economic context, the framework for which conditions their opportunities and limitations in promoting their own changing definitions of development. Although this book has neither the focus nor the space for full analysis of the postwar global political economy and the changing intellectual meanings of development, it is important to establish the context for women's program birth and nurture.

This chapter is organized into three parts. First is a brief account of changing postwar international relations. Second is an outline of the major changes in thinking and discourse about this contested term, development. These sections provide the basis for the last and primary focus of this chapter: changing conceptions and differentiations of the field once called women in development (WID), a field bursting with new labels, as is evident below.

The Postwar Global Economy

At the close of World War II, competition among major world powers divided the world into East and West, establishing a cold war. Military alliances formalized these coalitions in the form of the North Atlantic Treaty Organization (NATO) and the Warsaw Pact. Foreign ministries managed the diplomatic side of international relations, and bilateral technical assistance agencies provided a material exchange to solidify these relations.

Bilateral Assistance

Although universally committed to promoting "development," in all its meanings, bilateral technical assistance institutions are not a

Table 2.1   DAC Countries: Net ODA

Country	% GNP	Current $billion
Denmark	0.97	1.6
Sweden	0.89	2.0
Norway	0.87	1.24
Netherlands	0.80	3.3
France	0.55	8.4
Canada	0.39	2.1
Belgium	0.38	1.03
Luxembourg	0.38	0.07
Australia	0.34	1.14
Switzerland	0.34	1.08
Austria	0.32	0.75
Finland	0.32	0.39
Germany	0.31	7.5
United Kingdom	0.29	3.2
Japan	0.28	14.5
Ireland	0.27	0.14
Portugal	0.27	0.27
New Zealand	0.23	0.12
Spain	0.23	1.3
Italy	0.14	1.5
United States	0.10	7.3

Source: Based on data from OECD, "Financial Flows to Developing Countries in 1995: Sharp Decline in Official Aid; Private Flows Rise," press release (Paris: 1996).

monolithic group. Their missions vary from export promotion to genuine concern about reducing poverty and implementing structural change. Steven Arnold's comparison of European models, the institutional characteristics of which are outlined later, provides us with some flavor of these differences.[1]

Institutions also vary in meeting the United Nations' target of 0.7 percent of gross national product (GNP) for official development assistance (ODA). The Scandinavian and Dutch agencies have regularly surpassed this target since the mid to late 1970s. In absolute terms, however, those national agencies are not among the biggest donors in the Organization for Economic Cooperation and Development, Development Assistance Committee (OECD/DAC) group. In recent years, the giants have been Japan and the United States, although the U.S. position has diminished, as shown in Table 2.1.

Some institutions selectively use development criteria to identify recipient countries, and others include political criteria. Historically, West

Germany, for example, had as a criterion the nonrecognition of its eastern neighbor, but now that neighbor is part of a united Germany. Political winds change frequently.

Several bilateral agencies run worldwide programs, and others concentrate on a select few or on former colonial territories. They exercise some leverage when their total assistance represents a proportional "critical mass" (20 percent or more) in a recipient country. Sweden concentrates its assistance.

The institutional arrangements for bilateral assistance range from inclusion in the state department or foreign ministry to cooperation between the ministry and an autonomous aid agency, which is not generally headed by an executive of cabinet-level rank. (The terminology is ministry and minister for parliamentary forms of government, and department, secretariat, and secretary for presidential forms of government, to be contrasted in the next chapter.) Even with such rank, the minister is rarely equivalent to the foreign minister. Institutions also vary in terms of their centralization. Few bilateral assistance agencies fund field offices in Southern countries; instead, they rely on diplomatic or commercial officers among embassy staff. Development expertise is not likely to be extensive among those who promote business and diplomacy.

Politically, bilateral assistance institutions vary in terms of their permeability to nongovernmental organization (NGO) influence. Some institutions are insulated from external influence, whereas others seek engagement with NGOs through advisory committees and through contracting arrangements for research or project implementation. Some European countries have the reputation for strong church-related NGOs with a humanistic orientation that counters the commercial and foreign policy interests in development assistance decision making. Public support for development assistance is strong in several European countries, aided by public education, strong civil society, and internationally minded NGOs. The Netherlands stands out in this regard.

Among many so-called developing countries of the South, nonaligned nations pursued independent foreign and domestic policies, and others allied themselves with East or West under conditions over which they lacked full control. (The respective terms for these country groupings, invented in 1950s France, were third, second, and first worlds.) Support for these alliances occurred through technical assistance for development, among other relations. Intellectuals in the "world system" or "dependency" schools of thought traced ties as far back as the emergence of global capitalism in the sixteenth century, solidified in stark ways with the establishment of colonialism.[2]

As might be imagined, on maps, "foreigners" drew boundaries around large land masses in Latin America, Asia, and Africa, for as long as a century or two, to extract resources and develop markets. The major colonial powers included Britain, France, Spain, the Netherlands, Germany, Portugal, the United States, and Belgium. Colonization left historical legacies that continue to affect economies and institutions even now. Among those historic legacies are state or political institutions and development ideologies that privilege men, widening or narrowing gender gaps.[3] For many of those Southern spaces, neocolonial relations persist.

The Cold War's Impact on Economic Strategy

The global division of East and West had ramifications for national economic systems. In the West, market-driven or capitalist economies prevailed; the East was characterized by centrally planned economies (called socialist economies by some) in which the state took the active lead in development initiatives. The difference also had political characteristics: allegedly democratic for the West, and authoritarian for the East, although the meaning of democracy for women will be taken up in other chapters.

As newly emergent nations, then called the "third world," gained their independence, the debate over capitalist versus socialist strategies fueled cold war–like debates. On occasion, these debates turned normal political contestations into civil wars with international allies for opposing sides. The tentative peace of this cold war for NATO and Warsaw Pact allies produced tragic consequences for the many who died in and after third world conflicts, from eastern, southeastern, and western Asia to the Caribbean and south-central Africa. Since World War II, 20 million people in the developing world have been killed in the supposed peace of the cold war.[4]

Whether conflicted or not, it is important to be attuned to the ideologies that guide policy choices. One categorization identifies three "thought-worlds": conservative, liberal, and radical, further differentiated by state orientation.[5] Although those situated in the United States (only 5 percent of the world's population) might view "liberal" as reformist and activist, the term's larger global meanings refer to limited states that oversee open market economies.[6]

Multilateral Development Assistance Institutions

Under the umbrella of the United Nations, development institutions operate, each with distinctive missions. Major bodies include the following:

- Food and Agriculture Organization (FAO) (created in 1945)

- United Nations Children's Fund (UNICEF) (1946)

- World Bank (IBRD) (1944, made operational in 1946)

- United Nations Development Programme (UNDP) (1965)

- UNIFEM, successor to UN Voluntary Fund for Women (1976)

- World Food Program (1963)

- International Fund for Agricultural Development (IFAD) (1974)

- United Nations Fund for Population Activities (UNFPA) (1969)

- International Labour Organization (ILO) (which in 1919 actually pre-ceded the UN's creation but became its first specialized agency)

All these organizations spawned women (or gender) units in the late 1970s and thereafter. What sort of difference they make in people's lives (from the chapter's epigraph) is a question. Their institutional commitments to "human development"—which the UNDP's *Human Development Report* defines as spending on primary education, health care and family planning, and mass-supply water and sanitation—range from a low 10 percent in the World Bank to 78 percent in UNICEF.[7] Budgets are bottom-line statements about priorities and missions.

Multilateral institutions are staffed with geographic representation in mind, although chief executives traditionally come from particular world regions. Their decision-making procedures are thought to privilege certain world regions or development conceptions. Nowhere is this more evident than in the international banking institutions, wherein economists promote open, market economies.

Institutions and Their Founders in Specific Eras

The conceptions prevalent during the founding era for these institutions had formative influences on their missions, staffing choices, and internal procedures. Once imprinted with the founding ideology, professional staff established institutional cultures and structures that became difficult to change.

The founding ideology reflected gender conceptions of the era. Institutions, by and large, privileged men as staff and constituents. Women's advocacy offices and their meager staff struggled in these hosts, seeking to transform them even as they were treated like political parasites. The trappings they developed—technical guidelines, gender training, and the like—

can be understood in this light, as we shall see in later sections and chapters. Yet in power relations terms, most of those offices were lacking, without authority to transform institutions.

The North-South Divide

Even as the cold war prevailed, North-South issues increasingly dominated international debates during the 1970s. Northern countries include the rich countries of North America, Europe, and Japan and the geographically anomalous Australia and New Zealand (what some called the "first world"); Southern countries include most of Asia, Africa, and the Latin American and Caribbean region (the "third world"). Examined in North-South terms, international inequalities were glaringly wide, as measured by a host of economic and social indicators. These inequalities widened in obscene ways over the next two decades.

Since 1990, the UNDP has published an annual *Human Development Report*, a counterpoint to the World Bank's *World Development Report*, begun in 1978. They provide data on shocking inequalities, which others have featured (if readers can imagine) as a wide champagne glass of wealth in the low-population North, supported by the slim stem of wealth but massive population in the South, with its 80 percent of the population.

> The poorest 20% of the world's people saw their share of global income decline from 2.3% to 1.4% in the past 30 years. Meanwhile the share of the richest 20% rose from 70% to 85%. That doubled the ratio of the shares of the richest and the poorest—from 30:1 to 61:1.[8]

In the late 1970s, increasing oil prices fueled spending, deficits, and inflation. Third world countries borrowed capital from private and international banks, and some continue to carry the debt burdens. Proponents of a new international economic order outlined ways to reduce structural biases and to provide a fairer arena in which to trade.[9] International conferences of the 1970s, on topics central to women, such as population and the environment, assumed acrimonious North-South dimensions; women's centrality dropped through the cracks.

Development thinking emphasized economic growth, especially industrial and urban growth. Alternative voices called for "growth with equity" and the need to meet "basic human needs."[10] Pioneering approaches, however paltry the funding, aimed to turn charitable droppings for women into equity projects. Major world powers such as the United States and Britain promoted government spending cuts (except for the military), open economies for freer trade, and deregulation, albeit within the rule of law. From this, as the phraseology of the time would have it, the "magic of the marketplace" could prevail.

International banking institutions negotiated structural adjustment and stabilization policies to pave the way for this paradigm. They put pressure on Southern countries to cut tariffs, civil servants, and government spending (meager as it was in some countries). "Trade, not aid" became the buzzwords of the time. Europeans negotiated a series of short-lived Lomé agreements to stabilize Southern countries' export earnings. Free trade, enshrined in the General Agreement on Tariffs and Trade (GATT), was in ascendancy, however. Ironically, regional blocs negotiated agreements on trade liberalization, such as the North American Free Trade Agreement (NAFTA), the Asia Pacific Economic Forum (APEC), and an expanding European Union.

Governments' social spending cuts had predictable consequences for health and well-being. UNICEF sponsored several studies that made the social costs of these cuts more visible, especially costs to women and children.[11] Some called the 1980s a "lost decade," registering declines in per capita income for Africa and Latin America, although gains in infant survival and life expectancy. Agencies justified their little attention to women on efficiency rather than equity or justice grounds. Donor "fatigue" had set in for a number of countries, with consequences for contributions to multilateral assistance institutions.

The Cold War and Aftermath: Democracy?

The most significant global changes, in the turn toward the 1990s, involved the end of the cold war and the transition toward market economies and fledgling democracies in what was called the Eastern bloc (or now defunct "second world"). Ironically, women's representation in parliamentary institutions dropped markedly under democracy, diminishing the global proportional totals from 13 to 10 percent.[12] Both bilateral and multilateral institutions shifted some attention to these transitional economies, redistributing funds away from the South.

Ideologically, the world became less polarized on economic terms, though not on ethnic or cultural terms. In this "triumph of capitalism," argues Robert Heilbroner, ways must be found to make capitalism work better. Without political and policy intervention, capitalism's tendencies toward extensive inequality and government-elite collusion produce unacceptable costs for the majority.[13]

If we are to take Heilbroner seriously, democracy becomes a primary goal, along with the strengthening of civil society such as NGOs. Forces have converged in the 1990s over the political basis of development decisions and the consequent logical significance of democracy, as enshrined in the UNDP's *Human Development Reports* and even in the World Bank's *World Development Reports*. For the World Bank, however, "good governance" is often reduced to creating the legal and regulatory conditions for healthy commercial exchanges.[14]

As we approach the millennium, those who seek to extend democracy to women through women and women-friendly NGOs might seize the opportune discursive space of democracy and good governance. Remember Elson: A "campaign for democratic politics is at the heart of a transformatory approach to structural adjustment."[15]

Reality checks the success of such campaigns, given the concentration of wealth and decision making over trade and the movement of capital. The World Trade Organization, GATT's successor, emerged as a more inclusive and permanent office with greater enforcement powers. Those who fund, formulate, and monitor the new global trade are only distantly related to politically accountable institutions housed at the national level. Instead, transnational corporations, some 37,000, control 70 percent of the products in international trade; their ownership is largely in Northern, white male hands.[16] The speed of telecommunications and the multiple allegiances of corporations call national control, loyalty, and accountability into question. Hazel Henderson highlights computerized trading alone, in which over $1 trillion daily is exchanged "in the global financial casino," driving policies in many nation-states.[17] The unseen and unaccountable hands of markets and transnational corporations bear little responsibility for costs their investment and disinvestment incur for society and the environment. People do, and occasionally their governments support or regulate those costs through politically accountable institutions.

The ILO has long worked with governments, employers, and unions to establish clauses and conventions for labor standards and work protections. Among core conventions are those on "the freedom to organise, the right to collective bargaining, and the freedom from forced labour."[18] Gender perspectives on the routine and women-specific issues within the working world are muted, and conventions are selectively enforced. The specific issues are significant for governments, employers, and workers: gendered wage gaps, sexual harassment, and maternity and parental leave rights. Then and now, feminists debate over protective legislation on matters such as childbirth.[19] Do leave rights make certain categories of workers more expensive? Whose labor profile is the worker norm: those capable of pregnancy, or those incapable? Whose bodies undergo reproductive labor?

Labor standards are regularly ignored, not the least of which is one on equal remuneration. Should governments, international organizations, or NGOs penalize employers or tolerate governments that abuse or ignore such standards? Governments in the South often oppose linkages between labor-standards compliance and ostensible privileges of free-trade provisions.

> The strongest opposition is from the Bangkok group of Asian countries led by the Prime Minister of Malaysia. Cheap and disciplined labour is seen as one of their greatest assets. They claim that attempts to impose labour standards on the South is a form of cultural imperialism and cover for Northern protectionism.[20]

Great debates over economic growth and equity are part of the discourse on development. Those who believe economic axioms about the incompatibilty of equity with growth ought to revisit political machinery, in which the beneficiaries from inequity have special connections.

Changing International Discourse: "Development"

Shifts in development discourse ran parallel to shifts in the postwar global political economy, as well as to its contestations. WID analysts often positioned themselves in connection with these shifts in the hope of engaging "mainstream" thinking, as will be more fully evident below.

Theoretical Approaches to Discourse Analysis

The study of politics has long been attuned to language, discourse, and rhetoric, or what Murray Edelman has termed the "politics of symbolic action."[21] In the last two decades, this orientation has deepened with critical reflection on "modern" paradigms and the need to challenge the assumptions of those texts. The work of French theorist Michel Foucault is perhaps most closely associated with this approach. Feminist theorists have joined efforts to "interrogate" modern texts in Western political theory and in administration and bureaucracy.[22]

In the mid-1980s, colleagues at the Institute of Social Studies (ISS), the Hague, problematized development policy discourse as follows: "Discursive actions can be taken as an example of the capture and exercise of power by some sorts of people, arguments and organizations against others through specific happenings, in particular arenas, over various periods of time."[23] What makes development discourse different, they continue, is that "it justifies itself as being professional and scientific, and on that account socially and politically and altogether unproblematic." Yet well before the mid-1980s, WID analysis questioned the scientific and seemingly politically unproblematic nature of development.

With an even more penetrating critique than that of the ISS, James Ferguson problematizes technical assistance institutions (a "development industry," he calls them) that generate their own discourse, a discourse that constructs countries as objects of knowledge and then organizes interventions on the basis of that constructed knowledge. Even though planned interventions fail regularly on their own terms, they have "regular effects, which include the expansion and entrenchment of bureaucratic state power, side by side with the projection of a representation of economic and social life which denies 'politics' and, to the extent that it is successful, suspends its effects."[24] Like others in the social sciences, Ferguson believes that we need to study the institutional apparatus, its discourse, and effects, as much as we study "cultural groups."

Development from the Postwar Period and Beyond

Postwar development discourse in the West was based heavily on industrialization, the stages of which constituted economic development. Agriculture and rural areas were neglected with this approach, and environmental costs had yet to be counted. The social side to this sort of economic development was the degree to which people acquired "modern" attitudes—not coincidentally, idealized attitudes found in already industrialized societies. A flurry of behavioralist "scientific" studies conducted surveys with men on "becoming modern."[25]

Critics from Southern countries usually reacted to such discourse in light of the global economic context. Some critics emphasized import-substitution national strategies, to shore up a domestic capitalist class; others in the dependency mode emphasized national self-reliance and rejected national collaboration with international capital forces. The sort of data drawn upon in these strategies rendered women virtually invisible in terms of their contributions toward the economy, as later chapters will outline.

As global and income disparities became aggravated, mainstream critiques of industrialization focused on strategies that became known as "growth with equity" and "basic human needs" strategies during the 1970s. Those who promoted equitable growth justified an activist state that responded to a redistributive challenge, whereas basic human needs focused on food and shelter with a common phrase of the time, the "poorest of the poor." WID analysts during this era sought linguistic leverage from some of the major themes in this approach: gender equity and the concentration of women, or women-headed households, in poverty.

Economic crises as the 1980s approached led to major paradigm shifts, and international banking institutions began playing a larger role in the production of development knowledge. The World Bank dramatically increased its publications and thus its influence on the mainstream, especially with its *World Development Reports*, each with a thematic focus.[26] For reasons such as these, this "development industry" became an extremely important institution for development and for women. In 1984, the *World Development Report*'s thematic focus on population attended to women. In 1988, the report included its first "Women in Development" table.

As early as 1983, World Bank analysts emphasized problems of swollen states and their disincentives to open market economies. Through conditional lending, they negotiated and monitored stabilization and structural adjustment policies. Southern governments cut subsidies, leaving intact, however, military excesses.

By the end of the 1980s adjustment decade, voices called for resources to cope with the social costs of adjustment, in the name of "antipoverty" strategies. Even the World Bank's *World Development Report* focused on poverty alleviation in 1990. Analysts identified women and children as especially burdened by adjustment, a burden that threatened the success of adjustment itself.[27] Yet for bankers, said critics like Diane Elson, the state problem was to be "tackled by rolling back the state rather than transforming it."[28] Meanwhile, the debt burden continues to bear heavily on many countries in the South, with debt service consuming approximately a quarter to a third of export earnings in countries such as Argentina, Côte d'Ivoire, Brazil, Mexico, Morocco, Tanzania, and Nigeria.[29]

Multiple policy strategies are pursued in the name of "development," a word almost reified but commonly used. How is that development experienced? Gustavo Esteva says it well: The term development "appears mostly in jokes. . . . If you live in Mexico City today, you are either rich or numb if you fail to notice that development stinks."[30]

Changing Discourse: Women in Development

We can hardly begin this section without acknowledging the foremother of women in development: Danish economist Ester Boserup. A specialist and credible expert on agricultural development, she argued that modernization strategies undermined both women farmers and agricultural production in *Woman's Role in Economic Development*, published in 1970. As others would conclude in later tributes to her, Boserup made both an efficiency and a justice argument, but she did not take economic class into account.[31] The connection of diverse women to "women in development" must be understood in the contexts of shifting discourse and realities—some of it hardly "developmental," with its optimistic ring.

Women's work became the emphasis in WID analysis, a long-overdue counterpart to the more narrow focus of demographers and population experts who worried about controlling women's reproduction. The reproductive focus identified women almost solely with pregnancy and motherhood, particularly during the ages when women are "at risk" for reproduction.[32] Analysts problematized high population growth rates, not women's health.

Theory for Ideologically Differentiated Practice

Unlike Western women's or gender studies research, international women's studies takes theory and applies it to practice.[33] United Nations–sponsored international women's conferences provided forums in which recommendations and strategies could be articulated from Mexico City to Beijing, not to mention all the regional and preparatory meetings for these events.

WID's applied focus differentiated discursive camps. One highlighted possibilities for change in existing political economies; the other did not. For example, WID analysts of agriculture generally supported changes in laws, policies, and implementation to increase women's access to landownership, credit, and extension advice.[34] Other analysts criticized the economic model itself. For example, some analysts who focused on women in industrial production, increasingly in export-processing industries, criticized tainted connections with the global economic forces, women's participation within, and the legitimacy of the systems themselves. Others applauded increasing female labor force participation along with the skills and organizational connections women acquired. Still others bristled about the patronizing cues from Northern feminists, albeit concerned about exploitation.[35] The earliest differentiation of the 1970s was between so-called liberal-feminist and Marxist- or socialist-feminist camps, a differentiation that lingered in the 1980s.[36]

On a system that one theorist calls the "sex-gender system,"[37] both camps agreed: the hierarchical divide between male and female, in terms of control over assets (income, land, value accorded to labor), required elimination, not merely reform. Such critique posed major challenges to both existing political economies and their ostensibly revolutionary replacements. Topics like these were absent from most political agendas, and WID analysts helped put them on intellectual agendas. A decade later, these concerns manifested themselves in critiques of unitary household models (the "new household economics"), along with questions about not only the division and control of income within households but also subhousehold incentives for responding to policy incentives.[38] Intrahousehold inequalities have tragic consequences, as observers chillingly note in studies of sex ratios in Asia (discussed in a later chapter).

Yet WID analysts were late to address the explicitly gendered aspects of subordination, such as rape and domestic violence. Women's NGOs at the UN-sponsored international meetings helped shift the focus from economics alone to explicitly women's issues that cut across ideological, class, and national lines (a summary of the comprehensive Beijing Platform of Action was appended to Chapter 1).

Institutionally Differentiated Practice: Micro Level

From the 1970s through the early 1980s—the heyday of project-based technical assistance—analyses began to differentiate project types, focusing first on projects particularly for women, known as "women-specific projects." Critics of welfare approaches matched critics of mainstream projects oriented toward relief, service delivery, or charity; once funding ended, they generally could not be sustained. With this approach, women were viewed not as active participants in making their history but rather as victims. Pre-WID women's projects tended to be welfare oriented. Even as technical assistance and NGOs began gearing up to implement WID projects, bureaucracies persisted with welfare approaches, thus burdening WID with the reputation for project failure. As Mayra Buvinić would later label them, these kinds of projects "misbehaved."[39]

But project differentiation began to occur, and WID analysts classified projects into several types. One compared "equity" and "antipoverty" approaches to WID research and action. The equity approach was long associated with legal approaches to women's status in postwar UN work, whereas the antipoverty approach involved specific interventions for low-income women or female-headed households. There was a fine line, advocates learned, between women's characterization as victims as opposed to agents in change.

The early 1980s global political economy set the stage for an "efficiency" approach to emerge. Project and program performance improves with women's integration into ongoing sectors, according to this approach; efficiency approaches rarely result in questions being raised about restructuring the meaning and practice of "development" itself. When underpaid (or nonpaid) women become more efficient, who benefits?

WID advocates who struggled in resistant agencies often contributed to efficiency thinking, for their wary colleagues were not about to act on WID policies for equity or justice concerns, particularly in an era hostile to such notions. Moreover, WID advocates rarely exercised the kind of leverage or controlled enough resources to confront the mammoth task of challenging the overall development missions of institutions in which they were situated.

During the mid-1980s, analysts published a flurry of cases for use in training programs and courses. The first of such monographs was *The Nemow Case*,[40] a composite of integrated development project disasters for women through resettlement schemes. In 1985, a group affiliated with and near Harvard University developed the Harvard case study approach.[41] Ingrid Palmer oversaw a series of monograph-length cases on land, migration, agricultural policy, and resettlement policy and program action with Kumarian Press.

The mainstream of the "development industry," focused on sector-based assistance, helped elevate the micro- and project-oriented approach to women, thus paving the way for technical assistance institutions to move beyond women-specific projects to integrated or mainstreamed approaches that would influence all institutional operations. But sector-based thinking tended to compartmentalize action into such categories as health, family planning, and credit. People had yet to match the micro and middle approaches with global or macroeconomic policy trends that burdened or benefited women.

With the interest in mainstream integration came a shift toward the use of the word "gender" as opposed to "women." By gender, people call attention to the *social construction* of what it means to be male and female in different contexts. Gender emphasizes *relations between men and women*. In institutional terms, the word "gender" signals the spread of responsibility to men and to *gender gaps*; it underlines the significance of people's centrality to sectoral policies. Used as an adjective, it allows the word "sex" (still given to chuckles and jokes) to be avoided, as in "gender-disaggregated data." As Jahan remarks, however, gender terminology and meaning do not translate well into a variety of languages; also, the shift in labels caused confusion and instability in some institutions.[42]

Institutionally Differentiated Practice: Macro-Micro Links

WID's definitive turning point came in the Development Alternatives with Women for a New Era (DAWN) collective, a global group born in Bangalore, India, in 1984. The book *Development, Crises, and Alternative Visions: Third World Women's Perspectives* problematized development conceptions, challenged macro-level policies that caused systemic crises, applauded a diversity of feminisms, and offered alternative visions of a reconstructed development approach in which women's voice and power were central. The first chapter's opening heading claimed a "vantage point of poor women" and criticized "cultural traditions" that maintained female subordination.[43] One could also position DAWN's analysis within what remained of world-system or dependency approaches. DAWN's approach would later be labeled "empowerment," for it emphasized women's agency and collective organization.

Macro-level policy approaches also flourished, but outside the critical traditions of dependency or world-system approaches. Economists used language compatible with the mainstream discipline. For the UN International Research and Training Institute for the Advancement of Women (INSTRAW), Susan Joekes analyzed women in the world economy, and for the ILO, Palmer analyzed gender in population and agricultural and nonagricultural market structures, placing the work squarely within the context of structural economic change.[44] Rather than ask about the effects of structural adjustment on gender, she turns this around to the obstructions gender poses to market reform effectiveness. Mainstream decision makers may disregard gender, but can they ignore obstacles to the effectiveness of the policies they advocate?

Engagement with the discipline so dominant in development studies—economics—requires WID analysts to understand and critique its "male bias," as Elson terms it. Structural adjustment models assume that switching resources from nontradable to tradable goods and services is costless. Women carry the burden of nonremunerated work, and "what is regarded by economists as an increase in productivity or efficiency may instead be a shifting of costs from the paid economy to the unpaid economy."[45] Elson shows how households absorb costs of resource reallocation in ways that have repercussions for variables of concern to macroeconomists.

A distinction that cut across the macro-micro divide also clarified levels of change. Moser resurrected Molyneux's critique of Nicaragua based on the regime's attention to women's "practical" versus "strategic" interests. In a useful application to institutional technical assistance strategies, Moser defines strategic gender needs as those that "are formulated from the analysis of women's subordination to men," whereas practical gender needs are those that "are formulated from the concrete conditions women experience, in their engendered position within the sexual division of labor and deriving out of this their practical gender interests for human survival." Use of the term "gender," she says, is preferred for its emphasis on social positioning and its implied heterogeneity.[46]

Yet another attempt to differentiate WID was based on the type of

people active in the field: advocates, practitioners, and scholars. According
to Irene Tinker, long associated with the "equity" approach, advocates consisted of political appointees and lobbyists, practitioners, bureaucratic insiders and consultants, and scholars were a more autonomous and diverse
group.[47]

The international Association of Women in Development (AWID) also
makes use of a tripartite grouping of policymakers, academics, and practitioners, the latter more broadly defined to include grassroots activists.[48]
Its conferences institutionalize "trialogue," and its organizational structure institutionalizes trialogue through rotating presidencies among the
three groups.

Such groupings permit a focus on the rhetorical strategies that exist for
different audiences and, as such, allow some sense to be made of the highly
differentiated WID discourse. Nevertheless, approaches do carry with them
constructions and images that have concrete effects on technical assistance
and research strategies.

Implications

The postwar period has produced enormous change in the discourse and context of development, in which WID discourse has sought
some space. Without WID analysis, the multiplication of development institutions and discourses would have occurred with little or no attention to
women, thus further marginalizing them.

WID language has aligned itself with these shifts in contexts and discourses, simultaneously clinging to and distancing itself from mainstream
development thinking. To "speak truth to power" has long been the goal of
policy analysts, but just how similar must the speech be to the master's language? WID analysts nearly tip over on a fine dividing line: on one side is
the unproblematized "development industry," which requires transformation; on the other side is the need to speak a common language without
buying into its basic assumptions and values. Some view efficiency and
macroeconomic policy languages as evidence of tipping.

WID advocates' national and bureaucratic experiences, covered in the
next chapter, will make clearer the context in which this communication
takes place. It is an institutional context that began under resistant conditions but that has more recently provided space for dialogue and action. Yet
these institutions, by and large, are permeated with male bias in thought
and action.

Notes

1. Steven H. Arnold, *Implementing Development Assistance: European Approaches to Basic Needs* (Boulder, Colo.: Westview Press, 1982).
2. Immanuel Wallerstein, *The Modern World System* (New York: Academic Press, 1976). Also see writers associated with the dependency school, many of whom write from Latin American vantage points, for example, Christine E. Bose and Edna Acosta-Belén, eds., *Women in the Latin American Development Process* (Philadelphia: Temple University Press, 1995), and Sharon Stichter and Jane Parpart, eds., *Women, Employment and the Family in the International Division of Labour* (Philadelphia: Temple University Press, 1994). For a book that focuses on African self-sufficiency rather than global integration as a solution (and addresses women therein), see Bill Rau, *From Feast to Famine: Official Cures and Grassroots Remedies to Africa's Food Crisis* (London: Zed, 1991).
3. For literature on gender and the state internationally, see Sue Ellen Charlton et al. eds., *Women, the State and Development* (Albany, N.Y.: SUNY Albany Press, 1989). An extensive literature on colonization traces negative impacts, though it does not differentiate among women and types of impacts.
4. United Nations Research Institute for Social Development (UNRISD), *States of Disarray* (Geneva: UNRISD, 1995), p. 110.
5. David Goldsworthy, "Thinking Politically about Development," *Development and Change* 19 (1988): 508.
6. See my discussion in Kathleen Staudt, *Managing Development: State, Society and International Contexts* (Newbury Park, Calif.: Sage, 1991), chap. 4.
7. UNDP, *Human Development Report 1994* (New York: Oxford University Press, 1994), p. 74.
8. UNDP, *Human Development Report 1996* (New York: Oxford University Press, 1996), p. 2.
9. Bernard D. Rossiter, *The Global Struggle for More: Third World Conflicts with Rich Nations* (New York: Harper & Row, 1987).
10. UNDP, *Human Development Report 1996*, chap. 2.
11. Giovanni Andrew Cornia, Richard Jolly, and Frances Stewart, eds., *Adjustment with a Human Face*, vols. 1 and 2 (Oxford: Clarendon Press, 1987). Also see Lourdes Benería and Shelley Feldman, eds., *Unequal Burden: Economic Crises, Persistent Poverty, and Women's Work* (Boulder, Colo.: Westview Press, 1992).
12. UNDP, *Human Development Report 1995* (New York: Oxford University Press, 1995), with a thematic focus on gender. The Intergovernmental Parliamentary Union (IPU) in Geneva keeps a running tab on women's representation.
13. Robert Heilbroner, "Reflections: The Triumph of Capitalism," *The New Yorker*, January 23, 1989.
14. In the *World Bank Policy Research Bulletin* "Ah, Governance," 1994.
15. Diane Elson, "From Survival Strategies to Transformation Strategies," in Benería and Feldman, *Unequal Burden*, p. 39.
16. Women Working Worldwide, *World Trade Is a Women's Issue* (Manchester: WWW, n. d.), pp. 1, 3. Also see various issues of the newsletter *News and Views*, published by the Women's Environment & Development Organization (WEDO); Susan Joekes and Ann Weston, *Women and the New Trade Agenda* (New York: UNIFEM, 1995). Robert Reich, in *The Wealth of Nations* (New York: Vintage, 1991), uses the deterritorialization of corporate loyalty to make the case for government investments in its people: the residents around which territories are drawn.

17. Hazel Henderson is cited in a review about her book, *Building a Win-Win World: Life Beyond Global Economic Warfare* (New York: Berrett-Koehler 1996), p. 196.
18. Women Working Worldwide, *World Trade Is a Women's Issue*, p. 11.
19. Linda Lim, *More and Better Jobs for Women: An Action Guide* (Geneva: ILO, 1996), pp. 43–44. She supports the ILO position to strengthen women's right to maternity protection, while periodically updating legislative protection with timely scientific and technological knowledge.
20. Women Working Worldwide, *World Trade Is a Women's Issue*, p. 12.
21. Murray Edelman, *The Symbolic Uses of Politics* (Champaign and Urbana: University of Illinois Press, 1964). Deborah Stone's comparison of political rhetoric is quite useful in *Policy Paradox: The Art of Political Decision Making* (New York: W. W. Norton, 1997), chap. 6.
22. Christine di Stefano, *Configurations of Masculinity: A Feminist Perspective* (Ithaca, N.Y.: Cornell University Press, 1991); Kathy Ferguson, *The Feminist Case against Bureaucracy* (Philadelphia: Temple University Press, 1984), and "Women, Feminism, and Development," in *Women, International Development and Politics: The Bureaucratic Mire*, 1st ed., edited by Kathleen Staudt (Philadelphia: Temple University Press, 1990); Catherine Scott, *Gender and Development: Rethinking Modernization and Dependency Theory* (Boulder, Colo.: Lynne Rienner, 1995); Marianne H. Marchand and Jane L. Parpart, eds., *Feminism/Postmodernism/Development* (London: Routledge, 1995).
23. Raymond Apthorpe, "Development Policy Discourse," *Public Administration and Development* 6 (1986): 377.
24. James Ferguson, *The Anti-Politics Machine: "Development," Depoliticization and Bureaucratic Power in Lesotho* (New York: Cambridge University Press, 1990), pp. xiv–xv, 17.
25. Alex Inkeles, *Becoming Modern* (Cambridge, Mass.: Harvard University Press, 1974). See W. W. Rostow, *The Stages of Economic Growth* (Cambridge: Cambridge University Press, 1960).
26. For a chart on this growth, see Kathleen Staudt and William Weaver, *Political Science and Feminisms: Integration or Transformation?* (New York: Twayne/Macmillan, 1997), p. 109.
27. See note 12. On the threat that the neglect of gender posed to structural adjustment, see Ingrid Palmer, *Gender and Population in the Adjustment of African Economies: Planning for Change* (Geneva: ILO, 1991).
28. Elson, "From Survival Strategies to Transformation Strategies," p. 33.
29. UNRISD, *States of Disarray*, p. 41.
30. Gustavo Esteva, "Development: Metaphor, Myth, Threat," *Development: Seeds of Change* 3 (1985): 78.
31. Jane Jaquette, "Gender and Justice in Economic Development," in *Persistent Inequalities: Women and World Development*, edited by Irene Tinker (New York: Oxford University Press, 1990), and Lourdes Benería and Gita Sen, "Class and Gender Inequalities and Women's Role in Economic Development—Theoretical and Practical Implications," *Feminist Studies* 1 (1982): 157–76.
32. Jane Jaquette and Kathleen Staudt, "Women as 'At Risk' Reproducers: Biology, Science and Population in U.S. Foreign Policy," in *Women, Biology and Public Policy*, edited by Virginia Sapiro (Beverly Hills, Calif.: Sage, 1985), pp. 235–68.
33. Aruna Rao, *Women's Studies International: Nairobi and Beyond* (New York: Feminist Press, 1991).
34. Kathleen Staudt, *Agricultural Policy Implementation: A Case Study from Western Kenya* (West Hartford, Conn.: Kumarian Press, 1985). Also see Chapter 5 of this book.

35. Linda Lim, "Women's Work in Export Factories: The Politics of a Cause," in Tinker, *Persistent Inequalities*, pp. 101–19.
36. Jane Jaquette, "Women and Modernization Theory: A Decade of Feminist Criticism," *World Politics* 34, no. 2 (1982): 276–84, who also identified a female-sphere critique (which falls within Chapter 1's maternal feminism camp); Asoka Bandarage, "Women in Development: Liberalism, Marxism and Marxist-Feminism," *Development and Change* 15 (1984): 495–515.
37. Gayle Rubin, "The Traffic in Women: Notes on the 'Political Economy' of Sex," in *Toward an Anthropology of Women*, edited by Rayna Reiter (New York: Monthly Review Press, 1975), pp. 157–210.
38. Daisy Dwyer and Judith Bruce, eds., *A Home Divided: Women and Income in the Third World* (Stanford, Calif.: Stanford University Press, 1988); Lourdes Benería and Martha Roldán, *The Crossroads of Class and Gender: Industrial Homework Subcontracting and Household Dynamics in Mexico City* (Chicago: University of Chicago Press, 1987); Kathleen Staudt, "Uncaptured or Unmotivated? Women and the Food Crisis in Africa," *Rural Sociology* 52 no. 1 (1987): 37–55.
39. Mayra Buvinić, "Projects for Women in the Third World: Explaining Their Misbehavior," *World Development* 14, no. 5 (1986).
40. Ingrid Palmer, *The Nemow Case* (West Hartford, Conn.: Kumarian Press, 1985).
41. Catherine Overholt et al., *Gender Roles in Development Projects: A Case Book* (West Hartford, Conn.: Kumarian Press, 1985).
42. Rounaq Jahan, *The Elusive Agenda: Mainstreaming Women in Development* (London: Zed, 1995), p. 26.
43. Gita Sen and Caren Grown, *Development, Crises, and Alternative Visions: Third World Women's Perspectives* (New York: Monthly Review Press, 1987).
44. Susan Joekes, *Women in the World Economy* (New York: Oxford University Press, 1987); Palmer, *Gender and Population*.
45. Diane Elson, "Male Bias in Macro-Economics: The Case of Structural Adjustment," in *Male Bias in the Development Process*, edited by Diane Elson (Manchester: Manchester University Press, 1991), pp. 164–90.
46. Caroline O. N. Moser, *Gender Planning and Development: Theory, Practice and Training* (London: Routledge, 1993), and her "Gender Planning in the Third World: Meeting Practical and Strategic Needs," *World Development* 17, no. 11 (1989): 1803.
47. Tinker, *Persistent Inequalities*, pp. 35–52.
48. The Association for Women in Development can be reached at 1511 K Street, NW, Suite 825, Washington, D.C. 20005.

3 Women Engaging Public Affairs
Institutions Matter

> ... politics is not a dirty word.
> —Vina Mazumdar

In the government, people make decisions about public values. They decide how to spend money, they struggle over program priorities in spending, and they decide how to extract revenue from people. Outside of government, people influence decisions about taxing, spending, and program priorities through individual and collective strategies. All too often, an overwhelming number of those people engaged in political action—whether inside or outside government—are men. And these men only occasionally "see the world through women's eyes," to use the phrase of the 1995 World Conference on Women in Beijing, China.

Women, both inside and outside of government, have tried to influence government spending, taxing, and program priorities. They do so with mixed success. Women's success or failure depends on the kinds of political institutions with which they engage. Institutional histories, legacies, and choices matter. Through institutions, people try to hold governments accountable to them. Representative institutions are more or less accountable and accessible to women's voices, along with policy visions "through women's eyes." Historic legacies of inaccessibility have led many women to disengage rather than engage with those institutions. Such political action also has consequences, for women and for effective public policy. In this chapter, I analyze both presidential and parliamentary systems, as well as electoral formulas and the possibilities those formulas offer for narrow to wide ideological political party agendas.

Representative systems, no matter their success or failure in responding to women, operate within and depend on bureaucracies to carry out the policies and laws they support. Bureaucracies are with us, for better or worse. And bureaucracies may or may not operate within rules of law that are consistently enforced. Thus in this chapter, we must also analyze bureaucracies. Across national boundaries, bureaucracies often operate outside of representative and accountable governance. These international agencies, therefore, are potential renegades, operating according to their own norms.

How can women and gender, then, be "mainstreamed"? This topic is taken up in the latter part of the chapter.

Representative Systems

At the outset of the United Nations, member nations numbered a mere quarter of the nearly 200 nations now part of the General Assembly. Even though national numbers have multiplied, those nations are a fraction of the thousands of cultural groups that claim—through leaders or mass political identity—social patterns distinctive enough to merit autonomy within nations or even self-government. These are the nations—and the external and internal boundaries—that men have made.

The majority of countries now claim the word "democracy" in their governance. By the mid-1990s, Freedom House had counted about one-third of countries to be full democracies and another third to be partial democracies.[1] By claiming democracy, the countries and their leaders point to periodic elections wherein voters can choose representatives to speak and decide on their interests within a constitutional and legal framework that spells out acceptable rules and procedures. Those choices frequently take the form of political parties that recruit candidates for office and mobilize support for electoral victories, based on personality, policy, and ideological frameworks. Party choices range from factions within one party organization to two major parties to multiple party choices. Democracy further means that people and the press can speak relatively freely.

Democracy has not traditionally been defined in other important terms. In economic terms, the claim of democracy exists without accountability from commercial and corporate structures or with massive economic disparity between rich and poor or between men and women.

Nor has democracy traditionally been defined in gendered terms. Historically, nation-states claim the democracy label coincident with denying women the electoral franchise or the opportunity to hold public office. (Just a handful of countries, located in western Asia, deny women the vote.) In contemporary times, total or near-total male political monopolies coexist with the democratic label, not to mention men's monopolization of the opportunities, subsidies, benefits, and patronage from the political process. Women in development—as a field of study and as a practice—was born with the documentation of male privilege in the distribution of public resources.

Let us return, nevertheless, to the conceptions of democracy based on choices, freedoms, and constitutional procedures. Two systems of representation exist—

parliamentary and presidential—along with two basic electoral forms that select single members to represent districts rather than multiple members selected in proportion to votes for their parties. Outside of these basics, some countries opt for combination or hybrid systems. These systems matter for women in two ways: they open or close space that women might occupy, and they provide incentives for multiple ideological parties, some of which can build their policy programs around women's (or men's) policy agendas.

Parliamentary government, the most common form of government, fuses the legislative body (or bodies, for many are bicameral, with two representative houses) with the chief executive, known as the prime minister. Often the prime minister heads the party with the majority of seats in the parliament. This chief executive is "prime" among ministers in the cabinet, many of whom are loyal and senior members of the dominant party who work with permanent secretaries—senior civil servants in government ministries. This fusion of power leads to efficient decision making, to the extent that party members are loyal, but it is so efficient that the fusion can take advantage of and abuse the power that rests on government resources.

In presidential government, a less common form of government but prevalent in the Americas, power is ostensibly divided among three branches of government. The chief executive, the president, heads the executive branch, where appointed secretaries head government departments. In the legislative branch, congressional representatives operate separately in a process that ultimately seeks compromise and compatibility for laws to pass. Decision making is inefficient and fragmented, but branch power abuses can be checked. A third, judicial branch is supposed to ensure compatibility with ever-changing interpretations of the constitution.

These brief outlines are the ideal, textbook versions of parliamentary and presidential systems. The reality often differs, depending on historical and institutional legacies. For example, presidents manage the most powerful of three ostensibly equal branches in the Americas. And the use of the term "secretary" for a chief appointee or civil servant in government agencies is ironic, for the feminization of the huge occupational group called secretary has disempowered and cheapened this advisory and support labor, once historically recognized for its value.

How do women fare as chief executives and cabinet ministers or appointees in parliamentary and presidential systems? The small pool of women chief executives (rarely exceeding a dozen at any one time) is almost evenly divided between both systems. Each system produces equally small percentages of women in cabinet positions, less than a tenth.[2]

However, if the parliamentary-presidential distinction is coupled with attention to electoral formulas, we begin to understand other important ways that institutions matter. The major divide in electoral formulas is based on single member (SM) versus proportional representation (PR) formulas. When a single member represents a district, electoral arrangements provide incentives for two big parties, each aiming at a presumed majority around the center rather than at the polar ideologies of Right and Left. When multiple members represent a district, electoral arrangements provide incentives for multiple parties to compete along an ideological continuum. The French political scientist Maurice Duverger identified these classic patterns nearly half a century ago, but it took feminist political scientists to explore implications for women's representation and policy agendas.

An examination of the relatively small group of established democracies consistently shows that women fare better under proportional representation. The pattern continues to hold with an examination of a larger pool of established and partial democracies.[3] Women have consistently higher rates of national parliamentary and legislative representation under PR.

Yet the skeletal structures alone tell little of the lengthy political struggles to occupy a larger space in parties and subsequently parliamentary and legislative representation. In Scandinavian countries with parliamentary PR, women worked within parties—the most receptive of them labor and social democratic parties—to install quotas of women on winnable parts of lists from which representatives would be chosen. European green parties, although never majority parties, have instituted the most far-reaching affirmative action in gender quotas, requiring that "every other seat" be female. Left-of-center parties such as these have ideological platforms in which redistributive social justice agendas are compatible with many women's issues. However, in many South American countries, despite PR and ideologically Left choices, women's names have generally sunk to the bottom of lists for unwinnable seats. However, Argentina passed a 30 percent quota law that it enforced for all parties.[4]

As subsequent chapters will develop, a woman's face or even several women's faces on cabinets and in parliaments can hardly build the basis for broader, gender-responsive policy agendas. Some of the 90 percent or more of men must support those agendas, and the differences among men often fall along an ideological divide. Under British conservative parliamentary rule (SM) for two decades, even with a female prime minister, the party nominated and supported few women for seats or cabinet posts. Labor party rule offered more space to women, but in the 1997 electoral triumph, not before.

Once women occupy political space in sizable numbers, they can no longer be pigeonholed and stereotyped, muting the gender agenda. However, women's own ideological diversity complicates the political agenda, and gender priorities will be negotiated among them as well. Will there be common ground? In several countries, women form caucuses and coalitions over issues such as health and violence, but they will be cross-pressured over other issues. Whether there is a coalescence and who coalesces over gendering policies to alleviate poverty and respect human rights will be critical for strengthened women's capacity. Women are disproportionately represented among the poor, and only recently have their rights been officially viewed as compatible with human rights.

Once laws and policies pass from the overt political process, they enter the more closed but still political world of bureaucracies, both national and international. Among the most common responses to women's political demands is a women or gender unit in bureaucracy or a full ministry devoted to women. To bureaucracies we now turn.

Bureaucracies: Nonrepresentative Systems

Two decades have passed since the first women's advocacy offices were established in government and international technical assistance institutions. In governments, they have been called women's bureaus and ministries of women's affairs. Strapped with low budgets, limited staff, and initial resistance to their mandate, women's program staff pursued various strategies with uneven effects on their home institutions.

Political forces outside and within institutions are at the heart of effective change. We need to examine the institutional settings of women's programs, along with the contexts within those institutions. But women's advocacy in institutions is different from other advocacy, given the ways in which men's interests have been institutionalized. To illustrate the sort of political energy necessary to confront institutionalized privilege, we review literature on women/gender advocacy, emphasizing both bureaucratic and political strategies.

Politics in Institutional Settings

More than half a century ago, it was common for people to assume that politics and administration were separate and distinct activities. In this idealized conception, political decisions and laws were delivered to public institutions, where impartial public servants enforced them in neutral and technical ways. In this conception, the particular character of institutions mattered little compared with institutional control over subordinates.

From the postwar period onward, few who studied government operated under the delusions of the politics-administration distinction. Rather, administration is politics through other means, labeled "bureaucratic politics."[5] Those inside institutions compete with one another for valued resources, authority, and the power to define and frame issues. To achieve their goals, they bargain, negotiate, and build coalitions. They develop procedures to enforce policies and laws. They also alter the incentive structures in which staff work. Outside the study of government, the political-administration distinction still prevails to mystify people; institutions promote the image that enforcement is technical and impartial. We examined the discourse of the development industry (James Ferguson's term) in the last chapter.

People also once assumed that governments were coherent, unified entities. At the international level, parallel assumptions exist about the coherence of United Nations–affiliated bodies. Governments (like the UN family) are never monolithic entities. Rather, institutions within government (or within the UN family), which emerge out of particular historic and ideological contexts, are autonomous entities worthy of analysis in their own right. Institutions compete with one another for budgetary resources, for authority over programs, and for the power to define and frame issues.

Institutions have been packed together around a hierarchical grid and a formal division of labor, labeled as bureaus, offices, and departments, among other names. One can visualize composite parts in an organizational chart or a telephone directory, but these provide only the most obvious of units around which to understand what goes on inside institutions and why. Analysts must further unpack institutions to examine power relations within and between institutional parts.

In some idealized models, institutional change works from top to bottom in a hierarchical system. First, a new policy is made at the level of chief executive. Second, it is made operational with a plan. Third, it is communicated to those who put policies into practice, reinforced with guidelines, procedures, and research that disaggregates data. Communication methods range from memos and booklets to seminars and short courses. Fourth, just to make sure that no laggards remain, checkpoints are in place at the start of design or implementation. Then policy advocates keep their fingers crossed, in the hope that all will go well. Evaluations, if completed, validate the extent to which these inputs worked.

The Organization for Economic Cooperation and Development (OECD) Development Assistance Committee (DAC) created WID guidelines that provide a framework around which to organize and compare advocacy units in bilateral institutions.[6] It is a top-down, input-oriented model that provides few hints about institutional power relations, competitive struggles, or coalition building within and outside institutions.

Gender/women's program work occurs in large, hierarchically organized bilateral and multilateral institutions. This is perhaps the worst possible space for effective and creative work that is responsive to users. In their ideal form, said "father of sociology" Max Weber, institutions are characterized by a division of labor, depersonalized rules and procedures, recruitment and promotion by objective standards, and ultimate responsibility concentrated at the top of its pyramidal, hierarchical formal structure. The top-down, input-oriented model, ideally, would work with machine-like efficiency.

Advocacy in Institutions

Institutions do not operate in their idealized form. Alongside formal structure, informal power relations operate, easing task completion for some, and mystifying work for others. Executive authority dissipates as it passes downward through the hierarchy; Anthony Downs calls this a "leakage of authority."[7] Executive policies are routinely ignored or undermined; frequently they are made for symbolic reasons anyway, to appease outside constituencies or to build a good image.[8]

Conditions like these should forewarn all new policy advocates, women/gender or otherwise. Institutional policies do not automatically imply institutional practice; however, the articulation of a policy can be used as leverage to promote practice.

Rationality, including the use of new research to inform decision making, is assumed to prevail, but administrative labor provides little time, space, or incentive for translating (from "academese") research to practice, absorbing insights along the way. Moreover, disciplinary blinders may lead toward a tunnel vision over findings deemed irrelevant, such as the blinders many economists wear about women and gender. Although bureaucracies may commission research from outside contractors, all too often, institutional goals frame research agendas.

Institutional policymakers struggle over budgets, authority, ideology, and jurisdiction. They use resources strategically in light of short- and long-term goals. In a vertical sense, they build bases of support within institutions; in a horizontal sense, coalition partners cooperate over tactics to achieve their goals. Coalitions may extend to outside constituencies, members of which share mutual interests and ideologies in particular programs or initiatives. Political dynamics like these are often obscured with the use of technical language and rationales.

New policy advocates, WID or otherwise, must develop political skills to maneuver and succeed in institutional politics. Yet they must also develop the technical expertise to legitimize themselves. Ironically, they must not appear too "political," for the myths of technical rationality still prevail. Advocacy skills are based on a diagnosis of organizational culture.

Organizational Cultures

Institutions have their own distinctive cultures. Organizational cultures are defined as norms, rituals, and values about appropriate work behavior, often drawing on unique language, including acronyms and justifications that have meanings for participants in institutional settings.[9] In essence, culture can be found in participants' everyday work lives. To understand this culture, one must understand the history of the institution, including its founders, professional staff, disciplinary training, and mission.

Cultures sustain themselves through recruiting and rewarding those who assimilate. Yet no culture is static. Cultures change in response to crisis, including budgetary crisis; to new executives and associated staff replacements; and to resistant subcultures whose members build coalitions for change. Those who seek to redistribute institutional resources, or to transform development paradigms, fall within such subcultures.

New policy advocates, women/gender or otherwise, must *diagnose* institutional cultures and formulate strategies for assimilation or change. They work in institutions staffed by professionals trained in disciplines wherein research about women or about gender hierarchy is virtually absent. Women/gender advocates often depend on chief executives; if support from them is not forthcoming, WID missions remain isolated and disconnected to the mainstream. Finally, WID coalition building, as later discussed, is underdeveloped.

Ann Therese Lotherington calls attitudes and beliefs the central elements in organizational culture, which she labels "deep core."[10] She distinguishes levels of change, WID approaches—drawing on Caroline Moser's typology, discussed in a previous chapter—and barriers. At secondary levels of change, welfare, efficiency, and antipoverty WID approaches can effectively confront technical barriers. However, equity and empowerment approaches are necessary to confront the political and ideological barriers in near- and deep-core change levels, respectively.

"Development" Institutions

Development bureaucracies have special characteristics that undermine their effectiveness. First, their work is implemented on territory not their own, involving negotiation with sovereign governments that may or may not be accountable to their people. Thus, the users of the development monies are not connected politically to the ultimate sources of funds or the decision makers; users lack political voice or even the ability to complain with voice.[11]

Second, the work of development bureaucracies is highly fragmented. Not only are their development partners in separate institutions (with all their own institutional politics), thus requiring always-problematic coordination, but it is a separation of enormous physical, intellectual, and linguistic space.

To simplify this complexity, development staff use a generic development discourse to justify interventions, devoid of historically specific knowledge. According to Karen Hansen and Leslie Ashbaugh, development schemes change little over the decades. "It takes a good deal of historical irony to explain why development packages look so much alike and seem so oblivious to the evolving local realities."[12]

Finally, development institutions suffer common bureaucratic ailments. Among these are fragmentation associated with division of labor in hierarchical institutions. This division separates design, implementation, and evaluation for tasks and contexts with highly uncertain prospects for success. Technical and operational divisions are organized by sector. As Lotherington asks: "How can a cross-sectoral approach be organised within a strictly sector-oriented organisation?"[13] She adds that hierarchy renders the problem even more complex, with about ten levels of authority in the larger United Nations agencies.

In institutions, incentives (and penalties) encourage (and discourage) particular behaviors. The incentive in many development bureaucracies is to "move money."[14] Consequently, institutional attention often focuses on proposal design and approval rather than quality implementation. Evaluation is belated and relatively underdeveloped; it rarely connects performance with funding decisions.

Secrecy and guardedness are also common bureaucratic problems in a work world that demands loyalty and team effort. Institutions build a protective shell beyond which seeps little documentation other than that of promoting a good image and defending institutional interests. All too often, development institutions operate in a secretive way, with "restricted" and "confidential" stamped on documents for "limited distribution." Combined with the closed, behind-the-scenes decision-making style, few independent studies exist that make internal process transparent in this sometimes Orwellian world.

Among international banks such as the World Bank, master country lending plans had limited distribution within recipient countries. "Even ministers of a nation's cabinet could not obtain access to these documents, which in smaller, poorer countries were viewed as international decrees on their economic fate."[15] An NGO called the Bank Information Center circulates once-confidential documents to groups around the world.

Women and Gender in Institutions

As the preceeding section makes obvious, daunting challenges exist for all new policy advocates. However, new policies associated with women and gender are likely to face even greater obstacles, for three reasons: demographics, power dynamics of underrepresentation, and the institutionalization of male interests in states and bureaucracies.

Staff Demographics. The staff demographics of many public institutions have historically been skewed. Men monopolize high-level decision-making positions such as cabinet and subcabinet posts, and until recently, men have been the majority among professional and technical staff. Men have rarely responded to the initial challenge to make women or gender central to their work, although they have become important allies in some institutions. Thus, we must ask: how much action will occur in bureaucracies that underrepresent women?

To the extent women are charged with advocacy responsibilities, they face the challenge of making Weber's ideal real: that is, recruitment and action on meritorious grounds, without prejudice. Equal employment opportunity is a policy that many countries and bilateral and multilateral institutions have yet to achieve.

The Dynamics of Underrepresentation. Additionally, women professionals working in male-majority circumstances encounter structural dynamics with global applications. A lone woman is burdened by prejudice in committee and institutional settings. First, she represents all women, and any mistake she makes (as with any professional) fulfills prophecies among the prejudiced. Second, with what Rosabeth Kanter calls "boundary-heightening" behavior, men distance themselves from her through jokes and exclusionary tactics. Third, she is frequently typecast into one of several female caricatures.[16]

The result of this performance pressure is one of three broad generic strategies, termed by Albert O. Hirschman "exit, loyalty, or choice." She leaves, she assimilates the caricature, or she outperforms her peers to build legitimacy and gradual acceptance. As a Latin American proverb has it: "whereas a man may be made of silver, a woman must be made of gold."[17]

For Kanter, the higher the proportion of underrepresented, the better the prospects for productive working relationships. In the early years of WID programming, women advocates were sometimes the lone woman on committees in bilateral and multilateral institutions. Gradually, the proportion of female professionals has increased, though their representation at the highest ranks is still minuscule. Women now number approximately a third of professionals in UN agencies, though these figures vary from agency to agency. Increasingly, men now join women professionals in gender/WID advocacy.

A second problem Kanter identifies is the separation of career tracks for women and men. Women's tracks tend to have a short ladder, and they get stuck in fields of lower priority, such as personnel. Women/gender work is one of the fields in which one gets stuck, unless mainstream offices have a stake in gender-fair outcomes and they recruit staff with related expertise.[18] This may be changing in the 1990s, with women at the helm in several United Nations agencies such as UNFPA, UNICEF, and UNHCR (not to mention the U.S. secretary of state). Gender expertise also exists at the vice-presidential level of the Inter-American Development Bank.

Institutionalized Male Interests. Until recently, gender ideologies rendered women, their work, and their voice irrelevant to development policy. Two assumptions have long been taken for granted: that men support women and children in families, and that a conceptual division of life into public and private would subsume women within a private realm in which law does not or should not reach. Historically, specific gender ideologies have been disseminated globally; Maria Mies labels this "housewifization."[19]

The production of knowledge itself bears some responsibility for perpetuating this ideology, as few disciplines legitimized, until recently, methodical analyses of women or gender. Those trained before the 1970s rarely had the opportunity to learn about gender or women's work in their courses.

But more than curricular deficiencies are at issue here. With increased attention to states, their histories, and the incorporation of ideologies into their structures, analysts have begun to uncover the institutionalization of male interests, which exists independently of the dominant class. Sue Ellen Charlton and coauthors focus on state policies, states' definition of policies, and state officials who bring their ideologies, conventional views, and material realities to bear on decision making. As the Western state form was transplanted throughout the globe, it spread a public-private conception of policies that relegated women to a private or family sphere. As they argue:

> The cruel irony is that these distinctions serve to exclude women from public affairs even as the scope of those affairs broadens. At the same time, the definition of family as private serves to justify the paucity of policies which would provide women greater equity and freedom within the private sphere.[20]

Once policies are in place, complete with procedures and implementation track records, momentum for their continuity exists, with mere incremental change. Politicians come and go, but those who "man" institutions continue with their same gender ideologies. Women's programs thus confront this policy wall. Given the relative autonomy of institutions, it takes more than pluralist groups advocating change from the outside. Major work must be done inside institutions to transform them.

With the exuberance of the international women's conference in 1985, resolution makers had high expectations for what state action could do. Charlton and coauthors had this critique:

> *Forward Looking Strategies*, the final document of the Nairobi conference which concluded the U.N. Decade for Women, is filled with recommendations that depend on government for implementation. The Nairobi experience suggests that state action continues to hold considerable allure for serving women's interests in many different societies.[21]

It soon became clear that women could not depend on states, or state feminism, to deinstitutionalize male privilege or make women's capabilities a political and budgetary priority. A decade later, after the Fourth World Conference on Women, activists developed strategies to follow up, monitor, and press states and bureaucracies to put policies into action. The titles of accessible books include *Holding Governments Accountable* and *Keeping the Promises*.[22]

Still, though, women/gender advocates confront enormous challenges in their efforts to work with bilateral, multilateral, and state institutions that routinely privilege men's interests and mute women's voices and visions. Such challenges are compounded by the location of male privilege in the ideological "deep core" of institutions, to use Lotherington's term. The change may be so deep as to require not just resocialization but also new staff and transformed organizational missions.

To promote these changes, political strategies are necessary, inherent in all policy changes, whether distributive, regulatory, or redistributive. As Theodore Lowi notes, policies cause politics; redistributive policy evokes broad political conflict patterns.[23] These politics can get personal.

> [WID] policies are viewed as redistributing goods, services, and power between men and women. . . . Policies that intrude into a perceived private family sphere, a special variant of [redistributive] policy, are personalized, thus intensifying and aggravating that conflict.[24]

Thus WID tasks are daunting.

Mainstreaming Women and Gender

Mainstreaming WID involves infusing women and gender in all program operations. Mainstreaming is thus concerned with overall institutional accountability and responsiveness to women. But do organizations continue their basic practices, or do they undergo serious change instead? In women's studies terms, people worried about adding women (a reading, a lecture), mixing, and stirring (disappearing the insights, probably), as opposed to really changing the organization of courses. Recall Rounaq Jahan's contrasts between integration and agenda setting in a previous chapter. The former is a modest goal, whereas the latter is ambitious, particularly in political terms.

A major shortcoming in most mainstreaming discussions is the inattention to politics: transforming organizations requires *political* constituencies to drive the change. A central feature, then, involves building or opening space to such constituencies as they interact with policymakers and bureaucrats.

Women/Gender Advocates Inside Bureaucracies

Before the declaration of the International Women's Year and Decade in 1975, a handful of technical assistance institutions adopted policies to integrate women into programs. Energetic outsiders, and precious few internal advocates, did not allow the policies to languish. But with few resources and staff, those offices survived rather than thrived.

No known case of mainstreaming exists, save the agency dedicated to this mission, UNIFEM (the former UN Voluntary Fund for Women). UNIFEM's program with multilateral institutions and governments promotes mainstreaming and strengthening women's collective voices.[25]

WID advocacy confronts the bureaucratic inertia that faces many new policy issues. Organizational theorists have developed typologies for staff that allow thinking to move beyond the gender divide in bureaucracy alone, for support comes from both men and women. Lotherington developed a gender-neutral typology that helps clarify bureaucratic responses:

> Innovators . . . , supporters of WID policy, . . . are mainly women . . . located at all levels [with the] majority at middle and lower professional levels. They have been active in putting gender-responsive technical cooperation policy on the agenda and keeping it there.
> *Loyal Bureaucrats,* . . . "ideal bureaucrats" in Max Weber's sense . . . , wish to execute their work professionally, and in line with the policy and

signals. Once [these men] become proficient at implementing WID policy, and can argue as to why they do so, they may serve as examples—even if they lack private enthusiasm for the cause itself.

Hesitators, mostly men, consider aims . . . proper, but . . . find it impossible to support implementation of the new policy. In this category [are] those who only pay lip-service to gender . . . [and those] who "live in the reality" of the welfare approach.

Hard-Liners are silent resisters to WID policy. Nearly always men . . . , they are not easily persuaded. . . . They feel threatened by the new ideas. They may relate the whole debate on gender orientation to their personal attitude to women.[26]

With typologies like these, advocates can diagnose organizational culture and plan for change.

Early Advocacy in Official Institutions

WID programs need a baseline from which to assess change. The review that follows begins historically, with the earliest of WID programs. In the final chapters, we revisit the change, and the body of the text examines government and international action and inaction in more recent terms. WID needs an institutional memory and history, not to single out any agency, but only to clarify the obstacles to change.

U.S. Agency for International Development (USAID). USAID was one of the first bilateral institutions to respond to a legislative mandate to adopt a WID program. Until 1994, it was the first and only case for which book-length treatment existed, from which the following comes.[27]

USAID is a creature of its environment, an environment of low public support for development assistance and considerable dependence on lobby organizations to support its program authorization and budget requests in Congress. It has long been criticized as crowding development goals, amid many competing, even contradictory goals, including political support for U.S. allies, export promotion, and special interests.

In 1973, Congress mandated that the institution "integrate women in national economies," among its many other goals. It did so at a time when USAID was going in what was known as "new directions" toward equitable development, a response to a failing legitimacy in the eyes of many in Congress. Contextual crises are one of many conditions that lead to a transformed organizational culture, as discussed earlier.

At the outset, USAID's chief executive, and others that followed in this high-turnover appointee position, provided little verbal support for WID. In fact, one said publicly about WID: "isn't that the silliest thing you've ever heard?"

Initially, the WID Office was placed in the chief executive's office, with the dual responsibility of implementing equal employment opportunity

(EEO). This dual role mixed the agendas of WID and EEO in the eyes of many professionals. Soon thereafter, the WID Office was transferred to the Program and Policy Coordination Bureau, charged with planning and budgeting.

By the late 1970s, the WID Office was headed by a political appointee and staffed with several professionals. Its budget was less than a million dollars in a multi-billion-dollar agency. It had few budgetary resources to leverage project action in the regional and sectoral bureaus and no authority to veto projects, so it relied on research and persuasion with WID representatives in other bureaus and country missions in this decentralized agency, with offices in more than sixty countries at the time. The other WID staff were chosen in the bureaus and the country missions rather than by or with the WID Office; they had many responsibilities, onto which WID was added.

The WID Office pursued bureaucratic politics with three strategies to accomplish its huge mission. In hindsight, these could be labeled mainstreaming strategies.

1. *Bargaining within the Institution.* WID advocates bargained with resources they controlled to stimulate the implementation of WID in light of the incentive structures in which staff worked. Among incentives, according to Eugene Bardach,[28] prescription is the weakest, enabling resources are moderately effective, and resources tied to performance are strongest.

First, WID advocates used expertise to supply studies to staff and to define, within the legislative mandate, WID projects in annual reports to Congress. The latter is an incentive tied firmly to performance. Monitoring efforts were relatively effective, but for labeling WID projects and designating amounts (particularly in integrated projects), WID advocates were dependent on staff in country missions and regional bureaus.

WID advocates also built ties with outside experts whose work documented women's work and participation in sector activities such as agriculture, forestry, and water. Yet supplying more studies in an agency drowning in studies was not enough. Staff sought to generate interest in and demand for these studies. Also problematic was the tendency of some agency staff to substitute studies for project action.

Second, WID advocates used the limited staff and budget. They did so, however, from an enclave office that some staff thought was established for public-relations purposes to placate outside critics. Lacking much money of their own, WID lobbyists convinced Congress to set a $10 million target, and thus USAID as a whole had to document its achievements in annual reports.

WID staff reviewed project proposals, a complex two-stage affair. Agency procedures required a "woman-impact" statement in each proposal, which quickly proved useless to WID advocates as proposers merely recycled a benign paragraph from one proposal to another. This toothless procedural requirement was later replaced with more specific requirements on gender-disaggregated data and strategies.

Third, WID advocates built allies in other parts of the agency, so that they would develop shared responsibility for the issue. Alliances with agriculture—logical, given extensive documentation of women's prominence—were belated, weak developments. In contrast, alliances with education and population staff bore much fruit. The WID focal points in other bureaus and country missions were uneven allies, given the often involuntary nature of their assignment to these extra tasks.

2. *Nurturing Constituencies.* The WID coordinator forged ties with a variety of external constituencies, including WID researchers, contractors, and lobbyists. With the limited WID budget, resources were also invested in building ties with women researchers and women NGOs in USAID-assisted countries. She did this at some risk, for agency staff expressed criticism of "women-specific efforts," arguing that WID was just political, rather than technical.

3. *Getting to the Agency's Technical Core.* Only through reaching the technical core will routine, integral, and stable practices produce mainstreaming. Paper compliance is meaningless. WID advocates must recognize the multiple layers and activity and the discretion that staff exercise in response to policies. Forces of inertia come in different shapes, as Lotherington called to our attention.

WID advocates worked to reform procedures, change agency handbooks, and infuse research on women into country programming strategies, used to justify project proposals. WID worked with a supportive but weak ally, evaluation, to document performance gaps and project improvements. But evaluation, in this fragmented agency, had limited people focus, much less women's focus. Moreover, even evaluators were often content to stop at the level of undifferentiated households, units that may mask gender inequalities. WID advocates tried to work on data retrieval and research contracting that would make women's work visible, to little avail. WID also participated in mainstream training events. Much later, the WID Office embarked on its own gender training programs, targeting more male than female staff.

Utilizing these three strategies, the WID Office at USAID had little to show for its efforts in the early years. It doubled USAID funding, an impressive statement, but this amounted to moving such spending from 2 to 4 percent of overall accounts. The overwhelming resistance and resilience of gender ideologies account for the lack of transformation in this institution.

It should be pointed out, though, that over time, some of these strategies reaped responsiveness (or vengeance, depending on one's vantage point). In the early 1980s, a WID policy paper defined an "efficiency" mission and linked WID to private-sector initiatives, including microenterprise development. Overall funding increased. Moreover, large numbers of staff, male and female, underwent gender training, a strategy discussed later. USAID now leads OECD/DAC member nations in the number of full- and part-time WID professional staff. Although this is no indicator of mainstreaming, it does demonstrate resource commitments in times of budget scarcity.

African Training and Research Centre for Women (ATRCW). Mary Tadesse and Margaret Snyder recently completed the second book-length treatment of a WID program housed in the UN Economic Commission for Africa (ECA). The following paragraphs are summarized and condensed from their analysis.[29]

ATRCW was born in 1971 as a partnership with United Nations organizations, NGOs, and governments. Regional women's meetings on the continent during the 1960s provided an African-driven agenda and network, which came into institutional existence with support from the Swedish International Development Authority (SIDA) for two posts.

ATRCW had enormous impact on the women and development literature. It pioneered the formatting of gender-disaggregated data by labor and time allocation. Its analysis was disseminated widely to activists, official organizations, and academics.

ATRCW's home was in the Economic Commission for Africa. ATRCW's position within the UN structure in Africa provided a strategic location and vantage point from which to interact with other units with breadth and depth. In the 1970s, for example, it challenged home economists in the Food and Agriculture Organization (FAO) to move beyond conventional ideas and focus on women's economic activities with support from the Voluntary Fund for Women (now UNIFEM). ATRCW also worked on innovative community revolving loan funds with the United Nations Development Programme (UNDP). ATRCW staff worked closely with women's bureaus throughout the continent.

ATRCW's relations with its host institution varied with ECA's executive director. Although early and more recent relations have been good, there was a time when ATRCW's existence inside ECA was called into question, a threat that later dissipated. A chronic problem during the first half of its existence involved temporary, multiple sources of external funding with complex reporting requirements. Despite a performance record that virtually outshined its host (it was known as "the star in the ECA crown"), ECA provided little permanent support to ATRCW in the form of posts.

ATRCW's leadership, external leverage, and sheer will finally led to ECA permanent post support and a regular budget.

A thriving ATRCW mainstreamed work in ECA. Decentralization in the 1980s brought ATRCW closer to the subregional level in Africa. ATRCW voices and networkers consistently spoke and acted in governments and in continentwide documents. The vast majority of governments took measures to enhance women's agricultural work. A report in the early 1990s indicated that half of ATRCW's work was implemented by other ECA divisions.

Parallels with Women's Machinery. Advocates within multi- and bilateral technical assistance institutions had parallels within governments, particularly those units called "women's machinery," in UN-ese. It is quite common to establish a bureaucratic unit in government to organize staff and budgets around a policy issue or rising public priority. Staff in these units pursue a wide range of activities, from collecting and reporting data to funding research and projects and transforming government. After World War I, the U.S. Department of Labor established a Women's Bureau. Unlike a number of other countries, however, the United States has no Department (or in parliamentary systems, Ministry) of Women's Affairs or, as in Scandinavian countries, Equal Rights Affairs. On one side of the debate are those who worry that a single unit will isolate and marginalize women/gender activities from other parts of government. On the other side of the debate are those who want focus and leadership (at the cabinet level, especially) for women, gender, and equality policies.

Few women's machinery–type units get the sort of authority, staff, and budgetary support to accomplish such an ambitious goal as transforming government.[30] The establishment of such units, though, does signify response to political constituencies. The danger of such units is that they represent symbolic politics, or the appearance of activity when little actually goes on, due to budgetary and other reasons. The subsequent danger is that the political energy of constituencies may dissipate once such units are established, unless leadership exists to sustain the constituency-government interactions. There is no guarantee that leadership for women's machinery will pursue the mission. After elections, mainstream leadership that is hostile to women's machinery can appoint an ideological foe. Such was the fate of equal opportunity efforts in the United States during the 1980s.

During the last two decades, 90 percent of governments established women's machinery, thus seeming to legitimize a progressive women/gender agenda. The bureaucratic resistance is daunting, as noted before by a minister in Zimbabwe who found such obstacles more difficult to overcome than those she encountered as a guerrilla fighter in the struggle for national independence.[31] Women's ministries can become vehicles to dispense political patronage to dominant party supporters.[32] Resistance is also faced at grassroots levels, such as those in rural cooperatives supported in Sandinista Nicaragua.[33]

UNIFEM supported women's machinery efforts to mainstream gender agendas throughout government, beginning in the late 1980s. In the Philippines, with support from former President Corazon Aquino, the women's commission helped develop a parallel plan for women, with chapters that corresponded to each government function. Focal point advocates worked within each department and connected with women's commission leadership and constituency interests on its advisory board.[34] In Uganda, focal points lacked expertise, prompting the women's ministry leadership to work with the Ministry of Finance and Economic Planning. Together they established a national policy on gender, with procedures for gender-oriented policy in all the ministries.[35]

Women/gender advocacy within bureaucracies staffed with economists face considerable difficulties, unless economic rationales justify action. Nüket Kardam studied WID implementation in the World Bank and the UNDP, documenting ideologies that privileged mainstream economies and national sovereignty, respectively.[36] (Readers should remember how men monopolize governance in their claims for sovereignty.)

Recent Advocacy

As the 1980s came to a close, WID advocates pursued staff resocialization strategies to increase responsiveness. They termed it "gender training." At a 1991 conference in Bergen, Norway, cosponsored by the Chr. Michelsen Institute and the Population Council, the Canadian International Development Agency (CIDA) and SIDA were featured as prominent "success stories" in establishing agencywide accountability for WID and doing so partly through gender training.

Gender training, according to Aruna Rao and coauthors, "is a way of looking at the world, a lens that brings into focus the roles, resources, and responsibilities of women and men within the system under analysis."[37] Gender training differs in the extent to which it stresses equity, efficiency, and gender subordination.

SOS Corpo is a women's reproductive health NGO in Brazil that, like many NGOs, pursued gender training strategies. It sought to increase consciousness among medical staff, using learning by doing and sometimes confrontational strategies. Staff report gratifying examples of attitudinal change among these strategic players in women's health, but also grim remarks that demonstrate hostility to the workshops, dramatizations, and plastic modeling exercises.[38]

Later chapters examine the extent to which training is used to expand awareness and change behavior in bilateral institutions. Analysts agree that gender training alone, without institutionalization strategies, is no panacea. It is a way to reach the "hesitators" and "loyal bureaucrats" from the above-mentioned typology, but they need follow-up, work plans, evaluations, and other incentives to infuse women/gender into their work. Holistic institutional strategies are necessary to integrate and transform institutions. But change cannot stop at the boundaries of bureaucracies alone. Political constituencies must sustain contact with and monitor what goes on behind closed bureaucratic doors.

Bringing Politics Back In

Technical, bureaucratic approaches no doubt reduce the anxiety about redistributing development resources and the personal complexity of such work with a long history of male monopoly decision making. But what about politics, inside and outside of institutions, at both international and country levels? More than technical planning issues are at stake here. Advocates and scholars need to build practical and intellectual coalitions over shared common interests.

Environmental advocacy is a case in point. Although the links between gender and environmentally sustainable development are clear in women/gender advocates' minds, the same cannot be said for environmental advocates. Yet environmental advocacy—involving a cross-cutting issue like women/gender for sustainable development—faces similar bureaucratic struggles. Procedures or impact statements that call for attention to environment (or women) are diminished in overall cost-benefit, economist calculations to move money.[39]

UNIFEM can be applauded for its foresight in attaching an advocate to the resolution-writing machinery of the 1992 Rio environmental meetings,[40] but why didn't gender emerge from within? Green parties do a good job of advocating gender fairness and representative balance at the national setting, but international linkage has yet to be made. The phrase-length or paragraphic attention to gender found in new environmental tracts is testimony to the limited comprehension among those who should know gender better. "What on Earth Should Be Done?" asks Bruce Rich in his last chapter, wherein women finally get brief, paragraphic mention.[41]

Major work is necessary in alliance building between WID and those issues for which there is common ground. WID can never stand alone; nor can the few women in decision-making positions (assuming, perhaps dangerously, that they all have interest in, responsibility for, and expertise on gender). As Vina Mazumdar pleads in the epigraph, politics is not a dirty word, but realistically opens (or closes) alternatives. If "democratic politics is at the heart of a transformatory approach to structural adjustment,"[42] then the same is true of gender mainstreaming.

Bilateral and multilateral institutions have more recently jumped on the bandwagon of promoting good governance and democracy. What do they mean by this? Do definitions of good governance incorporate a gendered understanding of policy and implementation? And do democratic criteria specify any minimal standards about women's voice in decision making or gender-fair policies? Women/gender advocates share some unease in using "the master's words in the master's house," to use Lorde's phrase, for whips and whipping posts that mask deeper agendas.

Thus far, this new rhetoric has not incorporated gender for institutions at the negotiation tables where men sit to talk about development loans. Although "good governance" was coined in the late 1980s, its usage goes back nearly a decade, to "institutional development" to improve the effectiveness of state institutions in using their human and financial resources.

Yet the UNDP's *Human Development Report*, issued annually as a counterpart to the World Bank's *World Development Report*, provides human development indicators and rankings that might serve as leverage for those who seek to increase people's capabilities—what we might define as development. When human development index rankings are adjusted with gender data, national human development rankings always drop.

Although women's human rights are rarely at the forefront of policy and international negotiation, the United Nations Educational, Scientific, and Cultural Organization (UNESCO) and the UN secretary-general both issued public criticism when the religious fundamentalists in Afghanistan ordered women's dismissal from the workforce, including war widows, medical doctors, and others. Perhaps only the most egregious cases merit attention, even though women's exclusion from rights and democratic process is quite commonplace.

The fuller meaning of good governance connects it with accountability, participation, respect for human rights, strengthened civil society, and transparency of decision making. What does all this mean for development institutions? Responses range all the way from aiding democratic regimes (or those making good-faith efforts) and tying aid to democratic reforms to using governance among the criteria for awarding aid and using rhetoric to legitimize change.

In one key upshot of good governance emphasis, NGOs and recipient countries have turned the rhetoric around to ask bilateral and multilateral institutions to practice what they preach. Among democratic countries with bilateral institutions, such practices may be in place. Among multilateral institutions, however, for which governing boards exercise only nominal authority, the challenge to respond to accountability and participation is profound.

In all these calls for good governance, gender is invisible. If democracy meant that a critical mass of women exercised voice in representative and cabinet bodies, or that gender-fair policy agendas were in place, or that women and women-friendly NGOs exercised voice, then few countries could be labeled democratic. Few if any reforms have tied specific gendered changes to democracy.

Implications

As the theoretical and historical analyses in this chapter make clear, WID advocates confront a complex institutional world of bureaucracy and politics. It is a hierarchical and fragmented world in which men's interests have long been institutionalized. Mainstreaming women is "nothing short of an ambitious attempt to de-institutionalize male preference"[43] while simultaneously raising questions about conventional development discourse and practice. It should not be surprising that change has been so slow and difficult, given these obstacles.

Notes

1. Freedom House maps countries annually, based on standard criteria used in defining liberal democracy, such as regular elections, election choice, and freedom of speech and the press. See Kathleen Staudt, "Political Representation: Engendering Democracy," in *Background Papers for the Human Development Report 1995* (New York: UNDP, 1996), pp. 21–70.
2. The UN/Division for the Advancement of Women (DAW) conference of 1989 put political representation on the agenda, and from then on, began monitoring cabinet representation as regularly as the Inter-Parliamentary Union (IPU) monitors legislative and parliamentary seats. On cabinet representation, see Kathleen Staudt, "Women and High-Level Political Decision Making," paper presented at UN/DAW Conference, September 1989, and Staudt, "Political Representation."
3. Wilma Rule pioneered the study of women's representation in electoral systems. For the latest iteration, see Wilma Rule and William Zimmerman, eds., *Electoral Systems in Comparative Perspective: Their Impact on Women and Minorities* (Westport, Conn.: Greenwood Press, 1994). For an extension to partial democracies, see Staudt, "Political Representation."
4. Mark Jones, "Increasing Women's Representation via Gender Quotas: The Argentine Ley de Cupos," in *Women & Politics* 16, no. 4 (1996): 75–98.

5. The classic study is Graham Allison and Morton Halperin, "Bureaucratic Politics: A Paradigm and Some Policy Implications," *World Politics* 24 (1972): 40–79.

6. The OECD/DAC began monitoring WID in bilateral agencies in 1983, gradually developing more elaborate indicators of inputs and process (though not outcomes). See OECD/DAC, *Third Monitoring Report on the Implementation of the DAC Revised Guiding Principles on Women in Development (1989)* (Paris: OECD, 1992).

7. Anthony Downs, *Inside Bureaucracy* (Boston: Little, Brown, 1966).

8. Murray Edelman, *The Symbolic Uses of Politics* (Champaign and Urbana: University of Illinois Press, 1964).

9. See Kathleen Staudt, *Managing Development: State, Society and International Contexts* (Newbury Park, Calif.: Sage, 1991), chap. 3, for a full discussion, including a form to diagnose such culture.

10. Ann Therese Lotherington, *Implementation of Women-in-Development (WID) Policy* (Oslo: University of Oslo, Centre for Development and the Environment, 1991), p. 100.

11. Judith Tendler, *Inside Foreign Aid* (Baltimore: Johns Hopkins University Press, 1975).

12. Karen Tranberg Hansen and Leslie Ashbaugh, "Women on the Front Line: Development Issues in Southern Africa," in *WID Annual*, vol. 2, edited by Rita Gallin and Anne Ferguson (Boulder, Colo.: Westview Press, 1991), p. 221. Also see the special issue of *Sociologia Ruralis* 28, no. 1/2 (1988), "Development Aid as an Intervention in Dynamic Systems."

13. Lotherington, *Implementation of WID Policy*, p. 64.

14. Tendler, *Inside Foreign Aid*; Janne Lenox and Desmond McNeill, *The Women's Grant: Desk Study Review*, Evaluation Report 2.89 (Oslo: Royal Norwegian Ministry of Development Cooperation, 1989). The World Bank's own 1992 Wapenhans Report, which made this critique, is cited in U.S. GAO, *Multilateral Development: Status of World Bank Reforms* (Washington, D.C.: GAO, 1994).

15. Bruce Rich, *Mortgaging the Earth* (Boston: Beacon Press, 1994), p. 85. For a devastating history and critique of the World Bank, see Catherine Caufield, *Masters of Illusion: The World Bank and the Poverty of Nations* (New York: Henry Holt, 1996).

16. Rosabeth Kanter, *Men and Women of the Corporation*, 2d ed. (New York: Basic Books, 1993). For global applications, see Kathleen Staudt, "Strategic Locations: Gender Issues in Business Management," in *Women at the Center: Development Issues and Practices for the 1990s*, edited by Gay Young, Vidyamali Samarasinghe, and Ken Kusterer (West Hartford, Conn.: Kumarian Press, 1993), pp. 127–42.

17. Albert O. Hirschman, *Exit, Voice and Loyalty: Responses to Decline in Firms* (Cambridge, Mass.: Harvard University Press, 1970). The proverb is found in Elsa Chaney, *Supermadre: Women in Politics in Latin America* (Austin: University of Texas Press, 1979), p. 110.

18. Karen Himmelstrand, "Can an Aid Bureaucracy Empower Women?" in *Women, International Development, and Politics: The Bureaucratic Mire*, 2d., edited by Kathleen Staudt (Philadelphia: Temple University Press, 1997), pp. 101–13.

19. Maria Mies, *Patriarchy and Accumulation on a World Scale: Women in the International Division of Labour* (London: Zed, 1986).

20. Sue Ellen Charlton et al., eds., "Introduction," in *Women, the State and Development* (Albany, N.Y.: SUNY Albany Press, 1989), p. 15.

21. Charlton et al., *Women, the State and Development*, p. 13.

22. These are published by the Women's Environmental & Development Organiza-

tion (WEDO), New York. It also publishes a useful (and free) newsletter.

23. Theodore Lowi, *The End of Liberalism* (New York: W. W. Norton, 1979). Another major theme running throughout this book is that politics also changes policies.

24. Kathleen Staudt, *Women, Foreign Assistance and Advocacy Administration* (New York: Praeger, 1985), p. 2.

25. Mary Anderson, *Women on the Agenda: UNIFEM's Experience in Mainstreaming with Women 1985–1990* (New York: UNIFEM, 1990); also see Margaret Snyder, *Transforming Development: Women, Poverty and Politics*, (London: Intermediate Technology Publications, 1995).

26. Lotherington, *Implementation of WID Policy*, pp. 73–75.

27. Staudt, *Women, Foreign Assistance and Advocacy Administration*.

28. Eugene Bardach, *The Implementation Game* (Cambridge, Mass: MIT Press, 1977), pp. 119–24.

29. Mary Tadesse and Margaret Snyder, *African Women and Development: A History* (London: Zed, 1994).

30. Oki Ooko-Ombaka, "An Assessment of National Machinery for Women," *Assignment Children* 49, 50 (1980): 45–61.

31. Cited in Kathleen Staudt, "Gender Politics in Bureaucracy: Theoretical Issues in Comparative Perspective," in Staudt, *Women, International Development and Politics*, p. 21.

32. Barbara Lewis, "Farming Women, Public Policy, and the Women's Ministry: A Case Study from Cameroon," in Staudt, *Women, International Development and Politics*, 180–200.

33. Center for the Investigation and Study of Agrarian Reform (CIERA), Rural Women's Research Team, "Tough Row to Hoe: Women in Nicaragua's Agricultural Cooperatives," in Staudt, *Women, International Development and Politics*, pp. 201–26.

34. Philippine Commission expert Remedios Rikken's remarks are summarized in Aruna Rao et al., *Gender Training and Development Planning: Learning from Experience* (Bergen, Norway, and New York: Chr. Michelsen Institute and Population Council, 1991).

35. Zoe Oxaal, "Changing Institutions in Women's Interests," *Development and Gender in Brief* 5 (1997): 2. This is a substantive, useful, and free newsletter, available from the Institute of Development Studies at the University of Sussex, Brighton, UK (bridge@sussex.ac.uk).

36. Nüket Kardam, *Bringing Women In: Women's Issues in International Development Programs* (Boulder, Colo.: Lynne Rienner, 1991). Kardam also has a chapter in Staudt's *Women, International Development and Politics* entitled "The Adaptability of International Development Agencies: The Response of the World Bank to Women in Development" (pp. 114–28). Her book offers yet another, more successful case: the Ford Foundation with its academic activists and progressive leadership.

37. Rao et al., *Gender Training and Development Planning*, p. 7.

38. SOS Corpo was present at the 1991 Gender Training Conference in Bergen, Norway, for which I was one of four moderators. Its gender training person responded to a lengthy questionnaire.

39. Philippe LePrestre, *The World Bank and the Environmental Challenge* (Toronto: Associated University Presses, 1989). Staudt, *Managing Development*, extends the comparison. USAID had moved further on the environment than on WID, in response to a lawsuit settled out of court (Staudt, *Women, Foreign Assistance and Advocacy Administration*). See also Rich, *Mortgaging the Earth*, and Caufield, *Masters of Illusion*.

40. Mary Anderson, *Focusing on Women: UNIFEM's Experience in Mainstreaming* (New York: UNIFEM, 1993).
41. Rich, *Mortgaging the Earth*, p. 295. WEDO has been very critical of the Rio resolutions. Headlines over the five-year anniversary of Rio detailed limited actions. See recent issues of *News & Views*. Also see "Five Years after Environment Summit in Rio, Little Progress," *New York Times*, June 17, 1997.
42. Diane Elson, "From Survival Strategies to Transformation Strategies: Women's Needs and Structural Adjustment," in *Unequal Burden*, edited by Lourdes Benería and Shelley Feldman (Boulder, Colo.: Westview Press, 1992), p. 39.
43. In Rao et al., *Gender Training and Development Planning*, p. 36.

Part II
Analyzing Substantive Policies with a Gender Lens

4   Education for Life and Capacitation

> Human development, if not engendered,
> is endangered.
> —UNDP

> [E]ducation . . . is political throughout.
> —Paulo Freire

> True liberation begins in a woman's soul.
> —Emma Goldman

The United Nations Development Programme (UNDP) repeated its stark declaration of the epigraph of this chapter in its 1995 and 1996 *Human Development Reports*.[1] In its measurement and national rankings of human development, the UNDP harnesses a composite index score based on literacy, longevity, and per capita income. It privileges people's increased capabilities to survive and to exercise skills and choices about their lives as the outcomes (ends) of development. The indicators that economists privilege (such as growth rates, increased exports, or increased productivity) are *means* toward the ends of human development. The *means-ends* controversies in development continue to persist, however.

Political decisions are made in governments and international bodies about policies and budgetary support that affect people's capabilities to survive, exercise skills, and make choices about their lives. This chapter focuses on some of those policy priorities—or perhaps better called nonpriorities—in the area of education. The UNDP estimates that governments allocate approximately 13 percent of their current expenditures to human development, a figure larger than the 7 percent average of bilateral donors or the 4 to 16 percent of multilateral and regional development banks (World Bank and Inter-American, Asian, and African regional banks).[2] That figure is far below the 20 percent the UNDP advocates for public investment in people's capabilities.

This chapter defines education broadly, from childhood through adulthood. It genders the understanding of education, particularly the (low) priority of budgets that distribute public resources to children and mostly feminized occupational groups. The chapter also examines controversial issues surrounding the content and different experiences of males and females in the classroom. Education is a mainstream public policy, central to human development. To increase human capacity, gendered understanding and action are fundamental.

Education, Broadly Defined

Education enables and expands human capacity. An analysis of education is therefore larger than reports on educational enrollments and achievements. Although it is worthwhile to attend to equal opportunity to participate, disaggregating males and females in reports thereof, analyses should include student treatment and the curricular content conveyed in classrooms and textbooks. The United Nations Educational, Scientific, and Cultural Organization (UNESCO) calls this more comprehensive focus "participation and process."[3]

But other agendas may be at play as well. Nelly Stromquist reminds us of the use of education in state hegemonic projects: it transmits "representations and beliefs about the 'appropriate' and 'natural' social order." For women, she says, it conveys "traditional messages about women's reproductive functions in household and family and about productive functions in 'feminine' occupations."[4]

Alongside the military, education consumes comparable budgetary and staff resources. Its importance in budgetary, population, employment, and capacitation terms makes it relevant to many fields, beyond those relegated to disciplinary specialists in colleges of education. A billion young people, or one-fifth the world's population, are currently enrolled in schools.[5]

Education should do much more than reinforce a gender-constructed social order. It should provide an atmosphere for intellectual development. Comprehensive education has great potential to facilitate awareness of structures of domination and subordination. Here I include conscientization, or the awareness that comes when people develop critical consciousness about their place in society, analyze and dialogue about that reflection, and put their ideas into action. Popular education is also included, for it puts class relations and educational power relations on change agendas.[6]

Education in and outside the classroom provides the space in which to develop solidarity relations for active involvement in community and social change. Just as national university networks facilitate subsequent contacts and support for members of Mexico's job-seeking political elite, so also can networks facilitate support for social change.[7]

For youth in secondary and higher education, public service and community activism can have lifelong impacts on their commitment to civic engagement and social justice.[8] All too often, researchers miss the opportunity to examine the gendered dimensions of such involvement and impact. Two academic activists from different parts of the world note how crisis and social justice movements privilege class and ethnic or racial inequalities over gender. One comment is about Peru: "The women's struggle [is] protracted . . . to be fought not only for a long time but also on the basis of day-to-day issues."[9] The other comment comes from South Africa, demonstrating how the resistance and defiance inherent in challenging the existing order can strengthen women's resolve. During Mamphela Ramphele's student activist days, she "became quite an aggressive debater," intimidating "men who did not expect aggression from women." Although her cause was not feminist at that time, she says, she and her colleagues insisted "on being taken seriously as activists in our own right amongst our peers."[10] Ramphele is now a high-level university administrator, attempting to dismantle institutionalized white male privilege.

Gendering Education

Several policy principles come into play in gender discussions about education: justice, equality, and efficiency. We can examine these in terms of access and content, or participation and process. Worldwide, women constitute the majority of people who are illiterate, defined as the inability to read or write short and simple statements, usually judged to be fourth-grade level. According to the UNDP and UNESCO, two-thirds of all illiterates are female, totaling 565 million people.[11] Girls are pulled out or drop out of school earlier than boys in several world regions. Gender gaps are marked in Asia and Africa, as Table 4.1 shows.

In all world regions, literacy rates have improved. Zimbabwe, for example, has taken several positive steps to promote girls' education. According to the Ministry of Education report of 1992–94, it:

- encourages unitary curricula without gender biases (such as "woodwork for boys, needlework for girls");
- publicizes "successful" females, as models for emulation;
- pursues "positive discrimination," altering conditions and criteria for admission to certain levels;
- sponsors scholarship funds for girls seeking the Advanced Level of the General Certificate of Education; [and]
- acts affirmatively in promoting women.[12]

Table 4.1   Changes in Adult Literacy, 1980 to 1995

Region	Percent of Women Literate 1980	Percent of Women Literate 1995	Percent of Men Literate 1980	Percent of Men Literate 1995
Sub-Saharan Africa	29	47%	52	67%
Latin America/Caribbean	76	86%	82	88%
Arab states	26	44%	55	68%
East Asia/Oceania	58	76%	80	91%
China	53	73%	77	90%
Southern Asia	26	37%	53	63%
India	25	38%	55	66%

Source: Based on data from UNESCO, *World Education Report 1995* (New York: Oxford University Press, 1995), p. 19.

But large gender gaps still remain, especially in southern and western Asia, Africa, and the Arab states. Gaps like these reflect an inherent gender injustice, worthy of attention in their own right. Despite these grim statistics, breathtaking advances have occurred: over a fifty-year span, the number of girls attending Egyptian secondary school grew from forty-three to half a million.[13]

Before we applaud these figures, we should be reminded of the lingering class inequalities in which girls are mired. Among the garbage settlements of Cairo, the Association for the Protection of the Environment educates girls in job skills and provides salaries, a contrast to the girl sorters' usual household work in knee-deep garbage recycling. Although Egyptian law requires school attendance to age fifteen, just 45 percent of school-age girls in the garbage settlements attend school. Child labor is the norm for household survival.[14]

International agencies have recently become interested in girls' education for instrumental reasons, with efficient payoffs anticipated in other parts of their development missions. First and foremost is the well-documented relationship between years of female education and lower fertility rates. Women with six or more years of school are "decisively affected" for fertility behavior.[15] Reports of these kind are commonplace, though I have never seen similar studies that examine the effect of schooling on male fertility behavior. Second is the expected impact that more educated women will have on earning power and contributions to households.

Latin America is the world region that shows relatively balanced female-male literacy rates and school enrollment. We must search beneath the overarching, basic gender-disaggregation veneer, however. Here one finds an overrepresentation of illiteracy among rural women and indigenous women in many Latin American countries. In countries where indigenous people represent a third or more of the population—such as Guatemala, Peru,

Bolivia, and Ecuador—indigenous women are among the most marginal of marginal peoples, historically relegated to assimilationist educational programs that undermine their language and culture.[16] As cautioned in earlier chapters, "women" is a huge category of diverse people.

Despite this diversity, educational curricula and textbooks frequently impose a monotonous regularity on the images and expectations of women and girls. An exhaustive Argentine study conducted over a century shows "a clear and harmonious sexual division of labor, which is justified by the 'natural differences' among the sexes"; it concludes on the note of a continued "century-long immutability" in those images.[17] Thus, equal participation rates may reinforce unequal content, cues, and learning. Women learn to be passive and dependent. Our understanding of equality becomes more complicated when we examine both access and content. Access is easier to address, and certainly more politically palatable to address than curricula and process that privilege males.

Gendering Education Budgets

International agencies often launch special initiatives to increase awareness of problems and raise funds for their resolution. Access to basic literacy education has been one of them. UNESCO sponsored the International Literacy Year in 1990, but it attracted just $375,000 to implement the effort.[18] Other international agencies have promoted campaigns to promote "primary education for all," but human development is a long-term investment wherein bottom-line profitability (that is, when benefits exceed costs) is not always transparent. Thus, education funding often diminishes as a budgetary priority.

Education is important in its own right. However, compulsory education is also linked to historical and contemporary struggles to reduce child labor. Of course, the Egyptian example cited earlier, like in many countries, shows the uneven enforcement of laws. Child labor is an enormous problem worldwide, not only for the way it zaps energy and life from youth but also for the way it cheapens all labor with miserable pay, exploitative conditions, and negative effects on developmental health.[19]

Poverty and limited resources put constraints on the availability of education and its quality. Consider all the lines in an education budget that plentiful resources could augment:

- Size of classes (twenty versus forty or sixty students per teacher)
- Buildings (their safety, the existence of floors, desks, equipment, heating and cooling)

- Technology to transmit skills (computers, labs)
- Teachers' salaries and benefits
- Books for students and for libraries
- Food programs (breakfast, lunch)
- Transportation for students
- Space for all students at primary, secondary, and higher levels
- Programs for children with special needs related to language, disability, and so forth

The UNDP ranks and categorizes countries in terms of their scores on the human development index (HDI): high—ranks 1 (Canada) through 57 (Russian Federation); medium—ranks 58 (Brazil) through 126 (Papua New Guinea); and low—ranks 127 (Cameroon) through 174 (Niger).

The pupil-teacher ratio in primary schools is twenty-five and twenty-four pupils per teacher for high and medium HDI countries, respectively. Low HDI countries show a ratio of forty-six pupils per teacher on average, with several countries exceeding sixty pupils per teacher (Bangladesh, sixty-three; Central African Republic, ninety; Malawi, sixty-eight; Chad, sixty-four; and Burundi, sixty-three).[20] Of course, averages like these distort the probable larger classes in rural compared with urban areas.

The maldistribution of food and lack of income to purchase food take its toll on children. Nutritional experts estimate that human beings need a daily intake of approximately 2,100 calories. Without that, undernourishment occurs. The world press occasionally covers famine and its tragic deaths, but not the banalities of routine undernourishment and its negative effects on childhood development, energy, immunity to disease, and longevity. At the United Nations Summit focusing on the plight of the world's children, it was estimated that 15 million children under age five die annually. Malnutrition is a major culprit, but so is the lack of medicine for easily remedied illnesses such as diarrhea, respiratory infections, measles, and tetanus.[21] Schools are places where the diets of hungry children can be augmented through break-fast and lunch programs.

The UNDP reveals patterns of overconsumption and underconsumption that can be compared among countries and world regions. In some countries of the North, reducing human fat caused by overconsumption is big business. Countries with a high HDI average a daily caloric supply of 2,889; those with a medium HDI, 2,731; and those with a low HDI, excluding India, 2,097. Countries that fall below 2,000 include Cameroon, Zambia, Haiti, Central African Republic, Nepal, Rwanda, Malawi, Liberia, Chad, Angola, Burundi, Mozambique, Ethiopia, Afghanistan, Somalia (the lowest, at 1,505), and Sierre Leone.[22]

Caloric intake and child survival itself require a gendered lens. Infanticide and neglect of girls take gender-selective tolls. Amartya Sen, in a piece strikingly titled "More Than 100 Million Women Are Missing," methodically examined "sex ratios" in census data. He found glaring gender gaps in South and East Asia, with as few as eighty-some women to every hundred men. Yet the examination of state-by-state differences within countries, such as India, reveals further insights, raising questions about the effects of regional government policies and "culture" (for want of a more precise term) on the very survival rates of women. In the southern state of Kerala, India, sex ratios are balanced, attributed to fairer gender policy implementation in health and education.[23]

As public civil servants, teachers usually earn stable salaries, with benefits attached. In some countries, teachers' unions provide collective organizational strength and political leverage, depending on the extent to which unions are independent groups. Teachers' salaries often absorb the lion's share of the education budget, as much as 98 percent in Bolivia,[24] leaving little else for children. Mexico's teachers' union is the largest in the country, but observers view it as weakened through co-optation by the dominant political party.

The teaching profession, historically, has served as a major channel of occupational stability and upward mobility for women. The content of such work, involving contact with children, was less threatening to male occupational privilege than many other professions. Historically, governments pursued cost-saving strategies with a female teaching staff, deemed less needy of merit-based pay amid gender ideologies that assumed men to be breadwinners for households. In fact, women are often deemed suited to work with children, for they have been rightly or wrongly viewed as nurturers. A statement like that can make a liberal feminist bristle but reinforce a maternal feminist who wants skills such as nurturing to acquire value and to spread.

Teacher salary levels send cues about the value of education and the extent to which teachers' skills are prized. Salary levels are sometimes based on the qualifications and certifications necessary prior to job entry. When it comes to teachers, however, salary levels seem to reflect the extent to which occupations are "feminized." Female teachers predominate at the primary levels in all world regions except Sub-Saharan Africa and South and East Asia.[25] Studies of comparable worth in the United States show links between valuation of work and the predominance of men or women in professions: high male majority occupations are overvalued, and high female majority occupations are undervalued.[26]

Although women are the majority of primary school teachers in most countries, they are less prevalent at the secondary school level. UNESCO figures show 38 percent women teaching at the secondary level in developing countries, but 58 percent in developed countries.[27] Mexico, for example, recruits women to fill 80 percent of its primary teacher pool. In higher education, men are not only the majority but the persistent majority. This persistence of feminized-child work is striking in countries of the North, despite decades of supposed affirmative action to recruit more diverse faculty.

The teaching profession is gender segregated, but by level of students rather than the essence of the work itself. Female and male majorities reverse themselves from low to high levels. Public school teacher salaries vary from country to country. According to the Foundation for Teachers' Culture, among members of Mexico's largest teachers' union, wages were so low that 52 percent held two teaching jobs in order to make ends meet. (The school day is divided into two shifts in some areas, morning and afternoon, for more efficient space utilization.) According to the foundation, 21 percent of Mexican primary school teachers earned less than three minimum wages (one minimum wage is equivalent to US$20 weekly) in 1994–95, 42 percent earned three to five minimum wages, 19 percent earned five to eight minimum wages, and 10 percent earned eight or more minimum wages. This was reported in the *Mexican Labor News and Analysis* of June 16, 1997.

Residents of rich Northern countries like the United States complain about the quality of education and inequitable funding patterns. States like Texas (a former country) rhetorically guarantee equal education in constitutional principles, but disparities in per-student funding were recently marked—doubled or halved, depending on where the child lived—due to its property tax base. Property-poor districts levy steep rates but still generate less revenue.

Despite inequities in the United States, within its regional and local governments, the funding per child is considerable. In 1989, U.S. spending per primary-level pupil was $3,700 annually, a marked contrast to the $100 spent annually in Latin American countries.[28] Absolute differences in the economies of American countries reduce the likelihood of diminished national gaps in the near future. But political decision makers in Southern countries bear responsibility for devaluing education as well. The relative proportion allocated to education in national budgets is low, suggesting a low priority for education. Table 4.2 is illustrative.

Not only are proportional dedications to education low in national budgets, but the per-pupil expenditures vary markedly within countries at the first, second, and third levels of education. In the poorest world region, Africa, average per-pupil expenditures are $44 at the first level, $131 at the second level, and $1,324 at the third or higher education level.[29] The relatively privileged students and their families generally exercise more political clout than the masses

Table 4.2   Public Expenditure on Education in Latin America and the Caribbean

Country	Percent of 1992 GNP
High HDI	
Barbados	7.0
Medium HDI	
Brazil	4.6
Ecuador	2.7
Belize	5.7
Suriname	7.3
Cuba	6.6
Paraguay	2.6
Jamaica	4.7
Dominican Republic	1.6
Guyana	7.8
Guatemala	1.5
Honduras	4.1
El Salvador	1.6
Low HDI	
Haiti	1.8

Source: Based on data from UNDP, *World Development Report 1996* (New York: Oxford University Press, 1996), p. 19.

of other families, even though they presumably have a greater ability to pay.

This section has shown some gender dimensions of education in the overall context of low political priorities for human development programs. However, more than money or poverty is at work here when viewed with a gender lens. Let us revisit educational content and the deeper meaning of gender equality in education.

Gender Baggage

Even if girls have equal access to education, their experiences in the classroom are often different from those of boys. Girls learn different content from boys, particularly in secondary and higher education. They are channeled into gender-stereotyped fields or silenced in classrooms in overt and subtle ways that reinforce gender hierarchy.

As early as the primary school level, parents may contribute to devaluing and differentiating their daughters' education. Girls are recruited to help in household tasks (like boys) and are sometimes discouraged from continuing school. In the context of gendered wage disparities, or lack of wage employment for adult females, parents may be more reluctant to invest in tuition, various fees, uniforms, and supplies for daughters than for sons, who are expected to support aged parents. Tsitsi Dangarembga writes a startling account of parental discouragement, daughterly will, and persistence in a rigidly hierarchical schooling system, crisscrossed with classism, sexism, and racism in Zimbabwe.[30] UNICEF, working in partnership with South Asian governments, has provided funds that compensate poverty-stricken parents for these costs, in the interest of girls' continued schooling.[31]

Gender gaps begin to emerge in secondary education in the areas of science, engineering, agriculture, technology, and math, with consequences for later employment. The female share of enrollment is always lower than the male at secondary levels of education, although considerable ranges exist within world regions. For example, in Asia, the female low for these scientific fields is in Indonesia, at 2.3 percent; the high is in Turkey, at 28.2 percent. Females specialize in the humanities, commerce, and service.[32]

Math is a particularly instructive field for gender constructions. In the United States, gender-distinctive math interests and scores have been popularly coined as reflecting girls' "math anxiety." International comparisons of math and science test scores, broken down by nation, show gender difference in some countries but gender neutrality in others.[33] The latter pattern affirms the social construction built into curricular expectations and student performance. Yet the gaps have diminished over the last twenty to thirty years. Girls' testing advantage in reading is also a likely social construction. Curiously, however, we hear little about boys' "reading anxiety." If biology was as essential to male-female intellectual skills as some believe, historical and national differences would be minimal.

Girls also experience classrooms and textbooks differently from boys. Extensive research has documented the ways that textbooks and their pictures portray males and females differently—as active and passive, respectively. As a review on Argentina summarizes, "males are portrayed as working people, while the females are shown cooking, taking care of children, and performing other household duties."[34] Stories often center around males far more than females. Now dated, a famous study in the United States of 134 elementary schoolbooks found strikingly imbalanced ratios: five boy-centered to every two girl-centered stories, six male biographies to one female, and even more imbalanced fairy tales and animal character stories.[35] Huge generational cohorts, employed (or unemployed) in workforces, experienced an accumulation of daily exposure to these overt and subtle messages.[36] If governments' censorship of the media resulted in such methodical patterns, people would cry propaganda! In a gendered world, such patterns were naturalized and normalized in ways that raised no questions for much of history.

Besides textbooks, classroom climates reflect subtle and overt differences for boys and girls. Teachers seem to expect obedience and good behavior from girls but clever, albeit sometimes disruptive behavior from boys. Boys and girls themselves send cues to one another that depress achievement and enthusiasm for learning. In some cultures, girls' safety and family honor may be called into question with integrated classrooms. If girls are to be educated, then segregated educational opportunities quell parental concerns. The recruitment of female teachers also does much to quell parental anxieties about protecting girls' modesty.

Concerns for girls' safety is not merely some cultural delusion. At St. Kizito secondary school in Kenya, a coeducational boarding school, boys went on a rampage in 1991 that resulted in the death of nineteen girls and the rape of more than seventy by individuals and gangs. The school had tolerated everyday violence against females.[37]

Educators and parents have grappled with the issue of segregated or integrated classrooms for boys and girls. Within single countries, shifts have occurred from segregation to integration to calls to return to segregation. And these shifts have not occurred only in military (boys') schools. Educators have pilot tested math education for girls in classrooms that stress supposed girls' learning styles (hands-on, group work). Specific interventions for gender equity often produce dramatic results in computer lab use, enrollment in advanced math and other sciences, and test scores. At a UNESCO conference in 1995, attendees discussed "Is there a pedagogy for girls?" Pedagogy consisted of the following:

- cooperative and interactive learning modes,
- math and scientific content linkage to societal issues,
- emphasis of discussion and collaboration along with competition,
- private and public teacher-student probing and questioning,
- provision of precise feedback, balancing criticism and praise (rather than bland praise, often given to girls), [and]
- avoidance of rushing and speed.[38]

Educators have also experimented with separate boys' schools and classrooms to instill obedience and structure and thereby avoid high dropout rates. Both these kinds of experiments shift the pressures of heterosexual banter to nonclassroom environments. Likewise, schools sometimes expel or separate pregnant girls and child-mothers (without regard to their intimate counterparts).

Is resegregation compatible with equality principles? Of course, the meaning of equal treatment is rarely answered with the treatment of sameness.

Deborah Stone offers a metaphor to consider distributional issues and construct meanings for equality therein: Suppose a luscious cake was to be divided in class. Should the division be based on equal parts? Among those who are hungry? By status or rank? The questions go on and on.[39]

In an intriguing research project on the effects of gender-segregated schools in Peru, Violeta Sara-Lafosse examines more than academic achievement and test performance. She acknowledges research that demonstrates how integrated (coeducational) classrooms may discourage female performance compared with segregated (single-sex) schools, with their usually higher percentages of female authority figures. However, she also examines the "hidden curriculum" of single-sex schools by asking students and teachers about their perceptions of equal abilities among men and women, levels of aggression, and beliefs about the sexual division of labor, such as housework as women's work. Although differences are not huge, the tendencies in all-male schools are that boys aggress more, perceive girls as less able (and boys superior), and affirm polarized versions of masculinity and femininity as real.[40]

At the same time that questions are raised about segregating girls and boys, adult education and popular education undergo the same debates. To the extent cultures separate men and women, adult literacy programs focus on women- or men-only classes. Otherwise, husbands or fathers might oppose such programs. If power relations—male and female, professional and nonprofessional—are also contested in popular education, separate groups provide climates in which to speak and learn freely.

Adult programs focus on literacy, critical consciousness, and skill-building activities. Their effectiveness in changing power relations—or empowerment—is not always clear. The actual experience of political struggle may do as much or more. In a women's center in northern Mexico, women participants in a consciousness-raising course (on gender, class, and national consciousness) were less radicalized than women strikers in an export-processing factory. In that same center, the consciousness-raising course was followed with skill-building courses for paraprofessional jobs.[41] Research showed women expressing personal empowerment from the experience, but not the sort of empowerment in which they actively engaged in networks or organizations to address larger power imbalances. Moreover, most could not find jobs in the paraprofessional jobs for which they were trained.

Vocational training, frequently devoid of critical consciousness training, supplies skills for jobs that may or may not be plentiful. For which kinds of jobs are women being trained? All too often, men receive training for a wide range of jobs and salaries, but women learn and relearn a narrow range of traditional skills. In northeastern Brazil, women took courses in hygiene and beauty, health, restaurant, and telephone skills, while men received computer training. Elena Viveros noted a segregation of feminine and masculine fields, with obvious consequences for job prospects.[42]

Education is a topic to be examined in contexts. But it is a topic relevant everywhere in the world. Readers might examine the following section, considering the kind of education that would capacitate displaced workers.

The mainstream policy on education has an enormous influence on all parts of life, work, income, and taxes. Over time, girls face a special access problem and accumulate ideological baggage that diminishes the ability of education to capacitate so that, in Emma Goldman's terms, their liberation can emerge from within their souls.

Inattention to education is tied more generally to the devaluation of spending for human development. If children and female teachers were not so obviously prevalent in education, perhaps those who monopolize political decision making would behave differently. As in other policy areas, new faces and constituencies in the political process are critical to transforming education and strengthening its budgets to capacitate human development.

For Further Reflection[43]

With a population of 600,000, El Paso, Texas, is a city of chronic double-digit unemployment figures, with a quarter of its households under the poverty level. Around 1960, development decision makers transformed El Paso industry from its heavy manufacturing, natural resource base to light industry drawing on garment manufacturing. Part of that transformation was El Paso's per capita income: once comparable to the national per capita income, it fell to three-fifths of the national per capita income.

El Paso sits just across the Rio Grande from Juárez, Mexico's fifth largest city and home to the largest number of export-processing (maquiladora) factory workers. One hundred fifty thousand people, about 60 percent of them female, work in the maquiladoras, earning the official minimum wage plus fringe benefits in the form of bonuses and cafeteria food. Before the 1994 peso devaluation, the minimum wage was the equivalent of US$30 weekly, but devaluation reduced wages to about half that value. Northern Mexican wages are a contrast to the U.S. minimum, currently around $200 weekly.

Garment workers, most of them female, earn wages that are minimum or slightly more. The industry consists of several types of plants, ranging from large to medium- and small-size firms. The latter are subcontractors, for which the term "sweatshop" is an apt description. Sweatshops went out and back into business under new names, thereby avoiding wage payments, until a local group, La Mujer Obrera (The Woman Worker), lobbied the state legislature to make nonpayment a criminal offense. La Mujer Obrera has also sought funds to upgrade small garment manufacturers and lengthen the life of an industry with diminished prospects in Northern countries because of their high wages in comparison with countries in the South.

With the North American Free Trade Agreement (NAFTA), officially embracing Canada, the United States, and Mexico on January 1, 1994, the garment industry was probably weakened even more. NAFTA gradually lowers tariff barriers in this regional trade block. To win congressional majority support in the mid-1990s, several compromises became part of the agreement, among them provisions to support both environmental programs at the border and worker retraining for those displaced due to NAFTA. In 1997, El Paso won the dubious distinction of having the largest number of NAFTA-displaced workers.

La Mujer Obrera estimates that 6,000 garment workers lost their jobs after NAFTA. Most workers have limited education and English proficiency. The U.S. Department of Labor makes Trade Adjustment Assistance Program funds available to equivalent state agencies, which in turn subcontract worker retraining for up to eighteen months to existing adult education facilities. These adult education facilities focus primarily on English and high school equivalency classes, but two El Paso facilities offer vocational training as well.

Erica Castro, who observed classes in these various facilities, interviewed teachers and students. The schools divided workers by English level, on a one to ten scale. For most workers, job skills are not being taught in Spanish or simultaneously in the English instruction.

Most of the teachers seemed enthusiastic and interested in their students, but students expressed some discouragement at the progress they achieved for their twenty hours a week. Some expressed embarrassment with the childlike role in which they were placed. At one of the vocational schools, adults learned with high school students, some of whom ridiculed the adults. Even the teacher used them for comparative purposes—to paraphrase: "If you don't motivate yourselves, you'll end up like them." Of the forty students, women constituted a fourth; in all but one woman's case, the training was in cosmetology, a stereotypical low-pay option. At no schools did students have books they could take home to study with. Students got dittos in class. Moreover, no programs came with counselors or job placement efforts.

La Mujer Obrera lobbied to improve job training. Through the federal

Job Training Program Act for unemployed workers, a pilot training program was established to serve 400 in eight private centers. This is a fraction of the officially unemployed, but the new effort promises to have counselors and vocational training available for the unemployed workers.

In the meantime, questions have been raised about English fluency and high school equivalencies as job prerequisites. Community activist Norma Chávez, recently elected to the state legislature, successfully maneuvered a bill through the Texas House of Representatives that would forbid temporary employment agencies from requiring a high school diploma or its equivalent unless the requirement was connected to job performance.

Notes

1. United Nations Development Programme (UNDP), *Human Development Report 1996* (New York: Oxford University Press, 1996), with a thematic focus on the compatibility of growth and human development. The 1995 report focuses on gender.
2. UNDP, *Human Development Report 1994* (New York: Oxford University Press, 1994), pp. 7, 74. Human development expenditures include basic education, primary health, mass-coverage water supplies, and family planning services.
3. United Nations Educational, Scientific, and Cultural Organization (UNESCO), *World Education Report 1995* (New York: Oxford University Press, 1995), p. 18.
4. Nelly Stromquist, "Introduction," in *Women and Education in Latin America: Knowledge, Power, and Change,* edited by Nelly Stromquist (Boulder, Colo.: Lynne Rienner, 1992), p. 5.
5. According to UNESCO, "nearly $800 billion was still being spent worldwide on armaments in 1994, a decline, certainly, from the estimated $1,200 billion of 1987, but still equivalent to around two-thirds of estimated world public expenditure on education" (*World Education Report 1995*, p. 88). The enrollment figures are on p. 19. In United Nations Children's Fund (UNICEF), *The State of the World's Children 1996* (New York: Oxford University Press, 1996), figures 2 and 3 show that educational spending exceeds military spending in industrial countries, but that they are comparable in developing countries, as a percent of gross national product. In both world regions, the percentage spent on education has increased, while that spent on military has decreased.
6. The late Paulo Freire was a prolific writer, but his most famous work was *Pedagogy of the Oppressed* (New York: Continuum, 1970). See Mary Fink's discussion in "Women and Popular Education in Latin America," in Stromquist, *Women and Education in Latin America,* pp. 171–93. bell hooks critiques his glaring obliviousness to gender in *Teaching to Transgress: Education as the Practice of Freedom* (London: Routledge, 1994), p. 49.
7. Peter Smith's analysis of the UNAM networks is the classic work; see *Labyrinths of Power: Political Recruitment in Twentieth Century Mexico* (Princeton, N.J.: Princeton University Press, 1970), chap. 9.
8. The most thorough review, for the United States, is found in James Youniss, Jeffrey A. McLellan, and Miranda Yates, "What We Know about Engendering Civic Identity," *American Behavioral Scientist* 40, no. 5 (March/April 1997):

620–31. They do *not* use engendering the same way as the UNDP.

9. Nelly Stromquist, "Feminist Reflections on the Politics of the Peruvian University," in Stromquist, *Women and Education in Latin America*, p. 159. The U.S. literature is replete with studies of feminist breakaways from civil rights, anti-war, and New Left movements from the late 1960s; see especially Sara Evans, *Personal Politics* (New York: Vintage, 1980), and Jo Freeman, *The Politics of Women's Liberation* (New York: David McKay, 1975).

10. Mamphela Ramphele, *Crossing Boundaries* (New York: Feminist Press, 1997), p. 66.

11. UNESCO, *World Education Report 1995*, p. 11.

12. UNESCO, *World Education Report 1995*, p. 44.

13. Patricia L. McGrath, *The Unfinished Assignment: Equal Education for Women* (Washington, D.C.: Worldwatch, 1976), p. 7.

14. Marie Assad and Judith Bruce, *Empowering the Next Generation: Girls of the Maqattam Garbage Settlement* (New York: Seeds #19, 1997).

15. UNESCO, *World Education Report 1995*, p. 26.

16. Nelly Stromquist, "Women and Literacy in Latin America," in Stromquist, *Women and Education in Latin America*, pp. 19–32.

17. In Gloria Bonder, "Altering Sexual Stereotypes through Teacher Training," in Stromquist, *Women and Education in Latin America*, p. 235.

18. Stromquist, "Women and Literacy," p. 30.

19. International Labour Organization (ILO), *Child Labor: Targeting the Intolerable* (Geneva: ILO, 1996), p. 35. On p. 8, the report discusses the ill effects of child labor on growth and health.

20. UNDP, *Human Development Report 1996*, p. 164–65.

21. Results of the United Nations Summit were reported in the *New York Times*, September 29, 1990, p. 6. UNICEF produces an annual *State of the World's Children*, published by Oxford University Press.

22. UNDP, *Human Development Report 1996*, pp. 162–63.

23. Amartya Sen, "More Than 100 Million Women Are Missing," *New York Review of Books*, December 20, 1990, pp. 61–66. For full scholarly treatment of the intrahousehold division of labor, see his "Gender and Cooperative Conflicts," in *Persistent Inequalities: Women and World Development*, edited by Irene Tinker (New York: Oxford University Press, 1990), pp. 123–49.

24. UNESCO, *World Education Report 1995*, p. 45.

25. UNESCO, *World Education Report 1995*, p. 108.

26. Comparable-worth studies in the United States are plentiful. See, for example, Helen Remick, ed., *Comparable Worth and Wage Discrimination: Technical Possibilities and Political Realities* (Philadelphia: Temple University Press, 1984).

27. UNESCO, *World Education Report 1995*, p. 11.

28. Stromquist, "Women and Literacy," pp. 21–22.

29. UNESCO, *World Education Report 1995*, pp. 50, 54.

30. Tsitsi Dangarembga, *Nervous Conditions* (Seattle: Seal Press, 1988).

31. UNICEF, *State of the World's Children 1996*.

32. UNESCO, *World Education Report 1995*, p. 65.

33. UNESCO, *World Education Report 1995*. The literature on the United States is voluminous.

34. Cecilia Braslavsky, "Educational Legitimation of Women's Economic Subordination in Argentina," in Stromquist, *Women and Education in Latin America*, p. 52.

35. Women on Words and Images (WWI), *Dick and Jane as Victims* (Princeton, N.J.: WWI, 1975).

36. See Myra Sadker and David Sadker, *Failing at Fairness: How Our Schools Cheat*

Girls (New York: Simon & Schuster, 1995), who discuss females in the curriculum as "spectators" rather than "players" and as being burdened by the subtle accumulation of everyday injustices over the full span of their educational lives. In some ways, theirs is a gender analysis, for chapter 8 discusses the "mis-education" of boys for whom education is an "initiation into manhood." Bernice Sadler has written various reviews of the classroom climate in U.S. higher education during the 1980s, published by the American Council on Education, Project on the Status and Education of Women.

37. For a grim, methodical, and theoretically illuminating analysis, see H. Leslie Steeves, *Gender Violence and the Press: The St. Kizito Story* (Athens: Ohio University Center for International Studies, 1997).

38. UNESCO, *World Education Report 1995*, pp. 69–75. See Sadker and Sadker, *Failing at Fairness*, pp. 232ff. and chap. 6 on test scores.

39. Deborah Stone, *Policy Paradox: The Art of Political Decision Making*, 2d ed. (New York: W. W. Norton, 1997), chap. 2 on the equality example.

40. Violeta Sara-Lafosse, "Coeducational Settings and Educational and Social Outcomes in Peru," in Stromquist, *Women and Education in Latin America*, pp. 87–106.

41. Gay Young, "Gender Identification and Working-Class Solidarity among Maquila Workers in Ciudad Juárez: Stereotypes and Realities," and Kathleen Staudt, "Programming Women's Empowerment? A Case from Northern Mexico," in *Women on the U.S.-Mexico Border: Responses to Change*, edited by Vicki L. Ruiz and Susan Tiano (Boston: Allyn & Unwin, 1987), pp. 105–28, 155–73.

42. Elena Viveros, "Vocational Training and Job Opportunities for Women in Northeast Brazil," in Stromquist, *Women and Education in Latin America*, pp. 195–229.

43. Sources for this section are Erica Castro, "Trade Adjustment Assistance," paper for Political Science 3414, Women, Power and Politics, and Kathleen Staudt, *Free Trade? Informal Economies at the U.S.-Mexico Border* (Philadelphia: Temple University Press, 1998).

5 Women's Work
Central to Economies

I worked in the fields at night, by moonlight,
or at times where there was the least likelihood
of being seen. I did any kind of work I could
find—resurfacing houses with mud and dung,
planting date palm and other fruit trees, paddy
husking and harvesting.
—Landless laborer, Bangladesh

I was reassigned to the stitching cap operation.
I had to stitch 64 dozen in eight hours. Every day
I was bathed in my own sweat since there was no
ventilation at all. We complained [but they just said]
… you can easily be replaced by a hundred more.
—Garment worker, Philippines

It seems this project is just like the Chinese one
when we suffered before. We aren't going to put up
with that again. … We were asleep then. But now we
are awake.
—Rice farmer, Gambia

Women work for food, money, and wages. The value accorded that work is more or less related to its worth, depending on the institutions that mediate gender subordination from household to national and global levels. One of the oldest feminist traditions stresses women's ability to work and to reap its just rewards. But there is more than socialist feminism at work here. Amartya Sen and Jean Dreze have shown a link between "gainful" economic activity and female life expectancy. Broken down by world region, the higher women's activity rate, the longer their life expectancy, with South Asia and North Africa the lowest in both categories.[1]

To think comprehensively about women's work, we can divide it into three categories. First, women labor in the home and field, often with neither pay nor official counts making that work visible. Second, women generate income through self-employment, in what is sometimes known as microenterprise. Third, women work in the official labor force for wages and, perhaps, for protection and benefits. When national and international statistical reports include figures on women workers, they generally limit their counts to wage labor force participation. This is a drastic underestimation of women's labor.

As we shall see in this chapter, women's work is central to agricultural, industrial, and what is sometimes called "informal" economies. Women support themselves and other household members, either in part or in full, the latter as female household heads, estimated to be a de facto quarter of households worldwide. Often those households fall disproportionately below national poverty lines, giving rise to the phrase "feminization of poverty."[2]

In this chapter, I focus on women's work in agricultural, industrial, and informal economies, drawing on research that documents their work. In particular, I examine politics and policies that encourage or discourage particular forms of work, earnings, and consequences for men and women. Whether women can claim the value from their own labor is another matter. Research has only just begun to document "homes divided," which calls into question those idyllic assumptions about shared household resources.[3] Do men control all members' earnings, providing allowances? Do women manage all earnings? Or do earners control their own earnings? Without power and autonomy in their everyday lives, these questions may have problematic answers for women.

Undercounted and Underpaid

One of the earliest contributions of so-called women in development (WID) research was to examine women's work more inclusively and to make transparent official ideologies that circumscribe women's work visibility through exclusive definitions, derived from industrial societies. Women were labeled "housewives" or as not being in the labor force.

Consider these occupational categories from the Venezuela census: sales, agriculture and livestock, artisan and factory, service, others not identifiable. Now consider this actual women's work: raises and sells chickens, sells to consumers; takes in boarders, baby-sits, operates a drink stand, makes shoes at home.[4] In what category does this women's work fit? In that large, critical mass of people who work for money, but in unregulated spaces, women and men informally support themselves and their families.

The mismatch between counts and agricultural labor is even more glaring. Ruth Dixon-Mueller notes some striking examples of distortions in counting and redefining women's proportion of agricultural workers, within nations over time and among national neighbors: Algeria, 37 percent in 1954 but 2 percent in 1966; Iraq, 2 percent in 1957 but 37 percent in 1977. Egypt's Population Census of 1960–61 counted only 4 percent women among agricultural workers, but its Agricultural Census that same year counted 20 percent.[5] Gender ideologies produce methodological blinders bound so tight that we hardly know who is doing what work.

Much of women's work is uncounted and unpaid. A gender division of labor exists in all societies, along with gender-distinctive values for that labor. Linda Lim reports that "women still earn between 50 and 80 percent of men's wages worldwide," despite "equal remuneration" having one of the highest ratification rates of all International Labour Organization (ILO) standards.[6]

Before we begin examining different types of women's work, readers should understand that women may not control their ability to make the choice *to* work. Women face discriminatory obstacles in the range of work for which they receive pay, from gatekeepers at the workplace itself to systemic education gaps that undermine their credentials and skills. It is not coincidence that many women are stuck at the bottom of work hierarchies. One study of maquilas in northern Mexico found a virtually pure inverse relationship between the rank of a position and the percentage of women therein: plant managers, production superintendents and engineers, and supervisors were all male (except for 10 percent of first-line supervisors), and operators and assemblers were 70 percent or more female.[7]

Women's double day—or *doble jornada*, as it is known in the Americas—influences the perceptions of both women and the gatekeepers about female labor force commitment. Women's reproductive labor—birthing children and rearing families—limits full participation but enables men's participation.

Martha Chen analyzed women's right to be employed in India and Bangladesh as a matter of survival and justice. As late as the 1990s, women were excluded by custom and law from working outside the home. Saleha Begum, the landless worker quoted in the epigraph, was refused employment at UNICEF-supported food-for-work sites after local officials said, "Women in Bangladesh should not work outside their homes. We have never hired women at food-for-work sites." Urban women worked at these jobs when UNICEF first introduced those projects in 1974. Research showed that a third of such women were married to men who could not earn enough to meet family needs, and the rest were widowed, deserted, divorced, or unmarried; almost half were principal family earners with an average of 3.7 dependents. Begum was finally hired, but afterward she and her coworkers organized group loans for self-employment.[8]

Wage Work

Women work in production and service processes, contained in national homelands with differently valued and regulated labor pools. They work in factories, shops, professions, homes (as domestics), "entertainment industries," and public and private agencies. Mostly, fellow nationals employ women, but foreigners also employ women in fragmented global assembly production, largely electronics and garment factories that produce goods for export. By the late twentieth century, export-processing factories recruited women at far higher rates than they did men. Women's labor force participation is on the rise.

According to Susan Joekes, women constitute a quarter of the industrial labor force in developing countries, versus a fifth two decades ago. Countries with high proportions of women workers therein demonstrate the most successful growth rates. Joekes continues, though: "Women's greater participation has also played a significant *causal* role in industrialization, related to their lesser status and rewards in industrial production than men."[9] Women are central to the industrial boom, especially the export-processing zones, not only as workers but also as vehicles for enhancing profit.

Structural Adjustment: Gender Bias?

The deterritorialized, fragmented labor process of the global economy coincided with a major push among international banks and state officials to open economies to freer trade and reduced tariff barriers. How do men and women fare in such circumstances? Although adjustment drew some women into the labor market, especially export-processing factory work, it also burdened women with covering cuts in social services through unpaid and informal work.

In the former centrally planned economies of the Soviet Union and eastern Europe, cuts or sales of public industries led to massive displacements of women workers. In the former second world, women's labor force participation rates were highest. A dubious distinction of market transition was higher unemployment rates for women than for men.[10]

Women in the second world and elsewhere did not always prosper under preadjustment economies, either. Certainly, men's educational and political advantages gave them prior claims and patronage for the bulk of government jobs, some of which got lost under adjustment. The promise of structural adjustment and free trade is that of spurred growth over the long term. But are the motors of capital growth transparent or accountable to people? (Recall Chapter 2.)

In an analysis focused on the Middle East and North Africa, Valentine Moghadam lists both the costs and the potential benefits of structural adjustment. Besides those costs already mentioned, she reminds us that "flexible" labor translates into low-paid, temporary jobs. The poverty induced by structural adjustment hits single heads of households hard, and they are almost invariably women. On the benefit side, however, Moghadam points out that economic liberalization associated with export-oriented manufacturing increases the demand for female labor, breaks down cultural proscriptions about occupational segregation, and potentially results in further feminization of banking, insurance, accounting, and computing jobs.[11]

Manufacturing Jobs

Several Asian countries have grown rapidly under policies to promote export-oriented industrialization, among them Taiwan, China, Singapore, and the Republic of Korea. Others have welcomed export-processing factories, among them Indonesia, the Philippines, Mexico, Ireland, the Baltic countries, and Caribbean countries. In those factories, women make up a majority of the export-processing workforce, even 80 percent or more in a variety of countries.

What kinds of women work in export-processing industrialization? Studies are plentiful. Many women are young, productive household contributors. Employers recruit women for light assembly, electronic, toy production, garment, and clerical tasks. In some places, women are attractive recruitment targets due to socialization that seemingly trains them to defer to authority.

Women's actual compliance or resistance to the demands of industrial management actually varies widely. Devon Peña's analysis in northern Mexico documents considerable resistance to speedups and ever-increasing production. Workers restrict output and thereby reclaim some control over their lengthy workweeks, averaging forty-six hours. Women also vote with their feet, exhibiting annual turnover rates that surpass 100 percent annually.[12] In studies of Malaysian women workers in export-processing plants, Aihwa Ong documents outbreaks of hysteria, also a reaction to the control, speed, and stress of the Fordist managed workplace.[13]

What kinds of working conditions exist, in pay and safety terms? Export-processing factories, many of them new and modern, offer a mix of conditions. Environmentalists charge that toxic materials in the workplace and wastes in the wider community make export-processing factories dangerous for public safety and health. Those who defend the industries acknowledge that plant conditions include the "good, bad, and the ugly."[14] Host governments, too, bear responsibility. Governments range from those that ignore safety and health considerations to those that promote noble policy intentions (or policy cosmetics), which may or may not be enforced.

Governments are often eager to stimulate jobs and attract foreign investment, so they offer concessions such as tax relief and public works subsidies for the jobs created and the money put in circulation. In that eagerness, governments may compromise health, safety, and justice for workers, most of whom engage governments in minimal to nonexistent ways.

Northern Mexico is home to hundreds of thousands of export-processing factory workers in maquiladoras, employed mainly in U.S. and some Japanese corporations. The vast majority of workers earn the legal minimum wage plus fringe benefits and bonuses, as well as access to Mexico's public health and pension systems. In a household study of neighborhoods, one of them a maquila bedroom community, both male and female workers averaged one to two minimum wages weekly, or $45 per week. Household members required multiple earners to cope with urban costs of living. After the peso devaluation of 1994, a boom for foreign investors, wages dropped to half those levels.[15] Elsewhere, women are regularly paid less than men, even for the same work, such as in the Philippines.[16]

Labor unions in the North worry about job loss. In the past, they have pushed for protectionist policies that would make it more difficult for corporations to move capital and jobs "offshore" (hardly the right metaphor for the Chihuahua and Sonora deserts of North America). Sporadic transnational union organizing occurs, but it faces obstacles associated with nationalism and consumer interest in lower prices for products. The insatiable appetite for consumer goods helps drive global production (overproduction?). Multinational corporations sometimes threaten to leave countries where they face bad publicity, as is the situation with Disney and its Haitian plants.

In the South, people pursue individual resistance, acquiesce, or join organizations for change. If unions are not outlawed, organizations offer the potential to use the power of collective action to negotiate better conditions. In some countries, such as Mexico, several large unions are notorious for the way they have been co-opted by the dominant political party (PRI) over pacts to keep inflation and wage rates low.

Domestic and Other Service Work

Although lots of attention goes to this growing number of jobs for women, they are employed in significant numbers in other settings. One of the most common jobs for women in the Americas is domestic service. To be a maid, often apprenticed as a child laborer, is to work in settings unregulated by wage and hour laws, rarely in potential solidarity with other similarly situated workers. Maids (*muchachas*, the term inscribing them to perpetual girlhood) often earn less than the legal minimum wage and are even paid part of their earnings in kind (used clothing and meals, for example). Live-in maids, paid by the week or month, sometimes find themselves in perpetual labor without time limits. In some countries, domestic workers organize for better conditions and for legal protection under wage and hour laws, as a fine collection by Elsa Chaney and Mary García Castro demonstrates.[17]

Sex workers labor under conditions that are among the most risky of all occupations, known euphemistically as the "entertainment industry." Girls and women earn from mere pittance wages to salaries that surpass those of factory jobs, particularly around foreign military bases. In parts of Asia, girls are conscripted or bonded to work in the sex-tourism industry, to which government officials turn their heads in toleration. The rate of HIV infection is generally higher among sex workers than other groups of women, subjecting them to treacherous health risks.[18]

Women's participation in wage labor is growing. Equally large numbers of women work in agriculture and self-employment, in what is sometimes called the informal economy and microenterprises. To these we now turn.

Food and Agriculture

If we look at societies with a household lens, women's connection to food is well established. On the whole, it is women who gather food for home consumption in subsistence economies, or they purchase food as consumers in commercial economies. It is also women who process and prepare food for household consumption. Less well known is women's prominence in food production and marketing.

People who reside in rural areas often grow food and tend animals to support themselves or to augment their incomes. The gender division of labor varies, but a comprehensive review of agricultural work reports gender balance (40 to 60 percent male and female contributions) in Africa,

Asia, and the Caribbean, with diminishing female participation in North Africa, the Middle East, and Latin America.[19] Women participate in livestock production, too; men and women specialize in different types of animal care. Whereas cattle herding is often men's work, women do dairy work and raise chickens, ducks, and goats.[20]

Women's contribution to food and agriculture is clear, but programs and policies have often been oblivious to female labor and return for labor, as well as to the public's stakes in sustainable agriculture for *all* farmers. This section focuses particularly on agricultural policies, institutions, and constituencies. For many countries, agriculture is central to the health of the economy. Agricultural crops are exchanged in the global economy, earning precious foreign exchange. For countries with insufficient food to feed themselves, or with a selective taste for nonlocal foods, food is imported at prices that not all can bear. Food occasionally becomes a tool of foreign policy.

Gender in the Agricultural and Forestry Environment

World Bank reports point to the declining share of agriculture in the total workforce, from 70 percent in 1950 to 33 percent in 1990.[21] But before we dismiss the significance of agriculture, we must understand that "workforce" is a suspect term, given the underestimations of female labor, particularly in unpaid work and subsistence economies.

In many countries of the South, including the most populous India and China (which, combined, account for two-fifths of the world's population), a majority of people live in rural areas and depend on agriculture in whole or in part for their livelihood. China's rural population was 71 percent in 1993, and India's was 74 percent. Although both China and India are industrializing, agricultural production consumes a considerable portion of gross domestic product (GDP) (a fifth and a third, respectively). In most countries with low human development index (HDI) scores, agriculture represents a quarter or more of the GDP.[22] To improve agriculture, then, has the potential to pursue antipoverty measures.

Those who study agriculture must grapple with the sheer challenges of documenting who does what work, with what returns, in rural economies at a distance from capital cities, roads, and the conveniences that officials and researchers would like to take for granted. A labor-intensive, costly method of understanding the billions of hours people devote annually to agriculture involves time-allocation studies among samples of residents: through direct observation, time-use recall, and informant record keeping, recognizing, however, the seasonal variation that might distort sampling.[23]

Figure 5.1   Gender-Disaggregated Community Seasonal Activities Calendar

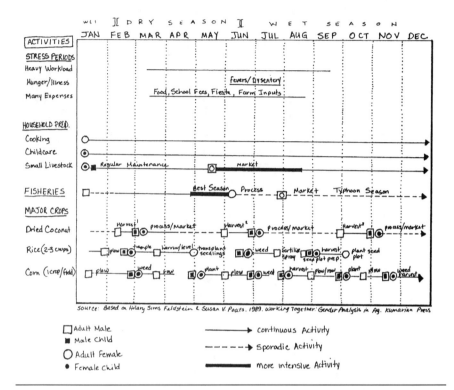

Source: M. Dale Shields and Barbara P. Thomas-Slayter, *Gender, Class, Ecological Decline, and Livelihood Strategies: A Case Study of Siguijor Island, the Philippines* (Worcester, Mass.: Clark University, 1993).

Time-allocation studies would confirm women's centrality to agricultural production in ways that grafts from industrial society census methodologies do not.

Clark University has pilot-tested methodologies in which to conceptualize gender in ecologically sustainable development. Several monographs allow readers to understand and to visualize seasonally specific tasks in highly condensed charts.[24] See Figure 5.1 for an inspiring but clear outline of these data.

In Africa, where agriculture is central to the economy and to rural dwellers, women are renowned for their predominance in food production. At the United Nations Economic Commission for Africa, the Women's Training and Research Centre developed a continental women's agenda, probably the first coinage of the phrase connecting women and development. It publicized striking figures about women's predominance in food production and marketing, at rates of 60 to 80 percent of labor. Economic crises gripped the African continent, where agricultural productivity decreased in per capita terms, unlike in most other world regions. Women persistently pursue their expertise in agriculture, even in cities. In Nairobi, a third of households cultivate and a fifth of households raise livestock in open spaces, rented or borrowed plots, and near homes.[25] As Jane Guyer's collection documents so well, mostly women handle the job of "feeding African cities," whether in rural or urban bases.[26]

Yet in most agricultural institutions, whether at the helm of ministries, among agricultural research faculty, or at mid- to low-level agricultural staff, men predominate and seem to operate with the working assumption that women and agricultural production are mutually exclusive phenomena. The development mainstream only slowly began to understand women's centrality in agriculture; by the 1980s, developers seemed ready to promote new practices among women and to thereby increase their labor, without regard for securing their claims on income therefrom or on the land they tilled. Agricultural policies are implemented with gendered consequences. Still, women lack control over land, agricultural subsidies and training, and the ability to trade their produce for a fair price, free from officials' and husbands' appropriation. As earlier chapters make clear, these gender matters are the result of political decisions. For Kenyan social scientist Achola Pala Okeyo, "women's advancement is highly political because it is an integral part of our quest for justice not only at the household level but all the way within the local, national and world economic order."[27] Women cannot ignore those gendered stakes, in the same way that officials cannot be oblivious to gender.

For many decades, development ideologies privileged urban areas and industrialization therein. Governments have a grim track record of response to the rural majority, especially small farmers and tenant and seasonable laborers. Rural people often flee to cities (also known as migration), beginning with men and then followed by women. For those who remain behind, a safe strategy is to keep a distance from government for some of the reasons outlined below.

Engaging Government

People's experience with government leaves much to be desired. Governments often give less to people than they take in taxes, bodies (conscription, inattention to maternal mortality), and symbolic support such as votes. Local officials have acted as much like police agents or arrogant civil servants as they have like bearers of knowledge that farmers might use to improve farm productivity and alleviate arduous tasks. Farmers' knowledge often gets ignored. In the late colonial era in Kenya, chiefs would uproot seedlings that women did not plant in lines, confiscate cattle to pay for cash crops such as tea bushes, and jail men who did not prune their coffee trees properly.[28]

The practice of local officials changed little after independence, although force and compulsion diminished somewhat. Male agents, book and school trained, often have little of the practical knowledge that women apprentices learn from their mothers. A rich ethnography of Zambia highlights people's skepticism about expensive fertilizer promotions or poor advice about when to burn weeds. When fire hazards are greatest, villagers avoid burning, although this is the time that extension manuals declare best. For villagers, the production of daily food is "too important to be experimented on."[29]

Studies of agricultural agents show appalling gaps in knowledge about appropriate planting and weeding practices for varieties of hybrid seeds. Farmers who respond—once known in the patronizing communications literature as "early adopters" (the polar opposite of "laggards")—may find themselves hooked in a cash economy, diminishing some of the self-sufficiency of their earlier practices.[30] Hybrid seeds, insecticides, and fertilizers must be purchased, not stored or dealt with through local means.

Staff in governmental machinery have so alienated people that many disengage, not the least of whom are those at the political margins, where women are overrepresented. African studies are replete with insights about how people distance themselves from authoritarian states. James Scott elevates this behavior to important political behavior, known as "everyday peasant resistance."[31] For example, Ruth Meena discusses women's refusal to grow cash crops in Tanzania. In Zambia, women questioned "why should we grow maize for the government?" Equally poignant was a question a farmer posed to Maud Shimwaayi Muntemba after her husband "gave" her the same payment for three times the output: "what is that but slavery?"[32]

With one foot or no feet in a commercial economy, rural people feed themselves through their own labor. However, public resources and policies can be brought to bear on farm productivity, security of returns, and burdensome labor. Perhaps engagement is in order, with governments accountable to more than those well connected to political and bureaucratic elites. Consider some of the government policies and programs with the potential to support farmers and alleviate their labor burdens: land registration and security, irrigation and potable water, marketing from isolated regions, farm-to-market roads, technical advice, loans, new tools and technology, cooperative authority, subsidized inputs to reduce risk, crop insurance, guaranteed purchases, and less regressive taxation, among others.

Let us begin with the larger structures that often privilege men over women in the control of assets and incomes. Governments have the authority to register, reform, and redistribute landholdings or use equality principles in such efforts. In many countries, landownership is highly concentrated: a small percentage of landowners own half or more of arable land, leaving the rural majority to farm small plots, to sharecrop as tenants, or to provide seasonable agricultural labor. But land concentration also has a gender dimension: in most land reforms, women's use rights have been incorporated into men's ownership, drawing on ideologies that assume men to be the household breadwinners. Land reform experts consult men about customary rules, silencing women's versions. As Zen Tadesse once starkly said about women after Ethiopia's postfeudal land reform of the mid-1970s: "tenants of former tenants." Crossing continents, Carmen Diana Deere and Magdalena León de Leal document the chronic problem of men's land reform in Latin America.[33]

Basic gender sense is rarely brought to bear in discussions of agriculture work, return on labor, and control over assets such as land. Women's control over land is minuscule, compounding their abilities to produce. The famous quote from the 1985 United Nations women's conference in Nairobi was that half the world's population (women) owned 1 percent of world land.[34]

Equality standards under rules of law have some potential to redress historic injustices. In weak states with large rural populations, plural laws allow men and women to negotiate, though he who controls the machinery of justice is the probable winner. Occasionally, women are able to make their claims in neutral courts of law. In Tanzania, for example, Holalia Pastory's case made its way to the High Court in 1989. A poor widow, she "inherited clan land. Her husband's relatives sought a court order to prevent her selling it, arguing that, according to Haya customary law, as a woman, she had no power to sell this land although she could use it for her lifetime."[35] Using international legal instruments (CEDAW) and national constitutional measures, the court decided that she could sell it on similar terms to those of men. A review of law cases in Africa plugs this into a liberal democratic rights framework—one we might term liberal feminism—in the way it challenged customary practices. Customary law, as historians document, was often an invention of elder men's material interests in early colonialism.[36]

The control and management of household income vary in ways that matter to farmers and policymakers. Developers often assume that men control all earnings and expenditure decisions or that household income is pooled. Instead, women manage household budgets in some cultures.

Moreover, men and women manage their own separate incomes in yet other areas. In parts of Africa, women control their own incomes, a corollary of which often means extensive household obligations. Whatever the customary practices, out-migration wreaks havoc on the norms. Most policies ignore the gender division of control over income or land.

A series of project interventions in the Gambia illustrates the persistent gendered ideological and material interests that drive implementation.[37] Government officials, with outside aid from sources of various ideological stripes (People's Republic of China, Taiwan, World Bank, United States, Britain), ignored women rice farmers, stripped them of indigenous resources, and produced project failure rather than more rice—Gambia's basic foodstuff, which it imported because local consumption did not fulfill national needs. Among the Mandinka people, men and women grow different crops on different land plots either for household consumption or for sale, the profits of which are cultivator controlled. With foreign assistance, developers designed rice irrigation schemes, based on the assumption that men household heads would own pumps and acquire credit through cooperatives. Developers also assumed that women would provide labor for men's rice production. According to local custom, women had the option to refuse, though some women worked for wages from husbands and other growers if that work did not compete with labor needed for their own crops and plots. Projects fostered intrahousehold conflicts. With new project funds, women acquired (after struggles, like those cited in the epigraph) cosmetic ownership, but the procedures threatened men, and backlash resulted in a perpetuation of past problems.

Resettlement schemes have often been catastrophic for people. In 1985, the World Bank and the government of India planned dam projects on the Narmada River, with great promise for water and irrigation. Dam projects—which a former prime minister called the "temples of modern India"—have forced millions of rural dwellers to resettle, with yet other promises of rehabilitation (that is, return to previous living standards). The majority of 1,500 large dam projects built since independence have failed, not delivering the promised irrigation, water, and help in daily life. The legacy of some dam projects, instead, is silt, destroyed fishing grounds, and breeding sites for malarial mosquitoes. India has been called "one of the most dammed nations on earth."[38]

Dam projects are attractive, however, to business and government. They provide opportunities to sell overvalued land for compensation, to purchase at inflated prices to sell to oustees, and to make business for contractors who may or may not comply with appropriate standards. For banks, dams offer the opportunity to move tremendous amounts of money; India has been the World Bank's most important client. One of the first organizers to mobilize residents against India's proposed Sardar Sarovar Dam was social worker Medha Patkar. Others followed her, resulting in residents refusing to move, public-relations disasters, pressure from other countries on the bank's board, and a face-saving request on the government of India's part to cancel the loan.[39]

Agricultural resettlement schemes have burdened women particularly, establishing structures of male machinery from administration to cooperative memberships through which payments are made, whether women labor or not. At the Mwea Rice Scheme in Kenya, women diverted produce from the official marketing channels and even fled these highly controlled schemes in large numbers. Ingrid Palmer summarizes the grim record of technical planners who designed modern resettlements with a composite case called "Nemow" (women spelled backwards).[40]

It has been widely documented that the largely male agricultural field staff focus on men farmers, even in areas where women manage farms in sizable numbers or perform most of the field work.[41] Because of widespread gender gaps in education, along with the patronage associated with those who successfully engage government, men predominate in extension staff, as the breakdown by world region strikingly shows: Africa, 97 percent male; Asia and Oceania, 77 percent male; Latin America and the Caribbean, 86 percent male; Europe, 86 percent male; North America, 81 percent male.[42]

My own research in western Kenya documented the tendency of agricultural extension officers to bypass women farm managers. Whether high or low income, on bigger or smaller pieces of land, the two-fifths of farms that women managed received fewer agricultural visits, training programs, and subsidized credit. The mere 2 percent of female field staff did home economics outreach—not always practical for farmers' needs. The lone woman credit recipient in a sample of 212 households was a widow of the subchief, who had borrowed money without her knowledge; she learned of her obligation to repay when extension officers visited her with threats of foreclosure. Of course, questions might be raised about the quality of advice among civil servants without much farm experience; other research documents surprising ignorance about the expert knowledge they are supposed to convey. Women farmers, too, are reluctant to associate with male strangers while their husbands are absent, laboring as migrant workers elsewhere.

Obvious implications to improve policy implementation would involve female staff recruitment, staff accountability to farmers, and *public* extension work. The government of Kenya has reformed its extension service, going so far as to integrate home economics and agricultural training for staff and farmers alike. But it leaves untouched the structures of gender subordination that perpetuate men's control over land and payments through male machinery. Disengaged from government machinery, women on their own trade or brew to earn income, to the extent that they can freely trade across district boundaries where officials at police checkpoints confiscate grain outside the marketing board's distribution system.

Engaged with government, women pursue strategies with the potential to dent those structures of gender subordination. In Zambia, the Ministry of Agriculture had long been a conservative, male-dominated branch that supported women's development in rhetoric but with few concrete operational programs.[43] With commitments from several strategically placed men and women, a women's extension program (WEP) was created to train women to plow, to mobilize women's groups for extension visits, and to generate a demand-driven agricultural extension system. A research project documented women farmers' work, the results of which opened up discussion about this group that male extension officers had ignored. Mary Masona, animal husbandry officer in the home economics section, persuaded colleagues in extension to create a people's participation project that built groups (mostly women) to advance their interests. WEP also encouraged the monitoring of training, setting goals on behalf of women and finally bringing gender parity to that effort. Actions of midlevel staff caught the positive attention of top-ranked Lusaka ministry officials. Outside women's constituencies, including women and development activists and officials in other agencies, vigilantly monitor the effort to prevent marginalization.

In India, the institutional machinery of agroforestry protection bears uncanny resemblance to institutions in other world regions, but it widens authority among men in the name of people's participation, as Bina Agarwal's research lays out so clearly.[44] In India, forests and village common land have declined, as a result of commercial development and individualized property rights. Women and men use forest products in different ways, for different purposes. Women gather fuel and fodder for everyday cooking needs, and it takes hours for them to travel by foot to collect these products. Landless people in particular depend on village commons for a large part of their income, fuel, and fodder, and landless women seek forest "famine food" for survival purposes. New forest management groups, many of which are government inspired, put cooperative members, who are mostly men, in charge of these institutions rather than residents, a more inclusive category that embraces women. Some all-male protection groups ban women's entry, even as they sell forestry products from their thinning and cleaning. Man-made rules are not efficiently communicated, as one women said: "Women often don't even know what rules the forest committee has decided upon. If more women were on the forest committee then they could pass on the information to other women and the forest would be better protected."[45]

Agarwal's research shows that groups with critical masses of women or separate women's groups result in better use of the forests. However, separation accommodates, rather than challenges, gender relations. But the lone, token woman can hardly challenge gender structures, either. Without critical masses, women cannot easily speak in male-only, potentially hostile atmospheres. Comanagement spreads stakes among all the users and potential abusers of the forest. It ensures that tree planting brings all relevant varieties to the forests, including those trees for fuel and fodder, and not just the men's preferred commercially profitable trees.

Engaging "Free" Markets

Free marketeers believe that governments have little to no business in the agricultural economy. Development experts once thought that crop prices ought to be stable—a stability that was best managed through bureaucratic fiat in the machinery of marketing boards. Farmers could thereby count on fixed prices, and governments could supply basic foodstuffs to consumers. Politically, urban and large farmer constituencies were placated at the expense of small farmers. In many countries, that practice became regressive taxation in disguise, as farmers received depressed prices for goods sold for higher prices in world markets. Consumer subsidies benefited rich and poor alike, adding to budgetary woes and deficit spending. State officials who "man" the marketing boards cost governments plenty.

Coupled with structural adjustment, market forces gained a freer reign, and governments cut personnel to increase efficiency, trade, and exports. By 1986, the slogan "getting prices right" turned into unstable but sometimes higher prices for those who received payment for crops.[46]

Reforms like these could conceivably work to the advantage of women farmers and others who were excluded from state networks of preference and privilege. Women consumers' interests are not identical to those of women farmers. Women farmers gain if they control proceeds or share control with other household members. But is structural adjustment working? The World Bank says yes for Africa, although it documents its answer through narrow, macro-level indicators of success. The current scenario is unsatisfactory—tragic in places—but Uma Lele says that the consequences of nonadjustment are worse. In a thick edited collection, voices from multiple vantage points provide a nuanced view of this complex situation.[47]

The rhetoric of free markets will take us through the millennium. Therefore, it seems appropriate to consider another compatible policy and program issue: microenterprise.

Informal Labor and Microenterprise

People make work for themselves to generate incomes, among other reasons. Self-employment is perhaps the oldest, most common profession. In the early 1970s, researchers began to name a form of work they called "informal,"[48] an everyday and common practice that occurs worldwide, especially in economies without widespread waged employment and tax and regulatory authority.

Although much ink was spilled over exactly how to define and measure informal work, most observers agree that it generates income outside the bounds of government authority; it also tends to be unregulated, untaxed, and undercounted. Some analysts thought that informal work would disappear with the spread of "modern" economies and strong states. Increasingly, though, analysts began to understand that informalization expanded in the late-twentieth-century global economy with these attendant characteristics: business downsizing, cuts in government spending, migration, wage rates that do not keep pace with inflation, and subcontracting to home-based workers.

The Two Faces of Informality

Informal work comes in two different varieties. One type tends to be small production and service operations, wherein workers use simple technology. They frequently use their labor or savings as start-up resources, whether by choice or by the credit squeeze they face from commercial banks and government loan programs. Credit squeezes are endemic in countries with a majority of illiterate people who lack assets such as land and wages to guarantee loans; women are particularly stuck in such circumstances. In Jana Everett and M. Savara's interviews with informal workers, one woman said: "If we go alone, who will listen to us? We don't know who to meet, what to ask for. People are rude to us, they think we are dirty and talk to us badly. They don't try and explain anything to us.[49]

Informal workers range from place-bound street vendors and long-distance traders (known as higglers in the Caribbean) to domestics, livestock raisers, and home-based seamstresses, among others. Informals establish small grocery stores in neighborhoods; they commercialize farm operations, such as poultry rearing or husking rice paddy. Even though women and men work informally at relatively balanced rates, especially if domestic labor counts as informal work, there is generally a gender hierarchy of earnings. Men earn more because the work in which they specialize reaps higher value.[50]

Another type of informal worker is found in subcontracted production processing. In the search for low-cost labor in a competitive global economy, firms fragment the production process to subcontractors who commission factory- and home-based workers, both categories of which enjoy little or no protection from wage, labor, and safety laws. In a study of 140 home-based workers in Mexico City, Lourdes Benería and Martha Roldán found that women earned paltry sums but persisted for not only the support the extra cash provided but also the negotiation and leverage ability that money gave them in household authority relations.[51] Studies in the United States show that this sort of informality occurs in global cities, including those at the border, particularly in immigrant and ethnic enclave communities. Ironically for some feminists, perhaps (though not for socialist feminists, who understand the significance of gender and class), even women sweatshop owners exploit a female majority workforce.[52]

Yet informality is so understudied in the United States, or stigmatized as crime and tax evasion, that we know little about the conditions for its emergence and profitability. At the U.S.-Mexico border, informality is extensive, documented in one out of three low- and middle-income households in particular neighborhoods of the 2-million-person metropolitan area of El Paso and Juárez.

The existence of informality in Mexico is no surprise, for government and academic studies show how it flourishes, particularly during times of economic crisis. Informality mystifies poverty, says Priscilla Connolly, for government advertises low official unemployment rates, with employment surveys counting people as economically active if they generate income, however minimal the hours or meager the income.[53]

Yet informality and poverty are not necessarily connected, as studies in Mexico and Venezuela show. The artificially low minimum wage in Mexico, along with the comparative advantages of leaky borders for informal "import-export" trade, makes certain kinds of self-employment more profitable than the booming export-processing factories at Mexico's northern border. Juárez alone has 150,000 industrial workers so employed, earning $30 weekly from these mostly U.S. firms before the 1994 peso devaluation, and $20 thereafter.[54]

Even in El Paso, informal work occurred as much among the better off and nonimmigrant households as among the poorer and immigrant households. El Pasoans, at the front lines of the global economy, seem to use what

Henry Selby and others call the "Mexican solution," or multiple household income earners in both wage and informal activities.[55]

The Magic of Microenterprise?

Only recently has attention to informal workers and their micro-enterprises emerged in development thinking and practice. Chapter 2 discussed the way post–World War II development thinking was preoccupied first with economic growth through industrialization, but later with spreading growth with equity throughout the countryside. Growth-with-equity approaches in the 1960s and 1970s tended to operate through government agencies and programs. With global economic downturns around 1980 and thereafter, along with significant pushes from conservative governments and neo-liberal economists in international banks, developers turned to entrepreneurship and marketplace strategies. Microenterprise finance was born in this context.

Microenterprise minimized government involvement and maximized people's autonomy and ability to succeed (and to fail) under the vagaries of the marketplace. Besides this value, microenterprise funds are replenishable when creditors repay their loans. Thus microenterprise qualified as sustainable development.

Two organizational strategies emerged through which to allocate credit: government and nongovernment. Choices over these strategies had some bearing on the extent to which women were able to use loans and to benefit therefrom.

In the early years of microenterprise lending, following the deep-set patterns of male preference in development spending, men predominated as recipients of credit. Even alternative funders, such as the Inter-American Foundation, focused on men in cooperative societies and small business. The focus on male breadwinners is at the foundation of much development policy and implementation. In government-allocated credit, men's monopolization of voice and representation in prevailing political machinery also works to male advantage. According to the UNDP, "in 1990, multilateral banks allocated $5.8 billion for rural credit to developing countries. Only 5% reached rural women."[56] The Inter-American Development Bank estimates that despite all the flurry of attention to microenterprise, only 2 percent of the microentrepreneurs have access to loans.[57] Some organizations pursue the strategy of disaggregating data on male and female borrowers to highlight discrepancies, set new goals, and channel more resources to women. In Quito, Ecuador, a nongovernmental organization (NGO) redistributed funds and used a specially earmarked fund, bringing women up to 65 percent of group borrowers and 35 percent of individual borrowers.[58]

During the 1980s, NGOs pioneered in efforts to allocate credit to women entrepreneurs. In some cases, their policies fostered group organization among borrowers with the potential for collective political power. NGOs tapped what was often a women's cultural tradition to save collectively and to rotate the saved sum to members in turn. In central Kenya, such groups are known as *mabati* groups; in Mexico, as *tandas*; and in Indonesia, as *arisans*.

Program Models

Program models born in South Asia acquired international fame and were later replicated in other world regions. One type offers comprehensive programs; another, a narrow focus.

In India, the Self-Employed Women's Association (SEWA) represents home-based, petty trade and casually waged women workers from the previously unorganized sector. Self-employment is central to India's economy and people's livelihoods, making up about 90 percent of its workforce. SEWA straddles "development and union activities, to address the problems its members face within the family as well as in the marketplace, as women as well as workers." It helps "members in cases of dowry, bride-price, domestic and sexual harassment, and rape," including filing court petitions and issuing summonses to husbands with police escorts. It lobbies for new laws and for enforcement relief, such as protection from police harassment. SEWA also facilitates price relief for members through low-price, collective purchases.[59]

SEWA is a liberal feminist organization that addresses women's practical and strategic concerns and embraces issues that were once marginalized as radical feminism. Yet SEWA was not always this way. As a textile union "women's wing" in 1954, it offered welfare activities to wives and daughters, such as sewing, knitting, embroidery, spinning, typing, and stenography; meanwhile, women factory workers were losing jobs, and lower-caste women worked in garment industries on casual piece-rate bases.[60] Organizations *do* change.

In Bangladesh, Dr. Mohammed Yunus initiated the Grameen Bank in 1976, a huge lender with 2 million members, most of whom have repaid their loans. The Grameen Bank was not designed to work with all women, but rather with those below nationally established poverty lines. The philosophy behind these efforts is that people with survival skills are willing to work hard; what they need is capital to increase their income and asset base.

Although national models vary, NGO-supported solidarity groups are organized along the following lines, similar to the Grameen Bank. Women form a group to support individual or group-based microenterprises through loans allocated and repaid in cycles. Savings are compulsory. If loans are not repaid, other members are responsible, or their ability to get future cycles of loans is in jeopardy. This "peer pressure" produces extraordinarily high repayment rates, averaging above 95 percent. In a multi-country comparison, Rae Blumberg reports that women have low rates of delinquency and default in Bangladesh, the Dominican Republic, Guatemala, and Indonesia.[61] However, a Colombian program, on which other programs have been modeled, shows a high dropout rate (around three-fourths) before loans are received. Through this "creaming" process, the group of borrowers who remain show low arrears rates (5.7 percent), higher incomes, and the creation of three to five jobs per microenterprise.[62] Of course, unpaid family labor is also implicated—uncounted in job creation, but potentially exploited as well.

How do program models vary? In some, NGO staff members interact extensively with borrowers in training programs for market identification and for accounting skills. In others, NGOs deal with the whole person. The holistically oriented Bangladesh Rural Advancement Committee (BRAC), with around a million members, supplements loans with literacy training and consciousness-raising sessions, aimed at women's empowerment. Ambitious activities like these broaden the staff mission and pose challenges to field work, especially female staff.[63] Yet the challenge is one with prospects to confront the larger structures that maintain female subordination.

The Grameen Bank, a focused organization, has a set of sixteen principles that women must memorize (see the accompanying box) that affect other aspects of their lives besides the microenterprise. At group meetings, women shout these principles in unison, complementing the more mundane computation and record-keeping activities of loan repayment. Women's compliance with these principles is mixed, with larger numbers opting for the health principles (including family planning) compared with non–Grameen Bank group members. However, the dowry refusal principle, supported verbally, is not yet supported in practice.[64] Daughters continue to be viewed as burdens, for which husbands' families are compensated, whereas sons bring resources into the household upon marriage.

During the heyday of family planning models, mothers' clubs emerged to provide social contexts in which to discuss reproductive health and methods. South Korea and Indonesia offered visible models. In order to attract women, organizations supplemented family planning with income-generating activities and credit. Other program models successfully pursued

Grameen Bank's Sixteen Decisions

1. We shall follow and advance the four principles of Grameen Bank—discipline, unity, courage, and hard work—in all walks of our lives.
2. Prosperity we shall bring to our families.
3. We shall not live in dilapidated houses. We shall repair our houses and work towards constructing new houses as soon as possible.
4. We shall grow vegetables all year round. We shall eat plenty of them and sell the surplus.
5. During the plantation season we shall plant as many seedlings as possible.
6. We shall plan to keep our families small. We shall minimize our expenditures. We shall look after our health.
7. We shall educate our children and ensure that we can earn to pay for their education.
8. We shall always keep our children and their environment clean.
9. We shall build and use pit latrines.
10. We shall drink water from tube wells. If it is not available, we shall boil water or use alum.
11. We shall not take dowry at our sons' weddings, nor shall we give any dowry at our daughters' weddings. We shall keep our center free from the curse of dowry. We shall not practice child marriage.
12. We shall not inflict injustice on anyone, nor shall we allow anyone else to do so.
13. We shall collectively undertake larger investments for higher incomes.
14. We shall always be ready to help each other. If anyone is in difficulty we shall help him or her.
15. If we come to know of any breach of discipline in any center, we shall go there and help restore discipline.
16. We shall introduce physical exercises in all of our centers. We shall take part in all social activities collectively.

Source: Helen Todd, *Women at the Center: Grameen Bank Borrowers after One Decade* (Oxford: Westview Press, 1996), appendix 3; originally developed in March 1984 at a national workshop of women center chiefs, Bangladesh.

family planning alone through neighborhood groups. Once group cohesion was in place, the context was in place for community bank trust. In Mexico, FEMAP's community bank members emerged a decade *after* neighborhood family planning groups had solidified trust and solidarity.[65]

Although repaid loans create the basis for sustainable development, top-heavy staff create the need for fund-raising to support staff salaries. The interest rate that borrowers pay is generally not sufficient to cover elaborate

Table 5.1   NGO Responses to Microenterprise Summit

Region	Total Groups Reported	Average Percentage of Women
Africa	125	80
Asia/Pacific	152	84
Europe	6	60
Latin America/Caribbean	78	66
Middle East/W. Asia	10	63
North America	16	56

Source: Extracted from *Micro-enterprise Summit Directory* (Washington, D.C.: Results, 1997).

staffing costs. NGOs typically distance themselves from the usurious rates of moneylenders and mafialike credit and extortion rackets.

NGO microenterprise finance has increasingly become the code word for women in development projects. In early 1997, a microenterprise finance summit was held in Washington, D.C., attracting heads of state, hundreds of NGOs, and international donor organizations. A directory showed a strong female majority among recipients in Africa and Asia (see Table 5.1 for details). My count of these project summaries represents those that responded to the directory's call rather than generalizations of the regions. Numbers are striking, however.

Evaluating Microenterprise

Although microenterprise programs have become a sort of panacea to respond to women in poverty during the era of minimalist government, a comprehensive analysis asks, without positive conclusion: "From Vicious to Virtuous Circles?" Small businesses fail amid limited skills and cash in saturated markets. Small project interventions begin to look like those "misbehaving" women's projects about which Mayra Buvinić warned more than a decade ago: make-work efforts for products without markets by overworked people. Or are solidarity group loans for the poor, with low interest and limited red tape, the "McDonald's of Third World credit projects to help the poor," as Blumberg once argued?[66]

Training programs are often attached to microenterprise programs in order to transfer knowledge and skills. But the evaluation of training produces mixed and uneven results. One review of Latin American programs found men's overrepresentation in "the formal training system offering preparation for the modern sector, whereas women predominated in short-term technical courses with a concentration in the service sector."[67] An evaluation of Central American projects, accounting for poor performance and closure of group enterprises, identified the absence of feasibility and marketing studies; for skills training to be effective, supplementary literacy and math training was established.[68]

At the core, microenterprise is served with the following types of credit programs:[69]

- *Commercial banks* (often reluctant to assume the administrative costs of large numbers of small loans unless mandated by law or set-aside funds).
- *Intermediary programs* (NGOs bear administrative costs and burdens, but linked to formal banks).
- *Parallel programs* (NGOs offer credit directly).
- *Poverty-focused development banks* (begin as parallel programs, but register as banks).
- *Community revolving loans* (government loans).
- *Savings and credit cooperatives/unions* (formal organizations, regulated by law, in which people pool work, savings, and lending, under their own governance).

Do microenterprise efforts work? A question like this begs other questions about the overt and implicit goals of microenterprise and about how we would measure these goals. Evaluation studies offer a mix of methodological approaches: from large to small, representative to purposive samples of members who respond to questionnaires over one to many units of time; observation and community immersion; organizational and staff analysis through the aforementioned techniques. An overarching distinction can be useful, drawing from Molyneux (as discussed in earlier chapters): efforts that address women's practical interests versus those that address their strategic interests in reducing female subordination within gender hierarchy. Still another distinction comes from Linda Mayoux, long-standing microenterprise analyst: market approaches that focus on increased incomes for individual women versus empowerment approaches that focus on income and power balance through group activity. Each approach has implications for evaluation criteria, as follows: "numbers of women reached, and increases in income and/or enterprise efficiency; cost-effectiveness for projects [the market approach, obviously]" and "impact on poverty and qualitative change in women's position; ultimately concerned with evaluation of clients themselves [empowerment approach]."[70] The economic and quantitative methodologies are quite common, formalized in tool formats such as the Harvard gender roles framework and adopted in bilateral agencies. But this is "essentially a 'static snapshot' and is not interested in any of the complexities of intra-household and intra-community decision making and power relations."[71]

Income data also pose challenges to evaluators, whether used in the narrow market approach or the Southern NGO empowerment approach. If the goal of microenterprise is to increase incomes, then we would examine before and after data on women's income and that of their families. Here, both inside and outside evaluations of the Grameen Bank show positive yet modest gains. Compared with similar non–Grameen Bank women, people's use of the credit "works" for the vast majority, with gains in income, assets, new production, and employment generation.[72]

But income is not a clear and easy figure to obtain. By what unit of time do we measure income—day, week, season? And how do we measure earnings in bartered or noncurrency terms? And about *whose* income do we inquire, within what responsibility contexts? In some societies, women exercise some autonomy over their income, accompanied by what is often extraordinary responsibilities. Several West African societies are the quintessential examples. In other societies, women's earnings are embedded within family earnings. Women's proportional contribution to those earnings appears to give them increased negotiating ability, leverage, and power *within* household contexts. While living in rural Bangladesh and getting to know the women personally, Helen Todd compared borrowers with a control sample. She found that the Grameen Bank women's contributions of more than half of household income (compared with a quarter in the control sample) made the real difference. She says that women "practice the power of termites . . . hollowing out male authority in the households."[73] As a woman named Gunjara put it, prefaced with remarks on her husband's love even before the bank *Taka* (currency): "Since I became a Grameen Bank member, because I am earning and taking the loans, the whole family treats me with more respect. I have more influence and when he sells my oil he gives me an account of his sales and puts the money back in my hand."[74]

To measure effectiveness, we would need to know about other family members' incomes and the extent to which the microenterprise credit enhances or relieves women from their earnings and responsibilities. Do husbands and extended family senior men view women's credit lines as threatening? Exploitable? Household dynamics are not always clear and predictable. Now that the Grameen Bank is more than a decade old, observers are beginning to document how women's credit is "pipelined" into the hands of husbands and senior male kin. Depending on the study and sample selection, analysts report pipelining of a tenth to a quarter of credit for women.[75] Another study reports no numbers but rather that some women's husbands "were beating them for not getting credit."[76] In BRAC, Aruna Rao and David Kelleher report that in close to a third of cases, women have little to no control over their loans. By excluding men, they ask, "is BRAC merely setting women up as conduits for credit to men and if so at what cost?"[77] BRAC has now begun to focus more on men (a gender lens that informs practice).

Evaluation studies like those cited above present a mixed picture when combined with others that conclude that women derive a sense of esteem and entitlement from participation. Indicators of these outcomes would likely vary from one culture or nation to the next, and those indicators are always subject to misinterpretation unless those doing the interpreting understand cultural cues quite well. Mahbub Ahmed found decreases in husbands' physical violence or threats of violence among bank members. Syed Hashemi and colleagues found that women whose male relatives pipelined loans were more empowered than nonbank members. Grameen Bank requirements that assets such as houses and surrounding land be put in women's names add to women's leverage within households as well; managing director Yunus views this "as an incentive for the husband to stay with the family, and the asset, rather than to walk out."[78] Readers should remember that customary laws legitimize gendered double standards in marriage and divorce in ways that advantage men.

Organizations themselves are part of what is evaluated as well. If a goal of microenterprise projects is to create efficient and effective NGOs to deliver services, to expand underrepresented voices in the political process, or to do both, then we would shift our lens away from individual members to groups, including the NGO bureaucracies themselves. David Korten warns about the mistake of assuming that all NGOs are independent people's organizations, accountable to their members; some are public service contractors that operate more like businesses.[79]

The first insight such studies offer is that organizations often do not operate the way they say they do. Community banks say that they form groups of particular sizes. They say that they approve loans for enterprise projects. Various studies of community banks raise questions about such organizations' compliance with their own rules, however. The studies raise questions about minimal staff oversight, which allows credit proposal diversion not only from the stated intent but also from the stated user. The question we need to ask is whether those diversions thwart desirable outcomes for members and for funders. If such outcomes are not thwarted, does it matter?

Diversion from intent appears to be commonplace in increasingly bureaucratized NGOs. Members apply for loans to husk paddy, and field staff know that midlevel management approves such loans, but the capital is used for other purposes. Is this problematic if income is earned and loans are repaid? At a minimum, efficiency seems to be reduced with paper compliance and pretenses. Organizations cannot learn lessons from their successes and failures if their "memory" (the red tape, the paper) is inaccurate.

Diversion from the stated user, however, can be devastating for many goals, including those based on the much used and abused term "empowerment." Pipelining, as discussed earlier, is one example of such diversion. In their nuanced title about community banks in Bangladesh, Anne Marie Goetz and Rina Sen Gupta ask "Who Takes the Credit?"[80]

As the Grameen Bank program matures, more and more studies are available to evaluate its effectiveness outside of the generally positive reports that organizations invariably produce about themselves. Some of these studies suggest that the common pattern that organizational theorists identified in the 1930s about modern bureaucracies have cropped up in microenterprise NGOs: goal displacement. Goal displacement occurs when the ostensible goals of the organization (say, credit to increase borrowers' incomes or to empower women) are displaced with the supreme goals of organizational maintenance and growth. Obsessions about repayment rates might be seen in this light, one consequence of which might be to focus on the better-off among the poor who are better able to repay. But even more troubling is Rosamund Ebdon's main point about how the Grameen Bank and BRAC encroach on other indigenous organizations in order to retain their role as central players. These central players set loan targets for their staff, along with pressure to perform with quantifiable outputs in accountability to their funders, exhibiting the "moving money" mentality noted in Chapter 3 for donor agencies and international banks. In Ebdon's words, they "were a business rather than an NGO, and therefore quite prepared to compete for clients."[81]

When field promoters are under pressure to move money and are accountable for repayment, the results might actually work in women's favor. This is what Blumberg argues in a Guatemala project. *Asesores* insisted that "the poor, the women, and the Indians . . . had the best payback record," perhaps because they "did not want to jeopardize the only chance at cheap credit they were likely to be offered in their lives."[82]

The most thorough independent study of the Grameen Bank, with nearly 14,000 staff, presents far more positive findings. Susan Holcombe concludes that Grameen has established an empowering management style for its mostly field-based staff.[83] Its organizational culture chips away at the authoritarianism, deference to hierarchy, and fatalism of the wider culture. (Yet other sources question the hierarchy and authoritarianism that seem implicit in insisting that members refer to Grameen field staff as "Sir." BRAC offers the options of "Brother" and "Sister." Both organizations recruit a largely male staff.) Holcombe, however, goes on to praise how

Grameen motivates its staff through a sense of satisfaction and pride in organizational achievements in poverty alleviation, rather than through money; training, quick promotions, and wage security solidify these incentives.

Pankaj Jain goes further in a seemingly negative evaluation of the Grameen Bank's noncompliance with its own rules. The group guarantee of repayment is not practiced. Yet the loan recovery rate is extraordinarily high, compared, for example, with the Indian government's 50 percent overdue rate. In a positive light, then, Jain attributes this to a focused and motivated staff.[84]

With individual and staff success, we might still wonder about other dimensions of empowerment. If microenterprise is evaluated on its ability to generate group power and civic voice, the record is not so positive. Of course, group strength and engagement with the political process are difficult to assess, however fundamental to power balance strategies. We would need to examine the informal and formal organizational networks in which women act, along with the receptiveness of the existing political machinery and its payoff to these formerly muted voices. The technical people involved in evaluations often steer as far from (that dirty word?) politics as they can. Yet it is *in* the political process where decisions are made about policy, implementation, and the allocation of public resources.

We can assume that women operating in groups acquire informational and network power. Todd's village-level studies show how "women use their social networks to advance their income-earning projects and in turn strengthen their networks by the way they use their loans. In turn, the alliances they make amongst their kin group as well as their membership of the center give them more clout within their own households."[85] Her studies do not demonstrate network transformation into collective political power.

In northern Mexico, too, a women's center course was evaluated on individual, network, and organizational empowerment terms. Although virtually all women gave voice to enhanced individual power and some to network power, just a few developed or used existing organizational power with new strength.[86] Such findings have implications for women's center course recruitment strategies, for organizational power could be enhanced through civic strategies to recruit grassroots women leaders. In Mexico, much organization at the neighborhood base rests on women's shoulders. The political machinery, along with the intermediaries who wheel and deal with officials in that machinery, tend to be men or privileged women rather than those women at the neighborhood organizational base.[87]

Hashemi and colleagues provide one of the most comprehensive lists of empowerment indicators and measurement scales for Bangladesh. Although they are not necessarily transferable elsewhere, the eight indicators may be adaptable:[88]

1. Mobility—places she had gone, and gone alone.

2. Economic security—house and land ownership, control over productive assets, cash savings, savings used for business.

3. Ability to make small purchases—points added to scale of items if husbands' permission not asked.

4. Ability to make large purchases—ditto on permission.

5. Involvement in major decisions—points added if woman's money used.

6. Relative freedom from domination by the family—freedom from money, jewelry, or livestock taken against her will; ability to visit natal kin; ability to work outside home.

7. Political and legal awareness—ability to name officials, knowledge of marriage and inheritance laws.

8. Participation in public protests and political campaigning—campaign experience, joint protest activity over wife beating, husbands' divorce or abandonment, unfair wages, unfair prices, misappropriation of relief goods, official high-handedness.

This comprehensive list includes no indicators of reproductive knowledge or control, which some might consider crucial empowerment factors as well.

In the end, can microenterprise programs empower women? The overview in this part of the chapter suggests some promising initiatives but lingering problems. Microenterprise occurs in political contexts where local, regional, and national decisions can make or break efforts through funding and/or regulation. Microenterprise also occurs in household contexts, with the potential to nudge away at rather than transform gender hierarchy. Our judgments about microenterprise might be couched in Molyneux's terms, contrasting practical and strategic interests. Successful microenterprise can meet everyday practical needs, but only when it is embedded in network and organizations is it capable of addressing strategic needs. Because the two go hand in hand, the differentiation might, in the end, be a false dichotomy.

Taken together, women's work in wage, agricultural, and informal economies presents research that complicates action. The expansion of paid work options open up ways for women to increase incomes and thereby improve their capabilities. In so doing, however, they participate in global economic forces that simultaneously cheapen the labor of all. Rather than draw conclusions, readers are invited to examine the following action-oriented appendixes in collective settings.

Applying the Insights

Urban Agriculture—Strategies for Food Security

Women's connection with food is fixed in the minds of many. In a commonplace gender division of labor, women process and cook food for home consumption. We are long accustomed to seeing women next to hearths and in kitchens. Pregnant women nurture life within them, and after birth, many mothers opt to nourish infants with food from their own bodies. Artists have often adorned paintings with idyllic pictures of such images.

Yet women's connection with food is far broader than this nature-nourish activity, in global perspective. Women grow food for home consumption and for sale in income-generating activities. They are farmers, as worthy of this occupational title as the mostly men so graced. In their farm work, women make decisions about the use and abuse of natural resources, with implications for sustainable resources. Women also buy and sell food as consumers and traders in income-generating activities. They do this work in both rural and urban areas. Food production and distribution are at the heart and soul of development, life, and nourishment. And within that process, women occupy central and strategic places.

The majority of agricultural work occurs in rural areas on land units of many sizes. And the majority of people live in rural or semirural locations around the world. Rural residents, many of them farmers and agricultural laborers, experience the common tendency toward "urban bias" in public priorities and spending. Rural areas are neglected, a process that stimulates rural-to-urban migration. Those who stay struggle in the form of arduous labor to gather firewood for cooking and heating, to gain spaces in schools and health clinics, and to carry water to their homes for cleaning and cooking. Most farmers depend on rain rather than irrigation and wells to nourish their crops. The huge rural population is central to human development strategies that would improve people's well-being and expand their options.

Yet we must break the common assumption that attention to agriculture is the same as attention to rural areas. Many urban residents also farm small plots, but in cities; city consumers depend on production therein to meet their food needs. A UNFPA study of food security provides vivid examples, as follows:[89]

- Dar es Salaam: one of five adults is a farmer.
- Cairo: 80,000 animals tended, mostly by women and children.
- New York: Green Thumb, an NGO, makes over 1,000 vacant lots available to community cultivator groups.
- Port Moresby: women constitute 70 percent of urban gardeners.
- Hong Kong: two-thirds of poultry, one-sixth of pigs, and nearly half of city-consumed vegetables are produced within urban boundaries.
- Singapore: 10,000 licensed farmers produced a quarter of city-consumed vegetables.
- Berlin: 80,000 community gardeners work small land plots set aside for horticulture.

Role Play. You are a community development officer (CDO) assigned to work in the west end of a large, sprawling capital city in a central African country. The area is filled with recent migrants from the countryside, seeking a better life. Many households are made up of women supporting their children through casual labor, trade, and food crop production on undeveloped land in the area. Houses are modest in size, usually one or two rooms, and constructed with scrap materials that people collect from nearby dumps.

As a CDO, you and your agency lean toward programming that supports group activities as ways to strengthen their buying, selling, production, and political strategies. In a recent work assignment, you visited households to learn about their needs, skills, and problems. You learned that the majority of household heads are women and that they have no regular income. You learned that they are not always able to put food on the table for their children more than twice a day. Yet residents impressed you with their cleverness and skills in identifying unused land on which they grew corn and beans for home consumption and occasional sales. Many women brought finely tuned skills in farming from their recent work managing small farms in the rural areas. Although the average level of education was grade three, most had solid arithmetic skills, though not literacy. A common problem that most women shared was harassment from city authorities and, occasionally, from private landowners. They farmed on public and private land without license or permit.

From your work as CDO, you know several strong neighborhood leaders. You also know that your agency is anxious to document some success stories for upcoming budgetary battles with parliament. You also know that there are some eager international funders who have monetary allocations they need to move before next year's budget cycle begins. UNICEF's mission is devoted to mothers' and children's well-being, including nutrition, whereas the World Bank's mission is income generation in efficient, legal land and licensure contexts. Next year, the city council will be holding elections, and most residents are eligible voters, though many residents are so cynical about the men who dominate politics that they have not bothered to register. Councilmen want first and foremost to win elections, but they also appreciate the city government's desperate need for revenue—dependent on fees from licenses and permits. Representatives believe that well-fed voters with regular incomes offer a contented electorate, likely to support their reelection bids.

After consulting with women leaders, you set up a meeting with some of the key movers and shakers with the leadership skills, budgetary resources, and authority to establish a program. At the public meeting, representatives from three neighborhood groups participate, along with UNICEF and World Bank staff members, the incumbent city councilman, and his challenger. You, the CDO, preside over the meeting, and you invite your supervisor to observe. Several residents also attend with their children. Your goal is to come up with some consensus about a plan that will build on residents' skills and respond to their problems.

Women's Work in a Global Economy— What Is to Be Done?

The class has just finished a unit on women's labor force participation in the global economy. Reading after reading made it clear that women sought paid employment, but that as a group they always earned less than men as a group. The wage gap is partly explained by women's labor in tasks deemed to have limited value. What's more, women's labor force participation is increasing everywhere with the expansion of export-processing factories. Visually, these patterns are brought home in *The Global Assembly Line*, a film on the Philippines and Mexico that you have shown to the class.

You have invited activists to class. Northern-based union organizers analyzed the grim decline in factory employment, leaving higher unemployment rates among women than men. Southern-based class members questioned the way these organizers privileged Northern over Southern workers, many of whom worked with fringe benefits for the first times in their lives. Northern-based class members wondered whether those Southern-based workers appreciated how fully exploited they were. Why didn't those workers press their own governments for higher minimum wages?

The class visitors who made the biggest impression spoke about transnational organizing activities. Transnational organizers once looked to the United Nations, and specifically to the International Labour Organization, for solutions to what they called "economic apartheid" in global investments across nearly 200 nation-states. Labor conventions, however, went unrespected, and no compromises had been reached on multinational codes of conduct for workers. However, their new and fledgling Transnational Women Workers (TRAWW) organization faces internal rifts over what are perceived as nationalist, even racist actions as members set priorities and develop their discourse and strategies for political action.

As the instructor, you notice the unease of some class participants who've rarely given a second thought to their own consumption strategies. They wear expensive sports shoes, assembled in Southeast Asia and peddled by athletes earning multimillion-dollar salaries. They dress in clothing assembled from lots of places, including those labeled "Made in USA." They search for the lowest-cost electronic equipment that virtually each and every one of them owns.

You, the instructor, lean back in the chair of your air-conditioned university office. You appreciate the freedom tenure has given you, despite the past gender and ideological infighting within your department, to explore significant topics such as these with students. The continued security of your position depends on university administrators' aggressive push to obtain outside funding from government and corporations. At least you haven't compromised on a consistent framework in your writing about women workers: global corporate hegemony prevails and sustains structures of gender domination and subordination.

Class participants seem overwhelmed at the end of the course unit. They wonder what can be done, from the personal everyday levels to the grand global structures. Do they engage or withdraw, at what levels, and in what institutions, from work to community and government? They hunger for meaningful and effective strategies, recognizing also the wisdom: choose battles carefully. The discussion begins.

For Further Reflection

Workers' Rights—Making Companies Responsible

Not all governments have the power to change working conditions. Not all governments seek to improve conditions or respond to workers with such claims. Women Working Worldwide lists strategies for action in nongovernmental arenas, a summary of which follows.[90]

Company Codes of Conduct. Given the failure of international institutions to develop and apply codes to multinational corporations, apply pressure to companies to adopt voluntary codes for public-relations purposes and to set themselves apart from competitors.

Fair-Trade Networks. Use consumer power to support workers' rights, through direct marketing of small producers' goods and campaigning for fair trade on specific goods such as coffee, flowers, toys, and garments. Buy goods with honest trademarks.

International Trade Union Strategies. Pursue international collective bargaining across national borders so that multinational firms cannot play one worker group off against another. Establish works councils such as those in Europe following the 1994 European Directive. Workers on those councils are in strategic positions to gain information and to influence corporate decisions about plant closures, for example.

Notes

1. Amartya Sen and Jean Dreze are cited in Martha Chen, "A Matter of Survival: Women's Right to Employment in India and Bangladesh," in *Women, Culture and Development: A Study of Human Capabilities*, edited by Martha Nussbaum and Jonathan Glover (New York: Clarendon/Oxford, 1995), pp. 37–61.
2. The term "feminization of poverty" is used by many. See Gertrude Goldberg and Eleanor Kremen, "The Feminization of Poverty: Not Only in America," in *Different Roles, Different Voices: Women and Politics in the United States and Europe*, edited by Marianne Githens, Pippa Norris, and Joni Lovenduski (New York: HarperCollins, 1994), pp. 136–44. Mayra Buvinić and Nadia Youssef estimate that de facto and de jure heads of households total a quarter to a third in *Women-Headed Households: The Ignored Factor in Development Planning* (Washington, D.C.: USAID, 1978).
3. Daisy Dwyer and Judith Bruce, eds., *A Home Divided: Women and Income in the Third World* (Stanford, Calif.: Stanford University Press, 1988); Devaki Jain and Nirmala Banerjee, eds., *Tyranny of the Household: Investigative Essays on Women's Work* (New Delhi: Shakti Books, 1985).
4. Jan Monk's case "What Counts?" (from a long list of census categories and jobs) is found in Kathleen Staudt, *Managing Development: State, Society and International Contexts* (Newbury Park, Calif.: Sage, 1991), pp. 94–95.
5. Ruth Dixon-Mueller, *Women in Third World Agriculture* (Geneva: ILO, 1985); Lourdes Benería, "Accounting for Women's Work: The Progress of Two Decades," *World Development* 20, no. 11 (1992): 1547–60.
6. Linda Lim, *More and Better Jobs for Women: An Action Guide* (Geneva: ILO, 1996), p. 17. As of 1995, 124 countries had ratified the Equal Remuneration Convention of 1951.
7. Devon Peña, *The Terror of the Machine: Technology, Work, Gender and Ecology on the U.S.-Mexico Border* (Austin: Center for Mexican American Studies, University of Texas at Austin, 1997), p. 65. Henry Ford actually used the "terror" phrase in his autobiography.
8. Chen, "A Matter of Survival." With support from her BRAC colleagues (the organization is discussed later under "Informal Labor and Microenterprise"), Begum ran for local political office and almost won.
9. Susan Joekes, *Women in the World Economy: An INSTRAW Study* (New York: Oxford University Press, 1987), p. 128. Also see her book with Ann Weston, *Women and the New Trade Agenda* (New York: UNIFEM, 1995), as well as

Guy Standing, "Global Feminization through Flexible Labor," *World Development* 17, no. 7 (1989): 1077–95.

10. Inter-American Development Bank, *Women in the Americas: Bridging the Gender Gap* (Washington, D.C.: IDB, 1995), p. 55. Women Working Worldwide, *World Trade Is a Women's Issue* (Manchester: WWW, n.d.), pp. 2, 4.

11. Valentine M. Moghadam, "Economic Reforms and Women's Employment in the Middle East and North Africa," *WIDER Angle* 1 (1995): 8–9.

12. Peña, see *Terror of the Machine*, p. 78, on workweeks; this compared with thirty-eight to forty in the United States or thirty-five in Europe. The environmental thesis is throughout, but see p. 57 and chap. 9. On p. 40, Peña reports that Ford Motor Company had turnover rates as high as 200 percent in early years, not to mention wildcat strikes.

13. Aihwa Ong, "Spirits of Resistance," in *Situated Lives: Gender and Culture in Everyday Life*, edited by Louise Lamphere, Helena Ragone, and Patricia Zavella (New York: Routledge, 1997), pp. 355–70.

14. Ellwyn R. Stoddard, "Border Maquila Ownership and Mexican Economic Benefits: A Comparative Analysis of the 'Good,' the 'Bad,' and the 'Ugly,'" *Journal of Borderlands Studies* 6, no. 2 (1991): 23–50. WEDO (Women's Environment & Development Organization) reports four million in export-processing work, 2.6 of them women, in *Codes of Conduct for Transnational Corporations: Strategies toward Democratic Global Governance* (New York: WEDO, 1995). WEDO's entire 1995 series on the global economy, the World Trade Organization, and transnational corporations is useful.

15. Kathleen Staudt, *Free Trade? Informal Economies at the U.S.-Mexico Border* (Philadelphia: Temple University Press, 1998).

16. Elizabeth Eviota, *The Political Economy of Gender: Women and the Sexual Division of Labour in the Philippines* (London: Zed, 1992), pp. 89, 122. See also June Nash and María Patricia Fernández-Kelly, eds., *Women, Men, and the International Division of Labor* (Albany, N.Y.: SUNY Albany Press, 1983).

17. Elsa Chaney and Mary García Castro, eds., *Muchachas No More: Household Workers in Latin America and the Caribbean* (Philadelphia: Temple University Press, 1989).

18. Sex-tourism is discussed widely; see, for example, Cynthia Enloe, *Bananas, Beaches, and Bases* (Berkeley: University of California Press, 1989), and *The Morning After* (Berkeley: University of California Press, 1993).

19. Helen Henderson, ed., *Gender and Agricultural Development: Surveying the Field* (Tucson: University of Arizona Press, 1993), p. 4, citing ILO figures.

20. Henderson, *Gender and Agricultural Development*, pp. 77–79.

21. World Bank, *Policy and Research Bulletin* 8, 1 (1997): 1–4.

22. UNDP, *Human Development Report 1996* (New York: Oxford University Press, 1996), from various tables appended to the text.

23. Henderson, *Gender and Agricultural Development*, pp. 12–16.

24. The Ecology, Community Organization and Gender (ECOGEN) project is located at Clark University, Worcester, MA 01610-1477. It produces various working papers, including the guide by Barbara Slayter-Thomas et al., *Tools of Gender Analysis* (1993), and case studies from Asia, Africa, and Latin America. The Institute of Philippine Culture also produces excellent case studies; for example, see Jeanne Frances I. Illo and Cynthia C. Veneración, *Women and Men in Rainfed Farming Systems: Case Studies of Households in the Bicol Region* (Manila: IPC, Ateneo de Manila University, 1988).

25. Donald B. Freeman, *A City of Farmers: Informal Urban Agriculture in the Open Spaces of Nairobi, Kenya* (Montreal: McGill-Queen's University Press, 1991).

26. Jane I. Guyer, ed., *Feeding African Cities: Studies in Regional Social History*

(Bloomington: Indiana University Press, 1987). Also see Nancy E. Horn, *Cultivating Customers: Market Women in Harare, Zimbabwe* (Boulder, Colo.: Lynne Rienner, 1994).

27. On low numbers of women in decision-making positions, see Cheryl R. Doss, *African Professional Women in Agriculture: An Analysis of Two Roundtable Discussions* (Morrilton, AK: Winrock International Institute for Agricultural Development, 1991), pp. 3–6 especially. On increased attention, see Katrine A. Saito and C. Jean Weidemann, *Agricultural Extension for Women Farmers in Africa* (Washington, D.C.: World Bank, 1990). On the dangers of more attention leading to more labor without necessary benefit, see Maria Nzomo and Kathleen Staudt, "Man-Made Political Machinery in Kenya: Political Space for Women?" in *Women and Politics Worldwide*, edited by Barbara Nelson and Najma Chowdhury (New Haven, Conn.: Yale University Press, 1994), pp. 415–36. Achola Pala Okeyo is cited in Cheryl Johnson-Odim, "Common Themes, Different Contexts: Third World Women and Feminism," in *Third World Women and the Politics of Feminism,* edited by Chandra Talpade Mohanty et al. (Bloomington: Indiana University Press, 1989), pp. 317–18.

28. Cited in Staudt, *Managing Development*, p. 231 (1981 figures). Also see note 41.

29. Else Skjønsberg, *Change in an African Village: Kefa Speaks* (West Hartford, Conn.: Kumarian Press, 1989), pp. 36, 65.

30. David Leonard, *Reaching the Peasant Farmer: Organization Theory and Practice in Kenya* (Chicago: University of Chicago Press, 1977). Communication theorist Everett Rogers had lasting impact on thinking with his diffusion of innovations model.

31. Naomi Chazan, "Engaging the State: Associational Life in Sub-Saharan Africa," and Michael Bratton, "Peasant-State Relations in Postcolonial Africa: Patterns of Engagement and Disengagement," in *State Power and Social Forces: Domination and Transformation in the Third World*, edited by Joel Migdal, Atul Kohli, and Vivienne Shue (New York: Cambridge University Press, 1994), pp. 231–93; Jane Parpart and Kathleen Staudt, eds., *Women and the State in Africa* (Boulder, Colo.: Lynne Rienner, 1989); James Scott, *Everyday Weapons of the Weak* (New Haven, Conn.: Yale University Press, 1985).

32. They are cited in Kathleen Staudt, "Uncaptured or Unmotivated? Women and the Food Crisis in Africa," *Rural Sociology* 52, no. 1 (1987): 37–55. Also see a special issue of *Issues* (1989), published by the African Studies Association, focused on the Nairobi meetings and beyond.

33. Zen Tadesse, "The Impact of Land Reform on Women: The Case of Ethiopia," in *Women, Land and Food Production* (Geneva: ISIS, 1979), pp.18–22. Carmen Diana Deere and Magdalena Leon de Leal, eds., *Rural Women and State Policy: Feminist Perspectives on Latin American Agricultural Development* (Boulder, Colo.: Westview Press, 1987).

34. A good estimate, but are the figures accurate? See the discussion by Sally Baden and Anne Marie Goetz, "Who Needs [Sex] When You Can Have [Gender]? Conflicting Discourses on Gender at Beijing," in *Women, International Development and Politics: The Bureaucratic Mire*, 2d ed., edited by Kathleen Staudt (Philadelphia: Temple University Press, 1997), pp. 37–58.

35. Ann Stewart, "Should Women Give up on the State? The African Experience," in *Women and the State: International Perspectives*, edited by Shirin M. Rai and Geraldine Lievesley (London: Taylor & Francis, 1996), p. 23. But also see women's use of pluralism in Laurel Rose, "A Woman Is Like a Field: Women's Strategies for Land Access in Swaziland," in *Agriculture, Women, and Land: The African Experience*, edited by Jean Davison (Boulder, Colo.: Westview Press, 1988), pp. 177–201.

36. See the literature reviewed in Kathleen Staudt, "The State and Gender in Colonial Africa," in *Women, the State and Development*, edited by Sue Ellen Charlton et al. (Albany, N.Y.: SUNY Albany Press, 1989), pp. 66–85.
37. Kathleen Staudt discusses the work of Jennie Dey and Judith Carnoy in "The Impact of Development Policies on Women," in *African Women South of the Sahara*, 2d ed., edited by Margaret Jean Hay and Sharon Stichter (New York: Longman, 1995).
38. Catherine Caufield, *Masters of Illusion: The World Bank and the Poverty of Nations* (New York: Henry Holt, 1996), chap. 1 (quotes, p. 16).
39. Caufield, *Masters of Illusion*, pp. 13–15.
40. Mwea is discussed in Staudt, "Uncaptured or Unmotivated." Ingrid Palmer, *The Nemow Case* (West Hartford, Conn.: Kumarian Press, 1985), leads a monograph series.
41. Saito and Weidemann, *Agricultural Extension*. Kathleen Staudt, *Agricultural Policy Implementation: A Case from Western Kenya* (West Hartford, Conn.: Kumarian Press, 1985).
42. See note 28 on figures. The next paragraphs are from my dissertation, condensed in Staudt, *Agricultural Policy Implementation*.
43. Janice Jiggins, with Paul Maimbo and Mary Masona, "Breaking New Ground: Reaching Out to Women Farmers in Western Zambia," in *Seeds 2: Supporting Women's Work around the World*, edited by Ann Leonard (New York: Feminist Press, 1995), pp. 17–40.
44. Bina Agarwal's work is summarized from "Environmental Action, Gender Equity and Women's Participation," *Development and Change* 28 (1997):1–44.
45. Agarwal, "Environmental Action," p. 24.
46. C. Peter Timmer, *Getting Prices Right: The Scope and Limits of Agricultural Price Policy* (Ithaca, N.Y.: Cornell University Press, 1986).
47. Uma Lele, "Women and Structural Transformation," *Economic Development and Cultural Change* 34, no. 2 (1986): 195–221. See selections in Christina H. Gladwin, ed., *Structural Adjustment and African Women Farmers* (Gainesville: University of Florida Press, 1991).
48. The literature on informal economies is huge. See Staudt, *Free Trade?* chaps. 2 and 4, for reviews. On women, see Marguerite Berger and Mayra Buvinić, eds., *Women's Ventures: Assistance to the Informal Sector in Latin America* (West Hartford, Conn.: Kumarian Press, 1989).
49. They are quoted in Naila Kabeer, *Reversed Realities: Gender Hierarchies in Development Thought* (London: Verso, 1994).
50. Alison MacEwen Scott, "Informal Sector or Female Sector? Gender Bias in Urban Labour Market Models," in *Male Bias in the Development Process*, edited by Diane Elson (Manchester: Manchester University Press, 1991), pp. 105–32. Rae Blumberg, "Gender, Micro-enterprise, Performance, and Power: Case Studies from the Dominican Republic, Ecuador, Guatemala, and Swaziland," in *Women in the Latin American Development Process*, edited by Christine E. Bose and Edna Acosta-Belén (Philadelphia: Temple University Press, 1995), pp. 194–206. In Berger and Buvinić, *Women's Ventures*, several writers, including one from ILO's regional office in Santiago, Chile (PREALC), take issue with the practice of including domestic labor in informal data. It is domestic labor that tips the feminization balance to this diverse occupational group.
51. Lourdes Benería and Martha Roldán, *The Crossroads of Class and Gender: Industrial Homework, Subcontracting and Household Dynamics in Mexico City* (Chicago: University of Chicago Press, 1987).
52. The immigration literature is reviewed in Staudt, *Free Trade?* chap. 4. On women in ethnic enclaves, see María Patricia Fernández-Kelly and Anna M.

García, "Informalization at the Core: Hispanic Women, Homework, and the Advanced Capitalist State," in *The Informal Economy: Studies in Advanced and Less Developed Countries,* edited by Alejandro Portes et al. (Baltimore: Johns Hopkins University Press, 1989). The material on the U.S.-Mexico border is from Staudt, *Free Trade?*

53. Priscilla Connolly, "The Politics of the Informal Sector: A Critique," in *Beyond Employment: Household, Gender and Subsistence,* edited by N. Redcliff and E. Mingione (London: Basil Blackwell, 1986).

54. On Venezuela, Vanessa Cartaya, "Informality and Poverty: Causal Relationship or Coincidence?" in *Contrapunto: The Informal Sector Debate in Latin America,* edited by Cathy Rakowski (Albany, N.Y.: SUNY Albany Press, 1994), pp. 223–50; on Mexico, Bryan Roberts, "Enterprise and Labor Markets: The Border and the Metropolitan Areas," *Frontera Norte* 5, no. 9 (1993): 33–66, and Staudt, *Free Trade?*

55. Henry Selby et al., *The Mexican Urban Household: Organizing for Self-Defense* (Austin: University of Texas Press, 1990). Staudt, *Free Trade?* makes the point that such solutions are spreading northward.

56. UNDP, *Human Development Report 1995* (N.Y.: Oxford University Press, 1995), p. 39.

57. Inter-American Development Bank (IDB), "Micro-enterprise Comes of Age," *The IDB,* April 1997, p. 3.

58. Inter-American Development Bank, *Women in the Americas: Bridging the Gender Gap* (Washington, D.C.: IDB, 1995), p. 75.

59. Kabeer, *Reversed Realities,* pp. 231–32, 242. Also see Pankaj S. Jain, "Managing Credit for the Rural Poor: Lessons from the Grameen Bank," *World Development* 24, no. 1 (1996): 79–90.

60. Kabeer, *Reversed Realities,* p. 232.

61. Blumberg, "Gender, Micro-enterprise, Performance and Power," p. 196. High figures are quoted for the Grameen Bank as well; see, for example, Susan Holcombe, *Managing to Empower: The Grameen Bank's Experience at Poverty Alleviation* (London: Zed, 1995), p. 5.

62. Cressida S. McKean, "Training and Technical Assistance for Small and Micro-enterprise: A Discussion of Their Effectiveness," in Rakowski, *Contrapunto,* p. 202.

63. Anne Marie Goetz, "Local Heroes: Patterns of Field Worker Discretion in Implementing GAD Policy in Bangladesh" (Sussex: IDS Discussion Paper no. 358, 1996). She demonstrates, though, that women staff make a difference at the local level, in terms of a more contact-friendly environment for female constituents.

64. Helen Todd, *Women at the Center: Grameen Bank Borrowers after One Decade* (Oxford: Westview Press, 1996), pp. 193, 204.

65. The Federación Mexicana de Asociaciones Privada (FEMAP) is an NGO to which I have provided service for four years. See Staudt, *Free Trade?* chap. 7. The mothers' clubs models from South Korea and Indonesia once circulated as project success stories.

66. Linda Mayoux, *From Vicious to Virtuous Circles? Gender and Micro-Enterprise Development,* Occasional Paper no. 3 (Geneva: UNRISD, 1995); Blumberg, "Gender, Micro-enterprise, Performance and Power," p. 204.

67. McKean, "Training and Technical Assistance," p. 212.

68. McKean, "Training and Technical Assistance," p. 213.

69. Mayoux, *From Vicious to Virtuous Circles?* p. 36.

70. Mayoux, *From Vicious to Virtuous Circles?* p. 6.

71. Catherine Overholt, et al., *Gender Roles in Development* (West Hartford, Conn.: Kumarian Press, 1985), but criticized in Shahrashoub Razavi and Carol

Miller, *From WID to GAD: Conceptual Shifts in the Women and Development Discourse*, Occasional Paper no. 1 (Geneva: UNRISD, 1995), p. 10.

72. Todd, *Women at the Center*, p. 221. Also see Syed M. Hashemi, Sidney Ruth Schuler, and Ann P. Riley, "Rural Credit Programs and Women's Empowerment in Bangladesh," *World Development* 24, no. 4 (1996): 635–54. Hossain is cited in Holcombe, *Managing to Empower*, p. 49.
73. Todd, *Women at the Center*, pp. 48, 188.
74. Cited in Todd, *Women at the Center*, p. 207.
75. Todd, *Women at the Center*, p. 222. Anne Marie Goetz and R. Sen Gupta, "Who Takes the Credit? Gender, Power and Control over Loan Use in Rural Credit Programmes in Bangladesh," *World Development* 24, no. 1 (1996): 45–64.
76. Rosamund Ebdon, "NGO Expansion and the Fight to Reach the Poor: Gender Implications of NGO Scaling-up in Bangladesh," "Getting Institutions Right for Women in Development," edited by Anne Marie Goetz. *IDS Bulletin* 26, no. 3 (1995): 50.
77. Aruna Rao and David Kelleher, "Engendering Organizational Change: The BRAC Case," in Goetz, "Getting Institutions Right," p. 75.
78. Ahmed and Yunus are cited in Holcombe, *Managing to Empower*, p. 51; Hashemi et al., "Rural Credit Programs."
79. David C. Korten, *Getting to the 21st Century: Voluntary Action and the Global Agenda* (West Hartford, Conn.: Kumarian Press, 1990), especially chap. 9.
80. Goetz and Sen Gupta, "Who Takes the Credit?" n. 81.
81. Ebdon, "NGO Expansion," pp. 53, 52.
82. Blumberg, "Gender, Micro-enterprise, Performance, and Power," pp. 209–10.
83. Holcombe, *Managing to Empower*, pp. 95, 37, 99, 125.
84. Jain, "Managing Credit for the Rural Poor."
85. Todd, *Women at the Center*, p. 92.
86. Kathleen Staudt, "Programming Women's Empowerment? A Case from Northern Mexico," in *Women on the U.S.-Mexico Border*, edited by Vicki L. Ruiz and Susan Tiano (Boston: Allyn & Unwin, 1987), pp. 165–76.
87. Staudt, *Free Trade?*
88. Hashemi et al., "Rural Credit Programs."
89. "Food for the Future: Women, Population and Food Security," UNFPA Web site (www.unfpa.org), [1996].
90. Women Working Worldwide, *World Trade Is a Women's Issue,* pp. 15–17.

6 Population, Overconsumption, and Reproductive Health

> ... our bodies have become a pawn in the struggles among states, religions, male heads of households, and private corporations.
> —Gita Sen and Caren Grown, DAWN

> It took Britain half the resources of the planet to achieve this prosperity; how many planets will a country like India require?
> —Mahatma Gandhi

In the last decade, a new group of activists has come to set the policy agenda in the area of population, the environment, and reproductive health. In the health and population fields, these new activists put the needs of users first, that is, those who use reproductive knowledge and techniques in their own contexts. For environmental activists, the adjective "sustainable" almost always precedes the word "development," by which they exemplify a sense of stewardship about the environment. Modern industrialization has destroyed many nonrenewable natural resources, and public policies have frequently subsidized that destruction, attaching little to no commercial value to once free goods such as air, water, and forests.

This chapter focuses on broad meanings of sustainable life and the shifting discourse and practice in population, environment, and family planning programs. It offers insights on evaluation and budgetary realities.

Sustainable Life

Over the long haul of history, most governments, religions, and cultures have fostered pro-natalism. Governments aimed to stimulate population growth in the "national" interest, to staff their militaries and to grow labor pools. With high mortality rates, people sought to replace and replenish their societies. Shockingly high rates of infant mortality are finally on the decline in most societies in the latter part of the twentieth century. To take just a few examples from several world regions, from 1960 to 1993, the number of infants per 1,000 live births who died before the age of one dropped from 99 to 37 in Colombia, from 179 to 66 in Egypt, from 188 to 116 in Equatorial Guinea, from 165 to 81 in India, and from 44 to 7 in Hong Kong.[1] When life is sustainable, people begin to lower their fertility, whether their governments want them to or not.

Besides the intrinsic celebration of birth in many cultures, children who survived supplied valuable labor in subsistence economies. Once adults, they supported parents in lieu of public support for welfare and pension. In economists' terms, the benefits of children exceeded their costs. In cultures like these, women's worth was valued primarily in reproductive terms, particularly the survival of sons, who assumed more value than daughters in patrilineal societies with exogamous marital patterns. Once daughters married, they left their birth homes.

In the latter half of the twentieth century, people benefited from advances in health and outreach. Some dreaded diseases, such as smallpox, have been eliminated, though new ones have emerged, such as acquired immunodeficiency syndrome (AIDS). Life expectancy has increased. People have been able to control their fertility more effectively and safely through low-dosage pills.

Governments were sometimes slow to catch up with contraceptive changes, leaving in place pro-natalist laws and policies. In the United States, only in 1964 did the Supreme Court outlaw Connecticut's ban on contraception for married couples, and in some states, single people's access to contraception was prohibited until 1972. Mexico's Population Law of 1947 banned contraception and made abortion a criminal offense. In 1972, however, Mexico adopted family planning policies, and vigorous programs reduced high fertility rates in this largely Roman Catholic county, from an average of more than six children per woman to half that rate.[2]

The rapid rise in the world population and the consequent burden on natural resources provoked action at the international level as well. Demographers have staggering figures to offer, evoking memories of the population control advocate of centuries past: Thomas Malthus's alarmist tract of 1798 predicted that food supply could not keep pace with population growth. Yet with a 1997 population at 5.8 billion, even the fiercest anti-Malthusian must grapple with quantumly different absolute numeric increases in minuscule time frames for each added billion people in our world of obscene inequalities. Remember that only around 1800 did the first billion people emerge since the beginning of humankind. According to the United Nations Fund for Population Activities (UNFPA), the world population took

- 123 years to go from 1 to 2 billion
- 33 years to go from 2 to 3 billion
- 14 years to go from 3 to 4 billion
- 13 years to go from 4 to 5 billion
- 11 years to go from 5 to 6 billion (expected, 1998)[3]

The maldistribution of global resources adds another dimension to the starkness of growth rates: almost a sixth of the world's population is chronically undernourished, according to the same UNFPA analysis. The United Nations Development Programme (UNDP) counts the increase in the number of people living in absolute poverty, by year and minute: nearly 25 million annually earn incomes of no more than $370 per year (the UN's definition of absolute poverty), and this increases by forty-seven per minute.[4]

Overconsumption and waste characterize another but different sixth of the world's population, most of whom inhabit the Northern countries. The drive to produce and consume, using energy and destroying resources in the process, is as destructive of the environment as the multiplication of people over time, if not more so. Gandhi's epigraph warns of the risks that rampant waste and overconsumption pose for sustainable development. Given these considerations, the quality of lives will differ if the world of the next few decades is home to, on the low end, 9 billion or, on the high end, 15 billion. And of course, the location of those billions will also make a difference.

Policies and programs will make a difference, as they have in the past, in the slowing of growth rates. But how much policy and program attention is given to slowing overconsumption and waste of natural resources? If anything, the mentality of capitalism's triumph and its associated downsizing of government seem to stimulate growth and natural resource use without regard for long-term costs that now go uncalculated.[5] The United Nations Conference on Environment and Development, also called the Earth Summit, momentarily called governmental and international attention to environmental destruction in 1992. The commitment to "life" is perhaps the common ground that health and environmental activists share.

In international law, persons who have been born are recognized as human beings. In this context, it may be useful to cite in full the International Planned Parenthood Federation's first principle in its 1995 Charter on Sexual and Reproductive Rights.[6]

The Right to Life
IPPF recognizes and believes that all persons have a right to life and that no one shall be arbitrarily deprived of their life. IPPF further recognizes that genocide is a crime under international law, and that this applies where measures including family planning are imposed which are intended to prevent births within a national, ethnic, racial, religious or cultural group with the

intention of destroying, in whole or in part, that group, and, therefore, commits itself to the following:

1.1   No woman's life should be put at risk or endangered by reason of pregnancy. This right refers in particular to avoidable deaths—especially to the need to reduce the risk factors for high-risk pregnancies, such as those which are "too early, too late, too close or too many."

1.2   No child's life should be put at risk or endangered by reason of lack of access to health care services and/or information, counseling or services related to sexual or reproductive health.

1.3   No person's life should be put at risk or endangered by reason of lack of access to health care services and/or information, counseling or services related to sexual or reproductive health.

AND further commits itself to taking all steps to ensure the attainment of the following right:

1.4   The right of all girl infants to be free from the risk of female infanticide.

The right to life in these broad terms must be understood in the context of the tremendous loss of female life associated with pregnancy. Each year, approximately half a million women die during pregnancy. Ninety-nine percent of these women are located in Southern countries. It is estimated that one-third to one-half of these women have died from unsafe abortions.[7] Table 6.1 shows striking regional differences in the strictness of abortion laws. Only women living in countries listed in the last column can make choices about their bodies in the early stages of pregnancy. During later stages of pregnancy, virtually all governments exercise public interest in the autonomous developing life through health and safety regulations.

Shifting Population Discourse and Practice

United Nations thematic world conferences have become vehicles to widen public policy agendas, stimulate governments to act, and inspire nongovernmental organizations (NGOs) to act on their own or to influence public agencies. The meetings draw official government appointees, along with representatives from national and international NGOs. The meetings produce consensus-like documents, although sometimes government appointees take exception to certain provisions in response to their foreign ministries or state departments.

International conferences are bully pulpits writ large, occasionally backed up with funding promises or commitments. The only certain outcome they produce is a mound of paper documents. After that, it takes sustained political action on the part of people in bureaucratic and government arenas to make those principles and funding commitments real.

Table 6.1 Types of Abortion Laws

Very Strict	Rather Strict	Rather Broad	Broad
Africa			
Angola, Benin, Central African Republic, Gabon, Kenya, Libya, Madagascar, Mali, Mauritania, Mauritius, Mozambique, Niger, Nigeria, Senegal, Somalia, Tanzania, Togo, Zaire	Algeria, Burkina Faso, Burundi, Congo, Egypt, Ethiopia, Guinea, Lesotho, Malawi, Morocco, Rwanda, Sierra Leone, Sudan, Uganda, Zimbabwe	Botswana, Ghana, Liberia, South Africa, Zambia	Tunisia
Asia/Oceania			
Afghanistan, Bangladesh, Burma, Cambodia, Indonesia, Iran, Laos, Lebanon, Oman, Philippines, Sri Lanka, Syria, United Arab Emirates, Yemen	Hong Kong, Jordan, Malaysia, Nepal, Pakistan, Saudi Arabia, Thailand	Australia, India, Iraq, Israel, Japan, Republic of Korea, Kuwait, New Zealand, Taiwan	China, Democratic Republic of Korea, Mongolia, Singapore, Turkey, Vietnam
Europe			
Ireland	N. Ireland, Switzerland	Finland, Great Britain, Hungary, Italy, Poland, Portugal, Spain	Albania, Austria, Belgium, Bosnia-Herzegovina, Bulgaria, Croatia, Czech Republic, Denmark, Estonia, France, Germany, Greece, Iceland, Latvia, Lithuania, Netherlands, Norway, Romania, Russia, Slovakia, Sweden
Americas			
Chile, Colombia, Dominican Republic, Guatemala	Argentina, Bolivia, Brazil, Costa Rica	El Salvador, Panama	Canada, Cuba, Puerto Rico, United States

Source: Adapted from "Reproductive Rights" (poster), IPPF, London.

Population conferences have acquired histories and track records that signal shifts in the international mood. The first environmental conference in 1972 in Stockholm, Sweden, formulated international and national recommendations for public policy and government action. The 1974 population conference in Bucharest, Romania, advertised the rift between advocates of population intervention and advocates of development that would trigger a demographic transition, whereby people would take action to lower birth rates once mortality rates declined and people's standards of living increased. In 1984 in Mexico City, powerful countries whose national policies and international monies pushed the "magic of the marketplace" idea further complicated action. By that time, religious and socially conservative political forces had gained strength to promote policies that privileged fetal life over pregnant women's death.[8]

Through these decades, a screaming silence would soon be audible that gave voice to women—about whose bodies policymakers debated, forged principles, and allocated funds. The inattention to women in mainstream textbooks on international affairs continues to amaze those who see the world through women's eyes.[9]

On what grounds do advocates promote family planning, for whom, and with what means? A special issue of *Conscience* in 1993 was devoted to the tensions surrounding means and ends: "if women are provided with family planning services, do the provider's motives matter?"[10] Means-ends dilemmas are multiple: Do the ends justify the means? Are the means compatible with the ends? And who decides these means and ends? The old adage "he who pays the piper calls the tune" takes a music metaphor into life and death issues. Does she who cannot pay have any voice in these matters?

A revealing chart on public expenditures for family planning and health shows how developing countries, with 78 percent of the world's population, account for just 10 percent of expenditures. In remaining countries, with just over 20 percent of the world's population, 90 percent of expenditures are made.[11] In most developing countries, less than half of contraceptive users meet their needs from private rather than public sources. In those private sectors, the prices vary dramatically; for example, IUDs are 17 cents in Indonesia but $300 in Côte d'Ivoire.[12]

Most public support comes with a demographic rather than a health or women's rights rationale. Yet prior to WID/gender advocacy, family planning programs were virtually the only ones that focused on women, viewed strictly in reproductive rather than productive or human rights terms. For population expert Sharon Camp, whatever the rationale, a quarter century of international population funding has saved a million or more women's lives. And demographics matter; although population growth does not cause poverty or environmental problems, she says that it "compounds the problems and complicates the solutions" in a world of many inequalities.[13] Yet new voices in new global arenas have begun to shift the demographic rationale.

Family planning programs took hold in some countries with public intervention. Demand-and-supply jargon from the discipline of economics characterized the opposing debates, with hardly a concern about women as primary users: on the one hand, development generates demand for contraception; but on the other hand, plentiful and accessible supplies of contraception increase their adoption. And why were women the primary objects, whether of service, of manipulation, or of intervention? Obviously, men participate in reproduction; their actions could be "targeted" as easily as women's. Certainly sterilization is far less complex in men's compared with women's bodies.

Of the majority of countries with strong to weak support for family planning, policy choices have been made or changed that promote reduced fertility.[14] These policies range from simple to complex, with direct to indirect signals about reproduction. Policymakers raised the legal age of marriage (thus limiting the years of assumed regularity in sexual activity), legalized contraception, and integrated family planning into health services. But on the whole, the people and their contexts remained submerged in analysis, particularly the social structures that subordinated and devalued women. Not surprisingly, family planning programs had limited success.

The contraception rates of married women are listed in Table 6.2. When indigenous practices exceed modern methods such as the pill, those figures are noted in parentheses, and they are striking in some countries. What this table fails to show are overall rates that include nonmarried women. Researchers can hardly get access to routine data on this obviously significant difference. Social conservatism inhibits discussion of these matters, much less programmatic action.

An indirect method to discourage birth involves widespread, better health care. Universal health care programs helped make China's one-child policy more palatable. But while reinforcing good health care—and the related higher survival rates of children—China pursued a methodical policy of incentives for having only one child, with draconian and consistently enforced penalties for noncompliance. These consisted of fines, loss of public benefits, and heavy peer pressure. Given the preference for sons that still prevails, this has led to increased female infanticide, as sex-ratio figures demonstrate.[15]

Governments spend surprisingly little on health care, as measured by the percentage of gross domestic product (GDP) that public health expenditures

Table 6.2   Percentage of Married Women Practicing Contraception

Country	Percent*	Country	Percent*
Albania	10	Latvia	19
Armenia	12	Liberia	9
Australia	72	Lithuania	12
Austria	56 (71)	Macedonia	39
Bangladesh	36	Madagascar	5
Barbados	53	Malawi	7
Belarus	30	Mali	1
Belgium	75	Mauritius	49 (75)
Benin	1	Mexico	45
Bolivia	18 (45)	Moldavia	24
Brazil	56	Morocco	36
Bulgaria	22	Namibia	26
Burkina Faso	4	Nepal	22
Burundi	1	Netherlands	72
Cameroon	4	New Zealand	60
Canada	69	Nicaragua	45
China	81	Nigeria	4
Colombia	55	Norway	65 (76)
Costa Rica	65	Panama	54
Cuba	68	Paraguay	35 (48)
Czech Republic	45 (69)	Peru	33
Denmark	71	Philippines	25 (40)
Dominican Republic	52	Poland	26 (75)
Ecuador	41	Portugal	32 (66)
Egypt	45	Romania	15 (57)
El Salvador	48	Russian Federation	13
Estonia	26	Rwanda	5
Ethiopia	3	Senegal	4
Finland	77	Slovakia	42 (74)
France	66	Slovenia	40
Gambia	7	Spain	38 (59)
Georgia	19	Sri Lanka	44 (66)
Germany	72	Sweden	71
Ghana	10	Tajikistan	15
Guatemala	19	Tanzania	7
Guyana	28	Thailand	64
Haiti	10	Togo	3 (34)
Honduras	34	Trinidad & Tobago	44
Hungary	62	Tunisia	40
India	36	Turkey	35 (63)
Indonesia	47	Uganda	3
Iraq	10	Ukraine	17
Ireland	60	United Kingdom	71
Italy	32 (78)	Venezuela	37 (49)
Jamaica	63	Vietnam	38 (53)
Japan	47 (64)	Yemen	6
Jordan	27	Zaire	3
Kenya	27	Zambia	9
Korea, Republic of	69	Zimbabwe	42
Kuwait	32		

Source: Based on data from "Reproductive Rights" (poster), IPPF, London.
*Numbers in parentheses are the percentages of women using indigenous contraceptive practices.

Table 6.3   Public Expenditures on Health versus Military

	Health % GDP 1990	Military % GDP 1985	1994
High HDI countries			
Republic of Korea	2.7	5.1	3.6
Argentina	2.5	3.8	1.7
Uruguay	2.5	2.5	2.5
Chile	3.4	7.8	3.5
Singapore	1.1	6.7	4.8
Medium HDI countries			
Brazil	2.8	0.8	1.6
Saudi Arabia	3.1	19.6	11.2
Iran	1.5	36.0	3.8
Algeria	5.4	1.7	2.7
Jordan	1.8	15.9	7.1
Low HDI countries			
Kenya	2.7	3.1	2.2
Ghana	1.7	1.0	0.9
Pakistan	1.8	6.9	6.9
India	1.3	3.0	2.8
Zambia	2.2	1.1	1.0

Source: Based on data from UNDP, *Human Development Report 1996* (New York: Oxford University Press, 1996). Listed are the top five countries in each category for which comparable data were available. This is meant to illustrate a range, not the universe of all Southern countries.

consume. Table 6.3 contrasts these figures with public expenditures for the military, categorized under countries with human development indexes (HDIs) that are high, medium, and low. Surprising about all three categories is the minute percentage spent on public health, ranging from 5.4 to 1.1 percent. The contrasting figures for the military range from 36 to 0.8 percent.

As structural adjustment policies began to take hold, the United Nations Children's Fund (UNICEF) commissioned a study with case studies of ten countries entitled *Adjustment with a Human Face*, as discussed in Chapter 2. Adjustment had been rather inhumane up until that point, resulting in cuts to education and health budgets for most countries, but leaving military budgets untouched. International banks claim to avoid politically sensitive, sovereignty-related policies, but people's security is bound up in public health, particularly in poverty-stricken countries where few privately funded alternatives exist.

Just as some governments use policy tools to discourage birth, others use policies to stimulate birth. Romania under Nicolae Ceauşescu was the most notorious example. The government prohibited contraception and outlawed abortion in 1966. After an initial spurt in fertility, people devised their own means to control fertility through subterfuge and sometimes tragic ways, for housing shortages and a meager standard of living provided contrary incentives to those of the legal machinery. Women sought underground abortions; unwanted children filled orphanages.[16]

Family Planning "Users"

In the context of the mid-1980s, which was still inhospitable to feminist discourses, a "user-focused" approach emerged, which, for all practical purposes, meant a women's focus. Such approaches broadened program attention beyond the delivery of contraception alone to a full range of services and an emphasis on "quality of care."[17]

User-focused programs also shifted evaluation criteria, methods, and outcome measures for specific programs. New outcome measures, such as number of cancer screenings and Pap smears, "client satisfaction," and "contraceptive continuation," however, sit side by side with "total fertility rate" (TFR), numbers of women reached "at risk" for reproduction, and "couple years of protection" (CYP) in rather instrumental and mechanistic form.

Public resources are always finite, so a key consideration in proposed expenditures is cost per user. The bottom-line consideration in competitive bids for project proposals may be based on these very factors. And certainly evaluation outcome indicators would incorporate cost-benefit calculations. In a chart comparing projected costs "per modern method user," figures range from the UNFPA's $1.10 to the World Bank's $19.55, figures for several NGOs range from $1.23 to $16.[18]

Consider the following case of user-focused, quality care. The program mission provides signals for evaluating such care. The Bangladesh Women's Health Coalition was established in 1980 to provide quality care for women. After a decade, it had served 97,000 women and children with approximately 145,000 services such as counseling, contraception, menstrual regulation, basic health care, prenatal care, immunization, and referrals for other services. It insists on several basic principles: treat each woman with respect, discuss each woman's particular needs, and provide each woman with sufficient information for her to make her own choices. The clinic provides female doctors and assistants, for it is unacceptable for women to be examined by male doctors except in emergencies. The clinic charges fees on a sliding scale, covering about a third of its expenses. Costs per client are low, under $5 for menstrual regulation clients who adopt contraception and return for follow-up services. Clients are often satisfied, returning for other services.[19]

Further consolidating the shift toward users was the preparatory work for the International Conference on Population and Development (ICPD), held in Cairo in 1994. The conference came after much thought, advocacy, and practice went into linking women and gender interests to the traditionally more narrow approaches of family planners. A women's development and population agenda included health, education, political voice, and income-generating opportunities. Advocates hoped to integrate objectives into mainstream agencies: increased human development expenditures (water, education, housing, and so forth), increased primary health care, legal reform and actions to recruit more women into decision making, decreased gender gaps in education, increased sexuality and gender education, increased attention to antipoverty policies. Cairo's consensus was to focus on a broad agenda, invariably a costly agenda. Advocates projected the need for far greater resource commitments, nearly double the 1994 figures. Some worried that the agenda was too broad, diluting attention to family planning services.

Once female life is respected and protected, we must also consider women's ability to know about and control their bodies. A common thread among most feminisms involves body integrity, whether that involves decisions to give birth or to prevent conception. And autonomy is obviously incompatible with policies that use compulsion, whether force or material rewards, amid poverty that offers few opportunities to those who "choose" rewards.

Top-down, mechanistic approaches to family planning calculate incentives and penalties to achieve hoped-for outcomes. These calculations are designed to influence staff as well as family planning users. In population policy terms, China is known for its methodical and vigorous rewards for one-child families, instigated in 1979, and its penalties for those with more.

Yet other countries build similar bureaucratic machinery. In India, for example, decision makers at the top, often located in capital cities, set targets or goals against which they judge the success or failure of staff who implement programs and those who monitor them. Staff may even be paid on a quota basis, counting sterilizations, IUD insertions, and condom and birth control pill deliveries. In circumstances like these, users may not get full information about the methods. Are pills necessary only on the days of sexual activity? Can pills be shared with friends? Answers to these and other questions are not so obvious to those without full information. Moreover, staff incentives exist to falsify data or to provide material for those without need, so that they can meet or exceed quotas. India's flirtation with authoritarian rule occurred in 1975, during the emergency that suspended civil liberties. According to Holly Sims:

> The wholesale violation of human rights yielded results: some 11 million people were sterilized during the Emergency, compared with only 1.3 million in the preceding year. However, there were costs beyond those borne by innocent victims of the body-snatching campaign. The government alienated millions of voters and cast a lingering pall on family-planning programs.[20]

Sims displays a chart with revealing gender differences for the decade thereafter: whereas male sterilizations decreased to levels below the emergency year, female sterilizations steadily quadrupled.[21] Do these rates have something to do with gender power imbalances?

For better or worse, most family planning programs focus on women—and on married women rather than all women with potential need. Among couples polled in a 1987 Secretariat of Health survey in Mexico, under 2 percent used condoms, 10 percent used IUDs, 35 percent relied on female sterilization, and 1.5 percent on male sterilization.[22] Program delivery often implicitly absolves men of responsibility, although scattered project models evince some shift, as discussed below.

Although there is an emphasis on the need for contraception, people should also recognize the value of birth and mothering. As Teresita de Barbieri so eloquently states: "In a world that offers women few routes to recognition apart from procreation, population control policies pose a dilemma. Women cannot afford to lose that avenue of recognition and power."[23] As maternal feminists would agree, the meaning and power of mothering across cultural boundaries are not always well understood. The metaphors of power in some cultures involve life-giving, reproductive images. Ultimately, local voices are the best interpreters of these meanings and their connections to reproductive health programs. For reasons like these, the global rise of women's reproductive health NGOs is noteworthy.[24]

Before we stray too far from overconsumption as the problem, it should be noted that some Northern and international NGOs have shifted emphasis from the planet and animal life to people's insatiable appetite for consumer goods. A birth in the North is fifty times more environmentally stressful than one in the South, in terms of energy use and waste disposal. With the mainstream approach to development measured in economic growth terms, such groups fight a hard battle, amid a crowded terrain of voices that promote consumption, related job creation, and overall growth without much regard for measuring damages to natural resources. Even seemingly environmentally sensitive analyses put resource destruction in dollars-and-cents terms, laying out the rationality of costs and benefits, with questionable values accorded the costs. "Ecorats" is the compelling label for such analysts.[25] (See "Applying the Insights" for the dilemmas of an NGO insider hoping to nudge reform.)

Reproductive Health Approaches

As more user-friendly activists became involved in reproductive health programming, the agenda widened to include women's ability to exercise power and control over their development. Activists like these problematized men's interests, stakes, and perspectives in reproductive decision making. User-friendly activists also subjected population and health institutions to critique and worked to transform them. Adrienne Germain and Jane Ordway outline requirements for reproductive health approaches:

- Reallocation of resources among existing programmes. Attention to currently neglected reproductive health issues.
- Changes in training and reward systems to enable and encourage service providers to offer choices and treat women with respect.
- Services for girls and women currently excluded (meaning young, unmarried, those not yet having a child).
- Commitment, not only to improving contraceptive understanding and use, but also to empowering women to manage their overall health and sexuality.
- Increased participation by women in reproductive health policy and programme decisions to build political will and institutional impetus for programme changes.[26]

Until the ICPD in 1994, predecessor conferences were best known as staging grounds for political and ideological posturing. Women became the target for planners, the means for them to achieve lower fertility goals. At Cairo, women's development became the ends, with reproductive health care the means.

Whichever the conference, the net result generally renewed commitments to developing policies in light of incentives and disincentives for population growth. During the 1990s, the world spent approximately $4 to $5 billion annually in developing countries. ICPD's Program of Action called for those monetary commitments to quadruple to $17 billion, though this has not happened. A recent *People and the Planet* article was titled "The Missing Billions," for the promises of Cairo had not materialized. (The writer also cautioned those surprised at the figures to remember that the world spends $40 billion annually to play golf.) States that lead in expenditures include Bangladesh, China, India, Indonesia, Mexico, South Africa, and Turkey;

others provide high per capita support, including Costa Rica, Jamaica, Nicaragua, Mauritius, Sri Lanka, Taiwan, and Tunisia. Among donor countries with large or increasing commitments, the article counts Denmark, Germany, Japan, the Netherlands, the United Kingdom, the United States (largest), and Australia.[27]

Male-Friendly Family Planning

In the area of population and family planning, gender analysts have perhaps moved the furthest. Not only does research detail the seeming "division of labor" in fertility, but it also connects findings to programs that address men's concerns. The UNFPA has produced several studies that report on country-level initiatives that offer promise for responding to the needs and perceptions of men users of and partners in reproductive services. Those initiatives dovetail with public health advocates who encourage more emphasis on condoms for protection from sexually transmitted diseases, including viruses associated with AIDS.

The analysis of men brings gender relations clearly into focus. Specifically, analysts ask us to consider how reproductive tools and the discourse of choice challenge power relations and threaten the gender status quo. Should the discourse and process soften the challenge? Will men's involvement spread stakes and support for use among those who seek contraception?

Deryck Onyango Omuodo argues that, in Africa, men are more likely to favor and to use family planning in men-only clinics with men-to-men educational programs. He stresses the importance of understanding "the level of male dominance and the significance of fears to their security" with the following quotes.

> A Kenyan journalist: "If you are a man you are the boss in the family. You decide what the family should look like."
> A Nigerian demographer: "The man . . . determines almost everything that happens in the family. . . . Even if she makes more money than the man, she is expected to submit to her husband."
> A Malawian finance official: "The man becomes more comfortable when he has economic power."

Omuodo says that programs should address men's fears, including the fear that contraception gives women too much freedom and reduces husbands' control over their sexuality. Rights language, he says, can imply militancy, so language must be coupled with persuasion and explanation. He cites family planning programs in Togo and Ghana that use media to address specific men, such as traditional and religious leaders, and encourage them to have positive attitudes toward family planning. He cites a historic Ghanaian program with a "Daddies Club" that aimed to persuade men to share parental responsibilities. The family planning association in Sierra Leone has successfully used drama, song, and other entertainment in workshops and presentations.[28]

Related to these approaches, Malcolm Potts cites studies that reported increased women's contraceptive use with knowledge of and support from men. For example, a prerevolutionary Iranian psychologist noted that only 12 percent of women who began using oral contraceptives sustained their use after six months. He changed the distribution system to work through husbands, who were informed of how the pills worked and passed them on to wives. Continuation rates after six months increased to 80 percent. Potts also asks that people reconsider coitus interruptus (withdrawal) as a pregnancy prevention measure. Clinics in Latin America offer treatment for sexual dysfunction and infertility and identification of sexually transmitted diseases.[29] An emerging consensus, however ideal, is that conception is a matter that ought to involve partnership and joint responsibility for consequences. In all too many societies, fathers' contributions to child care are irregular. When marriages end, fathers' failure to pay child support is strikingly high in a range of societies:[30]

- United States and Malaysia: up to one-half do not pay.
- Argentina: two-thirds do not pay.
- Japan: three-quarters do not pay.

More and more, activists and officials seek to cultivate men's support for family planning and women's reproductive health. Is this pursuit a practical or a strategic interest, or both? If women's development threatens men's interests, at what point should, or do, policymakers hold back? Some of the above recommendations seem to shore up male privilege. Holding back could be tantamount to facilitating backlash. Yet practical considerations may yield increased effectiveness for users and for programs. Elsewhere, men's perceptions of threat can result in damage to women in the form of violence, as the following chapter discusses in grim detail.

Perhaps the real issue is not just appeasement and support, but changes in notions of masculinity that depend on female subordination. UNFPA cites a project in the United States:

The Oakland Men's Project in California is devoted to eradicating male violence, racism and homophobia. Male mentors teach boys that violence is unacceptable and work on changing the stereotype that men must be tough, aggressive and in control. The group challenges the notion the males are naturally abusive and that females are natural targets of male abuse.[31]

Population policies are integrally tied to those relating to consumption and global inequalities. Women's reproductive health has finally acquired some value, and promising program models provide services compatible with users' complex and diverse lives. Only recently have these services expanded to address the broader, strategic interests that underlie gender subordination.

Applying the Insights

Institutional Transitions—From Population Control to Reproductive Health

You are a staff writer for a small, traditionally oriented environmental/population NGO. It is in the national headquarters, located in the capital city of your country. You join twenty other lobbyists, writers, and clerical staff in an organization that occasionally joins coalitions of organizations that work together to raise funds for population programs.

Your organization has long taken the "gloom and doom" approach to population growth. Its annual reports and press releases highlight the number of global births by second, minute, and hour. In the culture of your organization, successes have been achieved through this approach, measuring success by funds raised from private sources and by legislative victories for public appropriation bills that support population programs around the world. Several factors have led the movers and shakers of your organization to rethink its position. First, an increasingly powerful but opposing coalition organizes around the themes of both market-oriented "growth is good" and religiously inspired "pro-life" (privileging prebirth). Second, the amount of funds raised has dipped in the last two years. Third, a critical mass of new staff members (including yourself) is pushing from within for a broader organizational mission and image that reaches beyond population growth to reproductive health, development for those stuck in poverty (a feminized group worldwide), and the quality of life after birth.

Your supervisor has asked you to prepare a draft press release that announces a (possible) public shift in organizational mission. You know that she is taking a risk with you, for several long-term members of the organization's advisory board still believe fervently in the gloom and doom approach. You do your homework to better understand the discourse and programs of both the reproductive health and the growth/prolife coalition.

You check legislative hearings over the last few years. You surf Web sites as well. You are now ready to share your draft with the group, prior to turning it over to your supervisor.

Budget Cuts for the Women's Health Clinic

The Women's Health Clinic has come a long way since it was first opened two decades ago. Once run by the Ministry of Health, the former "Three Is Enough" clinic was a poorly ventilated, small space of last resort for beleaguered women. They used to arrive early, wait hours, and sometimes get told to return another day when it was less busy. Clinic managers required husbands' signatures for pills, which they issued for two months at a time, leading women to lend pills to one another. Some women complied, but others gave false names, left abruptly, or used brothers to forge signatures. A "we-them" hostile mentality prevailed amid delays associated with paperwork.

After pressure from the state women's council, you, Dr. Prima, were hired to streamline the clinic and make it more helpful to users. You ended the consent requirement, along with the ban on literature about family planning alternatives. You set up four divisions, all staffed with credentialed nurse practitioners: maternal/child wellness care, youth education, cancer screening, and family planning services. You got a grant that augmented your budget to expand services, but it recently ended, and the ministry says that it cannot increase your budget. In fact, the ministry was dealt a near-lethal blow when structural adjustments forced it to take a 20 percent cut, which it is now passing on to all clinics.

You are faced with dilemmas. About two-thirds of your costs are tied up in salaries for staff who haven't gotten raises for years. The salary of the highest paid is five times that of the lowest paid; currently, no volunteers are involved. The other third of the budget goes to maintenance and operations, lab costs, and pharmaceuticals. The ministry says that you might consolidate or eliminate some services, for duplication exists in the Ministry of Education (family life education) and in hospitals and clinics that people usually use for crisis rather than for preventive care.

You and your staff sit down to make some hard decisions. You've been applying for more grants, but nothing has come through yet in the competitive world of funding. You've also been negotiating with the Ministry of Education and other chiefs in your own ministry about transferring some of your programs. However, the staff in other programs have some of the same mentalities as in the "Three Is Enough," and the schools view your literature as too "explicit." You've been told to make a 20 percent cut, or the ministry staff will do it for you.

Notes

1. United Nations Development Programme (UNDP), *Human Development Report 1996* (New York: Oxford University Press, 1996), p. 148.
2. Mexico's 1947 General Law of Population evinces expansionist ideology (promote marriage and fertility, prohibit the sale and use of contraception, criminalize abortion). See Francisco Alba and Joseph Potter, "Population and Development in Mexico since 1940," *Population and Development Review* 12, no. 1 (1986): 61.
3. United Nations Fund for Population Activities (UNFPA), *Food for the Future: Women, Population, and Food Security* (New York: UNFPA, 1996).
4. UNDP Web site "Poverty Clock" (www.undp.org).
5. In preparation for the Earth Summit, the World Bank's *World Development Report 1992: Development and the Environment* (Washington, D.C.: World Bank, 1992) presents what it calls a market-friendly approach to sustaining the environment through incentives for environmentally friendly behavior, state subsidy reductions to wasteful water and energy users, and antipoverty measures. Of course, the overall thrust of the World Bank is to promote growth and consumption.
6. International Planned Parenthood Federation (IPPF), *IPPF Charter on Sexual and Reproductive Rights* (London: IPPF, 1995), p. 12.
7. These figures are regularly reported by UNICEF, UNDP, and IPPF.
8. See Jason L. Finkle and Barbara B. Crane, "The Politics of Bucharest: Population, Development, and the New International Economic Order," *Population and Development Review* 1 (1975): 87–114; Jason L. Finkle and Barbara B. Crane, "Ideology and Politics at Mexico City: The United States at the 1984 International Conference on Population," *Population and Development Review* 11 (1985): 1–28. For insights on global summits, see Hilary Charlesworth, "Women as Sherpas: Are Global Summits Useful for Women?" *Feminist Studies* 22, no. 3 (1996): 537–47. Although the answer to her question is a qualified yes, she identifies many obstacles, including the sustained political energy necessary to maintain and build on strong language. For example, Cairo's strong language on women's health was weakened in the subsequent Social Summit.
9. Kathleen Staudt and William Weaver, *Political Science and Feminisms: Integration or Transformation?* (New York: Twayne/Macmillan, 1997), chap. 8.
10. *Conscience: Women, Population and the Environment* 14, no. 3 (1993): 3.
11. Jennifer Zeitlin, Ramesh Govindaraj, and Lincoln D. Chen, "Financing Reproductive and Sexual Health Services," in *Population Policies Reconsidered: Health, Empowerment, and Rights*, edited by Gita Sen, Adrienne Germain, and Lincoln C. Chen (Cambridge, Mass.: Harvard University Press, 1994), p. 240.
12. Zeitlin et al., "Financing Reproductive and Sexual Health Services," p. 241.
13. Sharon Camp, "Global Population Stabilization: A 'No Regrets' Strategy," *Conscience: Women, Population and the Environment* 14, no. 3 (1993): 7–8.
14. Robert L. Lapham and W. Parker Mauldin, "Contraceptive Prevalence: The Influence of Organized Family Planning Programs," *Studies in Family Planning* 16, no. 3 (1985): 117–37.
15. China's almost infamous programs are covered regularly in media such as the *New York Times* and the *Christian Science Monitor*. The U.S. Public Broadcasting Service had a useful hour-long documentary on China's one-child policy that is good for classrooms, especially in its focus on front-line staff and their

incentives for enthusiastic enforcement. Conservatives in the United States have used UNFPA's support for China's program as a reason to withhold funds. See an insightful analysis in Barbara B. Crane and Jason L. Finkle, "The United States, China, and the United Nations Population Fund: Dynamics of U.S. Policymaking," *Population and Development Review* 15 (1989): 23–59. On skewed sex ratios (in 1987, 109.2 males to 100 females), see Naihua Zhang with Wu Xu, "Discovering the Positive within the Negative: The Women's Movement in a Changing China," in *The Challenge of Local Feminisms*, edited by Amrita Basu (Boulder, Colo.: Westview Press, 1995), pp. 42, 54.

16. The Romania material is summarized from Kathleen Staudt, *Managing Development: State, Society and International Contexts* (Newbury Park, Calif.: Sage, 1991), p. 251.

17. Judith Bruce, "Users' Perspectives on Contraceptive Technology and Delivery Systems," *Technology in Society* 9 (1987): 359–83, and Anrudh Jain and Judith Bruce, "A Reproductive Health Approach to the Objectives and Assessment of Family Planning Programs," in Sen et al., *Population Policies Reconsidered*, p. 196. Also see the fine series *Quality/Calidad/Qualite*, edited by Ann Leonard, published by the Population Council, One Dag Hammarskjøld Plaza, New York, NY 10017.

18. Zeitlin et al., "Financing Reproductive and Sexual Health Services," p. 237.

19. Bonnie J. Kay, Adrienne Germain, and Maggie Bangser, *The Bangladesh Women's Health Coalition,* Quality/Calidad/Qualité series, no. 3, edited by Ann Leonard (New York: Population Council, 1991). Menstrual regulation is legal in Bangladesh. It saves over 100,000 lives yearly (pp. 3–4). An estimated 750,000 women have clandestine abortions annually, about 7,500 of whom die.

20. Holly Sims, "Malthusian Nightmare or Richest in Human Resources?" in *India Briefing, 1992,* edited by Leonard Gordon and Philip Oldenburg (Boulder, Colo.: Westview Press, 1992), p. 25. For more grim details on implementation problems, see Donald Warwick, *Bitter Pills: Population Policies and Their Implementation in Eight Developing Countries* (Cambridge: Cambridge University Press, 1982), and Staudt, *Managing Development,* chap. 12.

21. Sims, "Malthusian Nightmare," p. 26.

22. M. Teresita de Barbieri, "Gender and Population Policy," *Conscience* 14, no. 3 (1993): 32.

23. de Barbieri, "Gender and Population Policy," p. 34. For a provocative (maternal?) feminist perspective, see Germaine Greer, *Sex and Destiny* (New York: Harper & Row, 1984). I cover some of the West African powerful meanings in "Integrating Women into Development Studies," in *Women, Development and Population: Revising Theories and Approaches* (Tucson: University of Arizona, Southwest Institute for Research on Women, 1986).

24. Claudia García-Moreno and Amparo Claro, "Challenges from the Women's Health Movement: Women's Rights versus Population Control," in Sen et al., *Population Policies Reconsidered,* p. 48. The International Women's Health Coalition works with scores of groups and thousands of individuals in southern countries. It can be reached at 24 East 21st Street, New York, NY 10010. Also see Sonia Correa with Rebecca Reichmann, *Population and Reproductive Rights: Feminist Perspectives from the South* (London: Zed, with DAWN, 1994).

25. World Bank, *World Development Report 1992.* Ecorats comes from a UNRISD title. In a 1994 video that the National Wildlife Federation prepared for the Cairo conference, the "fifty times" figure is cited.

26. Adrienne Germain and Jane Ordway, *Population Control and Women's Health: Balancing the Scales* (New York: International Women's Health Coalition,

1989), cited in *Gender Awareness for Population and Development* (London: IPPF, 1995), p. 7.

27. Shanti Conly, "The Missing Billions," *People and the Planet* (1996), reprinted on the UNFPA's Web site (www.unfpa.org). Charlesworth also cautions about the vague and voluntary monetary commitments of global summits ("Women as Sherpas," p. 542).

28. "A New Role for Men: Partners for Women's Empowerment," UNFPA Web site, accessed 1997. Also see focus group results that reveal male threats in Evelyn Folch Lyon, Luis de Lamacorra, and S. Bruce Schearer, "Focus Group Survey Research on Family Planning in Mexico," *Studies in Family Planning* 12 (1981): 413–15.

29. Malcolm Potts, "Family Planning: The Male Point of View," IPPF Web site (www.ippf.org), 1996. Also see Adrienne Germain, Sia Nowrojee, and Hnin Hnin Pyne, "Setting a New Agenda: Sexual and Reproductive Health and Rights," in Sen et al., *Population Policies Reconsidered*, p. 40, box 3.

30. "A New Role for Men."

31. "A New Role for Men."

7 Public Safety, Peace, and Violence against Women

> Human Rights are Women's Rights.
> —UN conferences, affirmed and reaffirmed

> War begins in the minds of men [commonplace saying in academic circles] . . . but ends in the bodies of men, women and children.
> —Judith Large

That human rights are and should be women's rights may seem obvious to most readers, but until the 1990s, humans and women were categories that overlapped little in international legal terms. Women, across the commonplace divide between the public and private spheres, occupied the private, domestic, and family sphere, but that dividing line varied from one society to another. Women's rights frequently went as far as the benevolence (or malevolence) of men with authority in their households. And those private authorities frequently drew from cultural practices that, along with other "inventions of traditions," served male interests.[1]

More than other social categories of people, women are situated in contexts of legal pluralism. Thus, the consistency, simplicity, and convenience of a single standard of law are not always operative. And the rule of law may itself not be operative, amid the whims and interests of politically and militarily powerful people. All too often, "might makes right" is the principle on which many countries operate, even with lengthy and verbose constitutions and international declarations that supposedly guarantee rights.

The delay in recognizing women's rights as human rights was present not only among mainstream national and international institutions. Even the women/gender in development researchers, policy analysts, and activists gave initial priority to issues relating to productive work and to reproduction. Attention to special crimes against women—among them rape, sexual assault and harassment, and wife battering—came much later after the 1975 international agenda of "development, equality, and peace," enshrined in Mexico City's World Platform of Action. Gradually, crime and violence became part of women's policy and collective agendas, not coincidentally as more feminists and women in nongovernmental organizations (NGOs) contributed their voices and occupied more spaces in the policymaking process. It is high time we put women's safety, health, and peaceful well-being at the center of the mainstream public policy agenda.

This chapter focuses on violence against women in so-called peacetime and war. To do so, I analyze the ways in which radical and liberal feminisms crossed the divide between public and private to broaden policy agendas to include violence. I examine the obvious topics of murder, rape, and domestic violence, showing the dilemmas of relying on a supposed neutral state, the enforcement of safety laws, or even state feminism. I also examine women in emergencies, from famine to war and refugee camps.

Besides these concerns, readers should be reminded of the methodical neglect of females, resulting in excessive death among girls and women. Previous chapters analyzed the waste of female life, evinced in uneven sex ratios and startling maternal mortality rates of half a million women annually. When women cannot control their own fertility, they are involuntarily forced into motherhood. Languages other than English make this stark realization more vivid: *maternidad involuntaria*.

Crossing Lines: Feminisms Merge

Previous chapters alluded to the delays in bringing violence against women to public policy agendas. How can we explain this? The answers are multiple, focusing first on women's movements themselves and second on official agendas.

First, violence against women has long been a priority of radical feminists, many of whom have been wary of engagement with governments and international agencies. Outside the realm of official institutions, they established shelters and crisis responses for victims. Without public resources, though, activists faced significant limits to large-scale response to this massive problem.

Wariness eventually gave way to some sort of engagement. After all, laws that privilege men and shield them from public responsibility and accountability for assault and murder burden all women. Even when laws are in place, they may leave much to be desired in the implementation process. Man-made laws are sometimes enforced with a virulence that denies women respect, agency, and justice. Periodically, insights emerge about antiquated laws that institutionalize double standards and treat women as little more than property—in some cases, male-damaged property to be unloaded on other men or on the damagers for the taking.

In 1997, international attention focused on two cases—single incidents that are usually so routine that they go unreported beyond specks in the local media, if even that. In Lima, a seventeen-year old woman was gang-raped. She insisted on pressing charges rather than conceding to her father's wish to kill them or her brother's wish to beat them. One rapist offered to marry her, and under a 1924 Peruvian law, a rapist goes free if he makes a marital offer and his victim accepts. A 1991 law exonerates gang-rapists' collaborators. Of an estimated 25,000 rapes a year in Peru, many are resolved through marriage, particularly when young poor women are involved. Said a man on the street about this case, who thought that post-rape marriage was "right and proper": "A raped woman is a used item. No one wants her. At least with this law the woman will get a husband."[2] Obviously, legal change is but one drop in the bucket toward filling society with attitudes that support gender justice.

In Mexico, a married woman with "permission" from her husband to go out with women friends was approached by a rapist early in the morning. She shot him, and he died after the ambulance took hours to get him to the hospital. She was jailed a year for murder until becoming a cause célèbre. The double standard of justice grants a victim of robbery freedom if he shoots his attacker. If the woman had received no media attention or had been more morally suspect, she would likely have remained in jail.[3] Until 1990, Mexico's law required women to be "chaste and honest" to qualify as victims of some types of rape.[4]

Feminists who leave such laws untouched miss the opportunity to address the larger public. Legal changes may bring justice to victims and perhaps provoke changes in consciousness about men's aggression toward women. However, feminists' attempts to engage the state means that they must use precious political energy for sometimes meager gains amid widespread tolerance of violence. In Kenya, parliamentarians openly laughed about not being able to chastise wives if an antiviolence law passed.[5] In Mexico, feminist activists who engaged with the state quickly became disillusioned with the meager congressional response of underfunded and unenforced efforts.[6]

A second reason for the delay in making the assault and murder of wives and lovers a crime has to do with classic liberal modern government. In classic notions, society is divided into public and private spheres. Standard political science textbooks draw contrasts between limited government (nearly equated with democracy) and expansive, totalitarian government. Limited government intrudes and interferes less in the private sphere, but expansive government permeates the nooks and crannies of everyday lives and decisions. In the category of despicable totalitarianism are countries such as Nazi Germany, the Stalinist Soviet Union, and China under the Cultural Revolution and one-child policies.

In the former Soviet Union and eastern European countries, the transition from authoritarian planned economies was associated with a hoped-for lift of state intrusion into people's personal lives. Thus, the feminist slogan from Western and some Southern countries—the personal is political—is one that progressive women recoiled against after decades of "political penetration" into household lives.[7]

Ironically, cosmetic state feminism did little to address the problem of male violence against women. In Russia, Sisters is a private center to aid victims of sexual violence, established in 1994. Before that, "the state did not see the need for such organizations . . . ; victims became outcasts," says its director Irina Cheren'kaia. Staff counsel victims, educate youth on sexual violence programs, promote crisis centers, and cooperate with law-enforcement authorities. Yet only 12 percent of victims go to the police, and 3 percent of cases reach the courts.[8] Figures like these raise questions about whether the social engineering of Russia's 1917 revolution created "new men," or whether that creation even intended to reduce male aggression toward women among the "old men."

Women's joys and burdens have long been centered in the private sphere of family and household. Until the twentieth century and continuing well into that century, women's public-sphere activities were limited in both polity and economy. If women were perceived to have political interests, those interests were represented by men and to men, with few exceptions. If women worked publicly, it was for the household, with earnings under fathers' and husbands' legal control.

Thus, historically, lines were drawn—in the interest of minimizing government—that conveniently excluded and maintained domestic violence behind the closed doors of homes and compounds. It was a crime for strangers to beat strangers, but incredulously, it was a family matter for intimates to beat intimates. Governments interested in maintaining safe and secure lives for the governed—including women—required action that crossed the line dividing private from public. Surely it is a far cry from totalitarianism for governments to "intrude" upon such crimes.

For decades, Latin American feminists have emphasized the connection between democracy in the country and in the home. Civil relations rather than violent relations are part of the democratic process. And violent, repressive regimes legitimize uncivilized relations from the top to the very bottom—the household base of society.[9]

These insights on national levels have been extended to international levels, with writing from feminists in international relations. Historically, the field of international relations has been the male bastion of political science that focused on war, conflict, and balances of power, which were upset with military might, shows of force, armament buildups, and verbal posturing. That sort of thinking permeates textbooks in the field. It took refreshing thinking from feminists to make visible the gender base on which nations relate to one another.[10] That visibility has emerged only occasionally, for example, when systematic rape is used as a tool of war and torture or when military officials acquire "comfort women" for soldiers. In recent decades, such visibility emerged for women in Bangladesh, Bosnia, and South Korea. Also infamous were the entertainment zones around former U.S. military bases in the Philippines.

Even under democratic conditions, wherein women and men rewrite constitutions and laws, vigilance is necessary to keep the spirit of new laws on track during enforcement. A case in point is the new South African constitution, ratified in a 1996 Constitution Court after two years of democracy under the 1994 Government of National Unity, with African National Congress (ANC) leaders at the helm (including a parliament that is an impressive one-quarter women). The constitution adopted broad principles of gender equality and human rights. Among those to protest ratification were traditional leaders who enforced customary law and with whom officials might compromise for political support. The new constitution, according to Margaret Burnham, a civil rights attorney who served on an ANC human rights panel, "addresses gender discrimination directly, but it is silent as to the discriminatory effects of customary laws." She says that it is not clear whether the law provides "relief to African women, who have the most to gain from aggressive implementation . . . occupying the subeconomy as domestics and subsistence agricultural workers and frozen out of the political and social mainstream by the policies of apartheid and the traditional tenets of customary family law." Women, Burnham continues, are "disproportionately the victims of violent crime, including domestic and sexual violence."[11]

Considerable writing about customary law demonstrates how fluid practices became codified under colonialism. And customary laws are far reaching, ranging from marriage and divorce to inheritance and property rights. In South Africa, customary law requires guardians' permission for women to marry, contract, and acquire property.[12] Bride-price (*lobola*) affirms women's reproductive value, but customary law deems women to be minors. Should a husband die, his estate goes to male relatives, and his widow may lose custody of their children.

Legal pluralism, double standards, and male-only human rights enforcement do not bode well for quelling men's aggression and violence against women. The Convention on the Elimination of All Forms of Discrimination against Women (CEDAW)—seemingly near world consensus—works only as well as national laws, judges, and local police make it work. And the makers and enforcers of such laws and practices are usually not women.

The machinery of governance still privileges men, making it relatively easy to inflict violence. We now turn to program initiatives that aim to alleviate the consequences of male violence against women in short-term, ameliorative ways.

Reducing the Damage: Programs against Battery and Rape

To address the form and content of violence against women, human rights and feminist frameworks for programs and laws are both gender-specific and seemingly gender-neutral. Should violence against women be addressed through specific laws and programs, such as women's police stations and counseling for recalcitrant men? Or should criminal offense be addressed under mainstream laws and programs and "human" rights? The latter mainstreams feminists' issues. No matter what the answer, we must understand the seeming neutrality of laws and programs and of their enforcers, whose gender ideologies will determine whether justice is served. Ultimately, laws must be gender-strategic, addressing the institutionalization of female subordination that exists in the climate of social, government, and media portrayals of gender relations.

In *Combating Violence against Women*, the International League for Human Rights provides categories for understanding and addressing violence.[13] It specifies four types: domestic violence, sexual harassment, sexual assault, and violence from tradition or culture. To this, however, we must add woman killing and the ease with which such killing is excused.

Gendered Perspectives on Murder

Jails are filled with real and scapegoated offenders against people and property. In repressive political systems, these offenses may be mere political criticism. Whatever the injustices of the criminal justice system, we must recognize that the world's prison population is by far a male population. For various reasons, most of which are related to a socialization process that encourages aggressiveness as the essence of multiple forms of masculinity, men commit many more criminal offenses than women.

Some of men's offenses are against intimates—supposed loved ones. Worldwide, women are more likely to be killed by their partners than are men. A study from New York City's Department of Health found more women killed by husbands and lovers than killed in robberies, sexual assaults, and drug and random attacks. Nationally, 40 percent of women are killed by partners, but only 6 percent of men are killed by wives or lovers.[14]

Men are sometimes legally excused for these offenses. In Brazil, women waged a two-decade struggle to challenge laws that allowed male killers to use the "honor defense" to absolve themselves of murder and penalty. Partners, from husbands to ex-husbands to boyfriends, were sanctioned to kill if they perceived unfaithfulness. A 1988 case absolved a murderer, and a state appeals court upheld the decision. But the Federal Public Ministry appealed to Brazil's highest court, which overturned the decision. Members of the tribunal declared that the honor defense defends not honor but the "self-esteem, vanity, and the pride of the lord who sees his wife as property."[15] Yet when the man was retried, he was again acquitted based on the honor defense. In the machinery of courts, gender ideologies continue to prevail.

Murder of women also occurs with support from the state. Women, like men, share abominable torture at the hands of repressive governments. But the torture of women has its special twists, relating to rape, pain inflicted on sexual organs, and routine examination of vaginal cavities at the pleasure of male guards. The 1993 Vienna tribunal on human rights offered grisly details of these atrocities. One speaker showed illustrations from the theocratic state of Iran of the proper size rocks to be used for stoning adulterous women: big—too large, would kill the adulterer without suffering; small—wouldn't inflict enough damage to lacerate the head; medium—just right.[16]

Among offenses against females, we could count those connecting sex-determination tests during pregnancy to abortion. India legalized abortion in 1969—relatively early among countries—for demographic reasons; India is now the second-most populous country on the globe. Feminist groups in Bombay are the often-quoted source for the striking figure that in the state of Maharashtra, all but one of 8,000 aborted fetuses were female.[17] Some clinic signs read: "Better to spend Rs500 today [on a sex-determination test] rather than Rs500,000 at the time of the girl's marriage [to meet dowry demands]."[18]

Female-fetus abortions were striking enough for several state legislatures to pass laws making it illegal to inform parents about sex determination. This prompted contentious responses, with some feminist critics arguing that such laws shifted attention from the oppressions women face during adulthood.[19] What should change: abortion laws, or women's oppression?

Dowry deaths, now reported regularly in India, numbered 792 in 1987 and 922 in 1988, according to official counts. The families of brides offer dowries to the families of grooms to relieve them of women's supposed burdensome dependency. This long-standing practice became highly commercialized during the twentieth century, so much so that in 1961, the Indian Congress passed a dowry prohibition law. Yet dowry continues, along with the retribution, threats, and death when dowries are unpaid or uncompleted.[20]

Lest we think that violence disappears in settings without dowries, it is useful to remind ourselves about the commonness of female death elsewhere. The United States, obsessed with counting, reports high female death rates at the hands of husbands, partners, and intimates. The New York City figures cited earlier are higher than the official (but probably vastly underreported) counts in India. According to law professor Elizabeth Schneider:

> Battering is the leading cause of injury to women in the United States. A woman is murdered by her husband or boyfriend every six hours. Somewhere between 2,000 and 4,000 women die each year of abuse. Between 30 and 40 percent of all women killed in this country are slain by a male intimate.[21]

Alarming in the United States, Europe, Mexico, India, and the countries to which they distribute their television and film productions is the frequency with which women are portrayed as objects and victims. The second edition of *The State of Women in the World Atlas* provides striking figures on the rapid increase in video and film productions that connect sex and violence.[22] Soft- and hard-core pornography offers societies mixed messages. On the one hand, they routinize relations of gender domination and subordination. On the other hand, they lift the sometimes centuries-old repression of sexuality. But pornography is also big business. In the United States alone, it is estimated that people spend $8 billion annually on "adult material."[23]

Murder is linked to assault. The intent of laws and programs on domestic violence is preventive: eliminate or reduce assault before it turns into murder. But can male aggression be reduced in the process? Can women's self-sufficiency emerge from such programs?

Domestic Violence

Domestic violence occurs behind the closed doors of homes and compounds, in a private sphere of life often shrouded from the gaze of government. Culture, tradition, and even law legitimized physical punishment until quite recently in most places. Peggy Sanday's anthropological analysis of 150 societies shows, however, the variation in violence against women, linked to gendered origin stories, economic context, and dominant cultural values.[24]

It is impossible to know the frequency of domestic violence, for in most places, it is a crime that goes unreported. A 1993 United Nations resource manual, *Strategies for Confronting Domestic Violence*, estimates that in one of three marriages, men are the "usual perpetrators."[25] Methodical studies in Papua New Guinea document a rate twice the "norm."[26] In a rich ethnography of western Kenya, 43 percent of ninety-four women said that their husbands physically abused them. Most of the rest said that abuse was increasing. Development strategies without opportunity for men's profitable labor seemed to render men relatively useless, even as cultural ideology celebrates their importance for household support. The assistant chief, one of the local leaders to whom victims come, says of husbands:

> [They] do not have employment; they do not work. Many leave early in the morning to go to groups with other people just to sit and talk; if they are drunkards they go to drink. They *kogotitsa lidiku* [lose the day]. When they come to their homes, because they have not brought any money or food they come home and begin beating their wives.[27]

In the area, agriculture is women's work, beneath men.

The UNDP chart on violence and crime reports no figures on domestic violence. A scant twenty-one countries, most of them in the North and with high human development rankings, report total rapes (with the United States leading the list).[28] For both domestic violence and rape, however, victims underreport crimes, and this undermines our ability to understand the scope and cost of the problem. Moreover, only a minority of countries obsess about numeric data collection or can afford to do so; the United States is one of those. Annual expenditures add up to $425 billion for jails, courts, and police.[29] The end of wars, cold and hot, can lead to peacetime dividends. Routine expenses on peacetime crime—a civil war in other terms—detract obscenely from public resources that could be spent to increase human capabilities.

Few countries bother to count, but even fewer add up the total costs of domestic violence and rape. Surely, economist-minded readers might wonder whether the benefits exceed the costs of intervention to reduce or end the violence. The UN *Strategies* report identified huge sums for police, court, and health and welfare services, along with women's emergency housing and social security benefits. Canadian estimates in 1980 added up to C$32 million.[30] To this, economists would add days of labor lost (paid and unpaid), along with declines in productivity. But if we could put numeric values on fear, untreated injury, and the replication of behavior by other household members, such as children, the overall cost would break budgets. Ironically, "safe-motherhood" initiatives among major international banks passed up opportunities to make mothers safe in their own homes.[31]

In cases of domestic violence, debates occur about whether to criminalize or decriminalize assaults. Should assaults between family intimates make a difference? Decriminalization stresses reconciliation, welfare, and therapy; it may offer relief as well, through grounds for divorce. Criminalization involves the police, the courts, and various tools of protection and penalty.[32] Such tools and protections establish distancing and adversary mechanisms that operate in complex ways in dependency relationships. Moreover, victims of violence depend on bureaucratic machinery, the staff of which may share gender prejudices. Without massive preprofessional or in-service training, the general tolerance of domestic violence easily continues.

In some cases, police themselves are perpetrators of violence against women. *Manushi* is a feminist magazine in India that began publication in 1979. Five years later, it had a circulation of 10,000. Madhu Kishwar and Ruth Vanita expanded that circulation through a book containing essays, editorials, and letters to the editors from *Manushi*'s first five years.[33] In a section on "Violence against Women," divided into three parts, they reprint six selections on police violence. Graphic accounts document how the police rape isolated, minor, and politically marginal women. If brought to justice— with an emphasis on the *if*—police officers face minor penalties. Among the most vulnerable to police abuse are sex workers (consider the case in the appendix).

In the rural areas of weak states, the absence of a police presence relegates legal and official response to a near-meaningless stature. Through their own solidarity structures, some women respond collectively, as in India, with occasional instances of attacks on abusers.[34] But often violence is a private crime that shames the victim and her family. Combined with a situation in which landlords are perpetrators of violence, lone women are unlikely to tackle those with political clout, even with laws and an official presence.

Several countries have established special women's machinery to deal with violence. Pakistan has several police stations, established under former prime minister Benazir Bhutto's leadership. But Brazil is the model country case.[35]

In Brazil, women's groups, along with the state council on women, pushed to establish *delegacias* (women's police stations) in 1985. Prior to this, violence against women was not taken seriously, even though later studies would show that in São Paulo, 70 percent of 2,000 battery cases involved women attacked in the home. Staffed with women, these stations respond to crimes of violence against women.

By 1990, Brazil had seventy such stations. In these all-purpose units, specially trained women police officers investigate crimes, provide psychological and legal counsel, and secure evidence from specially trained medical practitioners. Yet even with *delegacias*, about half the cases are not investigated and are eventually dismissed. The amount of resources devoted to the stations rises and falls with prevailing political and budgetary winds. The *delegadas* are stigmatized, called "the kitchen of the police." One attorney told Americas Watch that even at *delegacias*, a prevailing mentality exists that domestic violence is not a crime. "It's family, it's not a crime."[36]

Some violence against girls hardly reaches the stature of crimes. Nawal el Saadawi wrote painful memories of coming-of-age rituals that inflict violence on young bodies, with consequences for a healthy sexual and maternal life in adulthood.[37] Terms for the practice vary from genital mutilation to female circumcision. The latter terminology does not cover deeper operations such as excision (cutting the clitoris or all or part of the labia minora) and infibulation (cutting the clitoris, labia minora, and part of the labia majora, after which sides of the vulva are pinned together, except for a small opening that allows menstrual blood and urine to pass).[38]

Gender in Emergencies: War, Famine, and Refugee Camps

The tragedy of war, hunger, and displacement is shared by women, men, and children. However, women's experiences differ, because of the specific violence discussed earlier. Among recent war crimes, we count Bosnian women who face systematic rape (as did women in preindependence Bangladesh). In early 1997, an international court heard testimony relating to Yugoslav war crimes. Grozdana Cecez, forty-seven years old, was repeatedly raped in the prison camp. According to her testimony about the group rape (translated):

> I couldn't do anything. I was lying there and he was raping me. I had no way of defending myself. I didn't understand what was going on or what was happening to me. I was crying. I said, "My God, what have I come to live through."

Her perpetrators were young: "I could have been their mother."[39]

The mundane routine of famine and resettlement also situates women differently. As guardians of the children and responsible for food, women need a voice in the distribution system. If "male household heads" are targeted for food distribution, the supplies may never trickle down to women and children.[40]

The United Nations High Commissioner for Refugees is responsible for emergency relief. The agency has developed special techniques to identify gender interests through people-oriented planning, a quick method for relief workers to manage distribution and facilitate safety. Violence against women does not end in camps.[41]

In the latter twentieth century, war has different dimensions than those huge world wars of the not-too-distant past. Civilian casualties are more commonplace. Weapons are more widespread. Gun traffic gets far less media and budgetary play than does drug traffic.[42] The merchants of death, along with gun consumers, do their damage with a dazzling array of "antipersonnel" instruments, including land mines that linger long after fighting has stopped to kill and maim residents.

During civil and foreign wars, children's special plight is especially compelling. Because they have few to no political advocates, especially during wartime, UNICEF developed a special antiwar agenda in its *State of the World's Children 1996*. UNICEF highlights the reality of child soldiers and the trauma of sexual violence and rape. Idealistic as it may seem, UNICEF calls for commitments to mediation and conflict resolution, to the prevention of war, and to education to promote tolerance and peace.[43]

In times of so-called peace and war, women face special violence. It is a public safety problem of mammoth proportions, even though its costs are rarely tallied. Peacetime violence against women occurs within their own homes, and intimate offenders have historically been treated lightly (if at all) in a criminal justice system that drew the enforcement line at the private line of gender subordination.

Women are finally joining those categories of people for whom human rights are evoked. In the name of human rights struggles, women's practical and strategic interests have expanded the public agenda to include their safety in "peacetime" and the protection of their bodily integrity during war and rehabilitation.

Applying the Insights

Harassment of Sex Workers, Diluted Anti-AIDs Campaign, and Police Corruption

You are an organizer with a group of former sex workers in an aspiring global city in the middle Americas. In this city of more than a million people, foreign export-processing factories have been established that serve as magnets for migrants from rural areas. The factories pay only minimum wage, however, which amounts to the equivalent of $20 to $30 weekly. In household terms, this salary falls below the official poverty line.

The former sex workers have formed a community bank, and many have been able to move into equally profitable lines of work with small businesses. However, many continue their commitment to create and expand awareness about the spread of HIV and the scourge of AIDS. Little support exists in the public health agencies for treating the infected and supporting their final years with grace and dignity.

Whether sex workers or poverty-stricken factory workers, women exercise little power in local government. You, as a part-time organizer, seek funds for activities that would mobilize these and other women to speak and act in local politics. Yet you are profoundly cynical about prospects, based on past experiences and realities. Prostitution is a regulated occupation in particular zones of this city, for which licenses are granted and health inspections are required. Registration allows government to generate revenue officially. Unofficially, police harass workers, along with owners of the bars and brothels in which they work. Workers pay not only the bar owners but also the police for autonomy to earn their money. Occasionally, police roundups result in other abuses. Recently, several women were rounded up, put in a police van, and, based on a policeman's offer that couldn't be refused, performed oral sex through the hole in the board that separated the officers from the women in the back.

Group members serve as *promotoras*, preaching the wisdom of condom use. They put posters on the street, using startling language (*chingar*): "If you [crude verb for sexual intercourse], use a condom." At the order of the mayor, anxious about a visit of higher-level dignitaries, police tore down the posters. Group members are furious, wondering about the "free speech" provision that is supposed to be enshrined in the constitution.

Should you contest and confront the mayor? How? Leaders from a large NGO with which you occasionally work offer to set up a meeting with the mayor. Their stature and background virtually guarantees a hearing. But the condition is that you don't go to the press and thereby embarrass the mayor, who wants to keep things quiet.

Your group is looking for resources to sustain its work, but few are interested in public association with stigmatized workers. With group members' consent, your colleague puts out a query on an electronic listserv in which prostitute unions from a rich country to the north occasionally dialogue with catchy language and pleas to legitimize the occupation. Sex workers might be equal in the health and safety risks that their occupation poses, but not in compensation. You wonder whether anyone will put their money where their mouths are. What is to be done?

Notes

1. The classic book here is E. Hobsbawn and Terence O. Ranger, eds., *The Invention of Tradition* (Cambridge: Cambridge University Press, 1983). For the best source on elder men's manipulation of the process to serve material and control interests, see Martin Chanock, *Law, Custom and Social Order: The Colonial Experience in Malawi and Zambia* (Cambridge: Cambridge University Press, 1985).

2. Calvin Sims, "Justice in Peru," *New York Times*, March 12, 1997. Similar concerns were raised at the Rural Women's Labor Movement meeting in Bombay, India, 1990. See Rural Women's Labor Movement, "Women's Organizations against Rape in India: Report of a National Meeting Forum against the Oppression of Women," in Miranda Davies, ed., *Women and Violence: Realities and Responses Worldwide* (London: Zed, 1994), pp. 60–75.

3. Julia Preston, "Woman's Shooting of Attacker Rivets Mexico," *New York Times*, February 5, 1997.

4. Maria de la Luz Lima, special prosecutor of sexual crimes, Attorney General's Office, Mexico City, remarks in Ford Foundation, *Violence against Women: Addressing a Global Problem* (New York: Ford Foundation, 1992).

5. Phoebe Asiyo, former member of parliament (MP) in Kenya, writes an engaging account of failure (twice) to pass the Law of Marriage and Divorce. Men MPs talked about the necessity of disciplining wives and how beating was "a pleasure" to wives, a "way of expressing love" in custom. Her chapter can be found in the excellent collection on a Kenya conference addressing legal change: Mary Adhiambo Mbeo and Oki Ooko-Ombaka, eds., *Women and Law in Kenya: Perspectives and Emerging Issues* (Nairobi: Public Law Institute, 1989). The law movement, and women's voices within, has been important in the move to democratize Kenya. See an analysis of gendered policies in Maria Nzomo and Kathleen Staudt, "Man-Made Political Machinery in Kenya: Political Space for Women?" in *Women and Politics Worldwide*, edited by Barbara Nelson and Najma Chowdhury (New Haven, Conn.: Yale University Press, 1994), pp. 416–35.

6. Marta Lamas, Alicia Martínez, María Luisa Tárres, and Esperanza Tuñon, "Building Bridges: The Growth of Popular Feminism in Mexico," in *The Challenge of Local Feminisms*, edited by Amrita Basu (Boulder, Colo.: Westview Press, 1995), p. 343.

7. Barbara Einhorn, *Cinderella Goes to Market: Citizenship, Gender, and Women's Movements in Eastern and Central Europe* (London: Verso, 1993). I use the noun "penetration" deliberately; it was much in vogue in the male-oriented political development literature of the 1960s and 1970s as one of the stages through which countries passed.

8. Ekaterina Lakhova, "Women Should Participate in the Construction of Civil Society at All Levels," paper presented at Prospects for Equal Democracy in Russia, April 22–23, 1997, distributed by HURINet (Human Rights Information Network).

9. On Latin American feminisms, see selections in Jane Jaquette, ed., *The Women's Movement in Latin America*, 2d ed. (Boulder, Colo.: Westview Press, 1994); Alicia Frohmann and Teresa Veldés, "Democracy in the Country and in the Home: The Women's Movement in Chile," in Basu, *The Challenge of Local Feminisms*, pp. 276–302. *The Official Story*, a movie released on tape, makes this point well. It offers the vantage point of a military official's wife during Argentina's "dirty war," in which the authoritarian government disappeared

activists, critics, and others. *Las Madres de la Plaza de Mayo* is a documentary focusing on the mothers of the disappeared during the same period.

10. See various books by Cynthia Enloe, beginning with *Bananas, Beaches, and Bases* (Berkeley: University of California Press, 1989). Kathleen Staudt and William Weaver criticize international relations in *Political Science and Feminisms: Integration or Transformation?* (New York: Twayne/Macmillan, 1997). Another useful book is Georgina Ashworth, ed., *A Diplomacy of the Oppressed: New Directions in International Feminism*, (London: Zed, 1995). Judith Large's epigraph for this chapter comes from "Feminist Conflict Resolution" in that book (p. 23).

11. Margaret Burnham, "The New South African Constitution and Customary Law," *P*A*S [Program of African Studies] News and Events* 7, no. 2 (1997): 3.

12. Burnham, "New South African Constitution," p. 3. Also see Susan Bazitti, ed., *Putting Women on the Agenda* (Johannesburg: Raven Press, 1991), which brings together materials from a 1990 Lawyers for Human Rights conference relating to constitutional preparations for a new South Africa. Several chapters deal with Zimbabwe, Namibia, and Botswana as well. See note 1.

13. Cited in Jane Connors, "Government Measures to Confront Violence against Women," in Davies, *Women and Violence*, pp. 184–97.

14. Pam Bellick, "A Woman's Killer Is Likely to Be Her Partner," *New York Times*, March 31, 1997.

15. Dorothy Q. Thomas, "In Search of Solutions: Women's Police Stations in Brazil," in Davies, *Women and Violence*, pp. 27–31.

16. This is from a video that accompanies Elizabeth Fisher and Linda Gray McKay, *Gender Justice: Women's Rights Are Human Rights* (New York: Unitarian Universalist Service Committee, 1996). The four-part video is an excellent resource for classrooms and includes a British animation on the bank-instigated world debt crisis.

17. Sakuntala Narasimham, "India: From Sati to Sex Determination Tests," in Davies, *Women and Violence*, pp. 43–52.

18. Narasimham, "India," p. 45.

19. Jana Everett, "Gender Policy Reform in Maharashtra, India: Assessments of a Liberal Feminist Strategy," paper presented at the American Political Science Association meeting, Chicago, August 31–September 5, 1995.

20. Narasimham, "India," p. 45.

21. Elizabeth Schneider, in Ford Foundation, *Violence against Women*, p. 4.

22. Joni Seager, *The State of Women in the World Atlas* (New York: Penguin, 1997). The literature on media sex objectification of women is huge. *Killing Us Softly* is a video on U.S. advertising, updated in a speech and excerpted in the video accompanying Fisher and McKay, *Gender Justice*. On Bombay films, see Shamita Dasgupta, "Feminist Consciousness in Woman-Centered Hindi Films," *Journal of Popular Culture* 30, no. 1 (1996): 173–90.

23. Amy Harmon, "The Internet: For Parents, a New and Vexing Burden," *New York Times*, June 27, 1997.

24. Peggy Sanday, *Female Power and Male Dominance* (New York: Cambridge University Press, 1981).

25. United Nations, *Strategies for Confronting Domestic Violence* (New York: UN, 1993), p. 2.

26. Christine Bradley, "Why Male Violence against Women Is a Development Issue: Reflections from Papua New Guinea," in Davies, *Women and Violence*, pp. 10–26.

27. Judith M. Abwunza, *Women's Voices, Women's Power: Dialogues of Resistance from East Africa* (Peterborough, Ontario, Canada: Broadview Press, 1997), p. 119. Readers will recall my research from western Kenya in the 1970s, discussed

in Chapter 5. Reading Abwunza brought me back home, for Maragoli Location was just south of Idakho Location, where I lived for nearly a year.

28. United Nations Development Programme (UNDP), *Human Development Report 1995* (New York: Oxford University Press, 1995), p. 98.

29. The most recent U.S. figures, from Barbara Barkes et al., *American Government and Politics Today: The Essentials 1996–1997* (St. Paul, Minn.: West, 1996), p. 498.

30. Cited in Davies, "Understanding the Problem," United Nations resource manual, *Strategies for Confronting Domestic Violence*, p. 6.

31. Elizabeth Shrader Cox, "Gender Violence and Women's Health in Central America," in Davies, *Women and Violence*, p. 118, reminds us that the World Bank's safe motherhood campaign had little to do with mothers' safety from domestic violence.

32. Connors, "Government Measures," pp. 184–88.

33. Madhu Kishwar and Ruth Vanita, eds., *In Search of Answers: Indian Women's Voices from Manushi* (London: Zed, 1984), pp. 79–83.

34. Radha Kumar, "From Chipko to Sati: The Contemporary Indian Women's Movement," in Basu, *The Challenge of Local Feminisms*, p. 61.

35. The next paragraphs are summarized from Thomas, "In Search of Solutions." Also see Sara Nelson, "Constructing and Negotiating Gender in Women's Police Stations in Brazil," *Latin American Perspectives* 23, no. 1 (1996): 131–48. She reports on p. 139 that 200 stations operate throughout the country, most of them in São Paulo. On Pakistan (which only had two stations), see Tariq Butt, "Interrogate Lovingly," *Populi: The UNFPA Magazine* 21, no. 6 (June 1994): 5.

36. Thomas, "In Search of Solutions," pp. 36–42.

37. See Nawal el Saadawi, *The Hidden Face of Eve* (London: Zed, 1980), for a moving account of Egypt.

38. Erua Dorkenoo and Scilla Elworthy, "Female Genital Mutilation," in Davies, *Women and Violence*, p. 138, 141. They estimate that 74 million women are affected, mostly in Africa and the Arabian peninsula.

39. Gilian Sharpe, "Yugo War Crimes," distributed by HURINet, April 22, 1997.

40. From the BRIDGE publication *Development and Gender in Brief* (November 1996), edited by Sally Baden and Rachel Masika, with assistance from Zoe Oxaal. BRIDGE produces excellent newsletters and working papers. It can be reached at the Institute of Development Studies, University of Sussex, Brighton BN1 9RE, United Kingdom.

41. The UN High Commissioner for Refugees produces many useful monographs.

42. United Nations Research Institute for Social Development (UNRISD), *States in Disarray* (Geneva: UNRISD, 1995), pp. 111–14.

43. UNICEF, *The State of the World's Children 1996* (New York: Oxford University Press, 1996), p. 40.

Part III
Applying Context and Policy Analysis to Action

8 Bringing Politics Back in
Institutional Contexts for Mainstreaming

Teaching to Transgress
—bell hooks

With the approach of the Beijing World Conference on Women in 1995, technical assistance agencies sought to assess two decades of institutional efforts to mainstream women/gender into their programming. The focus on institutions dovetailed with the development community's belated emphasis on improved governance, accountability, and democracy. So far, this discussion had had little gender focus.

In this chapter and the next, I compare the mainstreaming strategies of bilateral assistance institutions in four European (Germany, Netherlands, Norway, Sweden) and two North American (Canada, United States) countries. Readers longing to "bring development home" might tackle the constituency, legislative/parliamentary, and executive politics that have heretofore marginalized gender in the bureaucracies that negotiate and implement bilateral technical assistance.

Readers struggling with institutions in their own countries will find parallels, for women's machineries (including women's studies programs) confront similar obstacles in their mainstreaming activities. Readers may very well wonder, as well, whether they live in democracies that work for women. By the close of these two chapters, readers may raise ethical questions about the masters' institutional tools with the core dilemma: are these mostly man-made institutions part of the problem or part of the solution?

Mainstreaming, using the pioneering definition of Rounaq Jahan, puts women "at centre-stage, part of the mainstream" in either an "integrationist" or an "agenda-setting" approach. According to Jahan, an integrationist approach "builds gender issues within existing development paradigms," whereas an agenda-setting approach uses gender perspectives to transform the existing development agenda.[1] Her distinctions can be applied to any institutional mission, within and across national borders.

Mainstreaming women is an activity that is embedded in bureaucratic and political contexts. Development paradigms differ from country to country, as does the foreign policy agenda that rationalizes a particular development paradigm. *Context matters*. I part ways with those who isolate mainstreaming from its context, yet I find Jahan's mainstreaming distinctions quite useful. Clearly, the integrationist approach is more modest: the dialogue over development is a Northern one, occurring primarily within the bilateral agency, its foreign policy host, and the national context in which it is situated. The transformative approach is ambitious: its development dialogue aims toward North-South partnership, wherein agency decentralization and development-as-empowerment conceptions shift the decision-making focus toward people in Southern countries.

Women/gender analysts would be remiss to ignore the transformation potential inherent in the context of hospitable donor development paradigms and agency operations. Were mainstreaming efforts situated within such contexts, a synergy between mutually supportive transformative missions would quicken and deepen the North-South partnership agenda. Mainstreaming strategies are more effective when embedded in hospitable agencies with transformative development paradigms that prioritize human development, Southern empowerment, and reductions in North-South structural inequalities.

The vision of transformative mainstreaming should not deter us from understanding integrationist mainstreaming. It too has potential, albeit slower and less effective. Mainstreaming improves under the conditions of democratic politics (wherein women exert their interests in critical mass numbers) and of accountability-directed institutional coalition-building strategies (wherein evaluation, personnel, and budgetary offices develop a stake in and responsibility for gender), as discussed briefly later. This chapter demonstrates that development assistance, a political project, requires nationally situated political analyses and strategies, in both donor and recipient countries and both inside and outside institutions.

Democratic Politics

Democratic voice and direction from the wider public must include critical masses of diverse women. For bilateral development assistance, the problematic issue here is this: which public? Taxing and spending authority comes from the public in the bilateral institutions' national contexts. The users of those funds in recipient countries, as Judith Tendler noted in her classic study two decades ago,[2] lack political voice in the funder country. As this analysis will demonstrate, bilateral institutions give minimal priority to funding female empowerment efforts in democratic countries. Yet women experience democracy in the national politics of bilateral institutions at minimal to impressive levels. Democracies differ, and their institutions give more or less space to women, gender interests, and ideologically compatible political parties.

My approach departs from those that would make women/gender a technical project alone. The antecedents of technical approaches are found in gender training, gender planning, and bureaucratic guidelines, as discussed in Chapter 3. Technical approaches are crucial in those agencies that operate with little public scrutiny. In the current world order, multilateral institutions are subject to far less public scrutiny than bilateral institutions situated in democratic countries.[3] Yet questions might be raised about bilateral institutions as well: Are seemingly democratic countries really democracies for women? How are women's voices expressed in public decision making?

Technical approaches are fundamental to mainstreaming, however. They help legitimize gender analyses in ways that foster coalition building inside bureaucracies. Technical approaches can also institutionalize policy changes that empower women with skills, authority, capital, citizenship, and human rights. Finally, technical approaches can protect and sustain women's gains when prevailing political winds would undermine them. Such winds blew strongly in many Northern countries beginning in the 1980s and continuing even now. Yet in democratic contexts, bureaucracies cannot and should not be insulated from popular will, that is, the political process. Democratic popular will, however, must represent women's and men's voices and interests.

Accountability: Evaluative and Financial

The rhetoric of development assistance can be dazzling and seductive. Rhetorical flourish emphasizes the transfer of resources to improve women's (and men's) lives. But bilateral assistance has many important objectives:

- It serves foreign policy goals, until recently bound up in the cold war among larger donors.
- It strengthens donor country businesses that supply products and expertise and that seek markets abroad.
- It supports country allies and ideologically aligned ministries in those countries.

To put resource transfers for improving people's lives at the top of such a list, it is imperative that institutions account for their outcomes—programmatically, politically, and financially. Successful coalition-building strategies foster accountability.

As we shall see, it is all too common for bilateral institutions, including women's units within, to measure and judge their performance with indicators of effort. OECD/DAC/women in development (WID) guidelines, most of them process- and input-oriented—with one exception (a statistical reporting system)—perpetuate this approach.

Institutional accountability is necessary to mainstream women, even in its most modest integrationist approach. Accountability has two dimensions. First, it refers to an ability to document program results and outcomes, frequently known as evaluation. Despite the common sense associated with evaluation—that is, of documenting results, learning lessons about what works and doesn't and why, and then applying those lessons to ongoing and future efforts—development agencies concentrate on "moving money" instead.[4]

Second, accountability has a financial dimension, in which institutions can document spending. We would expect accountable bilateral institutions to measure and account for their performance through evaluations and financial statements. After two decades, such accountability is limited, except for "women-specific" projects, which tend to be minor sidelines both programmatically and monetarily.

At the multilateral level, only one fleeting moment of the decades-long history of WID contained published (and therefore publicly accountable), precise, and comparable categories and figures. Projects of exclusive concern to women were 5 percent of all projects; projects designed to include women were 12 percent of projects; projects affecting women with no provision for their participation were 56 percent of projects but 63 percent of funding.[5] A decade later, we have no published documentation to determine whether this has changed.

Accounting for spending on women is admittedly difficult. Yet vague pronouncements about efforts, rather than results, are problematic for two reasons that relate to internal and external incentives for bureaucratic change. First, precise financial goals and objectives provide internal incentives for "resistant" and "hesitator" bureaucrats to change their ways (recall Lotherington's categories from Chapter 3). Second, reports on goal achievement provide crucial leverage for external activists to maintain vigilance on bureaucratic institutions and to push their executives to meet goals (and executives, in turn, to send cues to staff). To press for change, outsiders use resources in the wider public, such as interest group pressure, calls to appoint more responsive cabinet and subcabinet officials, supportive political party policy platforms, media visibility and public opinion expression, and ultimately votes to install new parties in power.

Greater bureaucratic openness is one among many principles of good governance, which the development community increasingly seeks in recipient countries. Presumably, bilateral assistance institutions should also meet good governance principles associated with open bureaucracies.

Bureaucracies often operate behind closed doors, making problematic open and full access to sources for research purposes. International agencies have their public-relations offices, through which the messiness of alleged development is filtered for external consumption. Staff generally speak through internal bureaucratic reporting relationships, or they speak cautiously, with anonymity, or not at all. In a comprehensive account of the biggest among development bank bureaucracies, Catherine Caufield acknowledges the "scores" of employees she cannot thank publicly, for it has always been clear, as stated by its current president, that "externally voiced criticism of the Bank is an indication of a desire to find alternative employment." She could also go to publicly released (or leaked) documents in this secretive organization, or to consultants who complain about how the agency distorted their analyses when inconsistent with the agency's agenda.[6]

In this chapter and the next, sources are multiple, moving beyond the academic institutional literature that provides some historical and baseline analyses. I also consulted OECD/DAC reports from its Women in Development Committee members; institutional documents (ranging from self-serving to descriptive and critically reflective reports); and an average of three United Nations Research Institute for Social Development (UNRISD)–sponsored interviews within four European institutions wherein institutional histories were reconstructed for Germany, the Netherlands, Norway, and Sweden (referred to in the text as Rs, for respondents). Interviews were not restricted to women/gender advocates alone.[7] Although the UNRISD survey instrument contained no questions about outcomes or coalition building, interviewees' responses provided information or made it possible for me to make inferences from the detailed institutional narratives. Nor did the UNRISD instrument pay heed to larger bureaucratic and political contexts. Nevertheless, secondary data are available to posit connections therein.

This chapter does not analyze the impact of bilateral assistance institutions on women's lives in those countries. Readers, however, can assume that policy legitimacy (or illegitimacy) and resources offer leverage to officials and nongovernmental organizations (NGOs) in country settings. There are several noteworthy examples of assistance that values and funds activities to empower women in their national politics. Unless such activities occur in political democracies (or those in transition toward democracy), however, such empowerment efforts will fall on deaf ears.

The remainder of this chapter is divided into several sections. First, I compare women/gender conceptions. Most donor countries (as they are frequently called) began with a separatist approach, but the preparations for and outcomes of the United Nations' 1985 Nairobi conference built the basis for mainstreaming claims. Second, I examine the institutions that host women/ gender mainstreaming, each with its own distinctive approaches and missions, which may or may not mesh with gender perspectives. In the next chapter, national political contexts of these institutions are compared, including women's political representation, gender policy discourse, women's movements, and the political structures that facilitate or impede female voices. From outside politics, we then move to inside strategies.

Conceptualizing Women/Gender Mainstreaming

Given the diverse bilateral institutions and national polities, it should be no surprise that women/gender mainstreaming is conceptualized differently. Still, all women/gender advocacy occurs in large bureaucracies, the classic characteristics of which include hierarchy, secretiveness, procedural complexity, and division of labor. Bureaucratic characteristics do not bode well for feminisms.

Caroline Moser analyzes five discourses on women/gender: welfare, efficiency, poverty alleviation, equity, and empowerment.[8] Although most terms are self-evident, there is some danger in reifying the rhetoric, for bureaucratic practice over time often varies and merges one or more discourses. Of course, too, bureaucrats frequently "package" their advocacy in language designed to maximize the greatest leverage in their political contexts, thus suggesting the danger of examining language alone. Yet discourse has consequences for vision (or its absence), including the extent to which program efforts reach beyond the "domestication of women."[9]

Bilateral institutions initiated what was invariably called women in development over a period that ranged from 1968 (Sweden) to 1986 (Germany). The agencies and their acronyms include:

- Canadian International Development Agency (CIDA)
- Bundesministerium fur Wirtschaftliche Zusammenarbeit (BMZ)
- Directorate General of International Cooperation (DGIS)
- Norwegian Agency for Development Cooperation (NORAD)
- Swedish International Development Authority (SIDA)
- U.S. Agency for International Development (USAID)

But whatever WID/gender's birthing era, bilateral institutions usually began from a similar vantage point: welfare. Even the now forward-looking and pioneering Nordic donors (Sweden; Norway, starting in 1975) reconstruct their histories as mired in welfarism, which viewed women as recipients of child care, maternal and child health, and training in housekeeping tasks. NORAD interviews indicate that 10 percent of overall spending went to women in this form (Rs). Anderson and Baud report that for the mid-1980s, just as Germany was about to declare its WID policy, 12 percent of funding went to women.[10]

From the early years to now, it is difficult to differentiate WID/gender spending on women's *practical* interests from spending on those *strategic* interests that reduce female subordination (recall Molyneux and Moser on language, discussed earlier). For example, Sweden took the early but risky step of supporting family planning projects. At the same time, Sweden had an institutional mainstreaming vision. Mary Tadesse and Margaret Snyder, in reconstructing the history of the African Training and Research Centre for Women (ATRCW) (of the UN Economic Commission for Africa), credit Sweden with foresight in funding two posts to build African-based networks for women's development.[11]

Another pioneer was USAID, with a 1973 congressional mandate to "integrate women in development." The WID Office's operational definition distinguished WID as "economic" rather than family planning oriented, but the understaffed office depended on untrained staff in the more than sixty far-flung field offices to report funding for "women-specific," "women's component," and "women-integrated" efforts for annual reports to the U.S. Congress. In this pre–gender training era, both underreporting and exaggeration occurred, but official totals indicated that 2 percent of funding went to women in 1978. All projects required a women-impact statement, but these were little more than paragraphs recycled from one project to the next; an understaffed WID Office could barely monitor a fraction of several thousand projects yearly with quality attention.

The WID legislation was the product of a politically savvy informal network of Washington, D.C.-based women who understood the outside political leverage that congressional reporting provided to advocacy offices, potentially buried in big bureaucracies. The WID Office languished with civil service coordinators until a 1978 political appointee, with ties to women's constituencies, put plans in action to facilitate women's empowerment in countries where USAID worked. She did this at some risk, for agency staff criticized the "women-specific efforts" as political rather than technical projects. Although the 1979 separate projects represented just a fifth of WID projects and a tenth of still-minimal WID funding, they provoked hostile reactions among staff. Yet the WID coordinator's work meshed with USAID's rhetorical mission under a Democratic president—to serve the "rural poor majority" through "growth with equity"—a mission that altered under Republican presidencies.

By 1982, as articulated in a policy statement, USAID's WID program became the epitome of an efficiency approach, grounded in microenterprise women's projects. The intent of this policy was to spread responsibility throughout the entire agency. Subsequent efforts to package the issue in USAID and efficiency terms documented how project effectiveness increased with women's inclusion.[12]

More recently, USAID discourse, with its democracy initiatives, legitimized funding for empowerment efforts, but at minimal levels. Notable projects include women and law networks, efforts to put women on national political agendas, and assistance to encourage municipal government accountability to women.

Germany's belated WID effort is a high-technology, high-volume bilateral effort, centralized in Germany but fragmented across several agencies and operating in more than a hundred countries. The BMZ's efficiency orientation joins an antipoverty approach. Its WID effort is careful to talk efficiency language and avoid women-specific approaches, believed to produce less resistance in the institution. A Women, Family, and Youth unit has developed an elaborate categorization scheme to differentiate the thousands of BMZ projects according to expected impacts: women positive, women risky, women negative, and unspecified effects (the latter of which characterizes "most" projects) (Rs). Neither numbers or percentages nor funding amounts are provided for the categories. The Women, Family, and Youth unit has the authority to countersign and delay project approval, a procedure intended to build more focus on women, to the extent that its staff can provide quality monitoring. BMZ staff emphasize women's integration into sectors that address practical development needs (Rs). Whereas most donors use WID or gender discourse, Germany couches women in family discourse.[13]

The Netherlands comes closest to an empowerment approach, which it calls autonomy. Drawing on university action-oriented research projects, the Netherlands conceptualized women *and* development in terms of emancipation from multiple inequalities, according to its report for the 1975 UN women's conference. Its directorate built ties to and supported the Women and Autonomy group at the University of Leiden, whose faculty developed participatory research methodologies. In a 1990 white paper to Parliament, it shifted to women's autonomy as active agents in development, with "autonomy" interpreted as individuals' authority, freedom, and opportunity to control their own lives and bodies. Autonomy has four components: political, physical, economic, and sociocultural. As DGIS staff articulate, and as projects to empower women's voices document, the Netherlands tries to take its cue from women in recipient countries (Rs). Some of these women are now part of a network of those trained at the world's largest women's development advanced graduate program at the Hague.

From its early years, NORAD staff called its assistance "women oriented." It was integrated and made a priority in an overall development strategy that questioned traditional economic growth and bureaucratic models. Its 1980s action plan used equal-opportunity language, drawing it to the equity approach, but it stopped short of the gender equity language that pervades Sweden's whole assistance after SIDA underwent the institutional diagnosis that constitutes a "gender planning" model (Rs).

Norway's equity approaches rely on specific women's programming through its 1984-instituted women's grant.[14] The grant provides flexibly administered seed money to support a wide range of pilot activities, activities with no other funding sources, and activities that strategically address the structures that maintain female subordination. For example, the grant funded the Ambedkar untouchables' social justice movement, as well as KALI, the first feminist publishing house in India. Norway's actions suggest that separate and autonomous women's programming is a legitimate stage toward, yet consistent with, mainstreaming.

Sweden's equity discourse makes it appear that gender mainstreaming is in place. SIDA views such equity as consistent with effective and efficient programming (Rs). Yet SIDA also pursues separate women's programming as a means toward mainstreaming. By 1992, Brouwers and colleagues reported that Sweden provided more than half the funds for all OECD/DAC-supported women's machinery.[15] If consistent with UNIFEM's changing philosophy of 1989 and thereafter, strong women's machinery activities pursue mainstreaming missions: they aim to spread responsibility for gender to other ministries.

Canada's WID policy, declared in 1984 (after steering committee work from 1977 on), took a partial cue from the limitations of separatist WID units, often sidelined from the mainstream of agency operations in early years. Its advocates developed a corporate-like plan of operations to spread responsibility to all staff in the name of gender equity. In the late 1980s, CIDA had the reputation as the most forward-looking bilateral institution in the mainstreaming mission. Upon more methodical reflection, admirably done at the instigation of its own evaluation unit, CIDA outcomes are judged more modestly. Gender equity does not resonate well enough with CIDA's agenda to promote "self-sustaining development" that "puts poverty first" (countries and people).[16]

The comparison of women/gender mainstreaming discourse shows that *no single conceptual line predominates*, even among like-minded donors. Although welfarism was the starting point, or the base from which institutions moved, none now claim this infamous approach. Yet if incrementalism truly prevails to the extent that most observers of government conclude it does, we would imagine some perpetuation of welfare, from which incremental change has occurred.

Moreover, the discussion shows the mix of discourses: Nordic countries pursue equity alongside empowerment; efficiency in the United States is considered an effective means to alleviate poverty, yet broadly defined empowerment projects coexist with these efforts. Without numbers and categorization schemes, which no European donors reported in interviews (Rs), we cannot fully know the predominant approach. Neither can the anecdotal success stories mentioned in interviews and documents clarify predominant activity.

Finally, conceptions shift across time. This is due partly to changing organizational and intellectual agendas: WID advocates learn what works and what doesn't in their bureaucracies; WID/gender conceptual thinking changes among activists and academics. These shifts are also caused by changing ideological and partisan complexions in government, as electoral results change the national cast of characters in power. Nowhere is this more marked than the shift from center-left to center-right and conservative party dominance in the 1980s and beyond. Conservatism frequently meshes with an efficiency discourse or one that couches women in motherhood and family terms (even as men are not couched in fatherhood and family terms) rather than as citizens or members of occupational groups. Although conservative parties gained strength over social democratic parties in most North American and European democracies in the 1980s through the early 1990s, women's official representation also gained (discussed later). No analysis details the links between changed bilateral policy (much less WID discourse) and specific female representatives and the groups to whom they are accountable. However, we can tentatively assume that more diverse women were elected who increasingly learned to use discourses compatible with prevailing political contexts.

Institutional Missions and Climates

National politics and culture shape the bilateral institutions under analysis in this chapter. The institutions themselves have their own history, culture, and mission, with particular ideological content. History shapes institutions. Paraphrasing a nineteenth-century theorist in a way that allows us to understand WID/gender advocates in bilateral institutions, Robert Putnam states: "Individuals may 'choose' their institutions, but they do not choose them under circumstances of their own making, and their choices in turn influence the rules within which their successors choose."[17]

Although universally committed to promoting "development," bilateral institutions are not a monolithic group.[18] Their missions vary from predominantly export promotion (United States, Germany) to poverty alleviation and structural change between rich and poor countries (Nordic region, Netherlands, Canada). The assistance mission is ideologically embedded in foreign policy, and the bilateral offices themselves are sometimes physically embedded in foreign ministries.

Institutions also vary in the extent to which they meet UN targets (0.7 percent of gross national product) for official development assistance. Whereas the Dutch and Nordic countries have regularly surpassed this target since the mid- to late 1970s, Canada, Germany, and the United States have not, although the latter two are among the largest donors in absolute terms (Japan leads donors in absolute monetary figures). Despite large absolute funding levels, the United States consistently funds Israel and Egypt at levels far above those justified by need (using indicators of per capita income or of poverty), owing to Middle East foreign policy accords.[19] The diverse bilateral missions make inevitable the diverse WID/gender mainstreaming efforts detailed earlier.

Germany's bilateral operation is fragmented at headquarters, yet it contains rigorous procedures, "border[ing] on inflexibility."[20] Historically, its comparative advantage has been high-technology project assistance in infrastructure such as dams, roads, and utilities. The Federal Republic of Germany once prohibited aid to countries recognizing its eastern neighbor, the German Democratic Republic. Parliamentary changes of the 1970s, including a female minister of economic cooperation in 1977, increased commitment to basic human needs and poverty alleviation. She presented a parliamentary paper outlining women's worsening position in conventional development (Rs).

More recently, Germany has proclaimed good governance and democracy as conditions for aid.[21] German unification has prompted Germany to look inward to meet its massive development responsibilities. (Indeed, former eastern European countries, in transition to market economies, have captured a segment of other bilateral assistance budgets once destined for Southern countries.)

Bilateral institutions vary in the extent to which decision making is centralized in their national capitals versus field offices in recipient countries. Those bilateral institutions with a strong presence in recipient countries should be more adept at understanding their national policies, politics, and NGOs. Country-specific knowledge and presence are preconditions for making North-South partnership work. The distribution of women/gender staff reflects that commitment as well. Headquarters-staff field commitments range from heavy field presence (Sweden and Norway) to heavy field and headquarters presence (Netherlands, United States) to heavy (Canada) and light (Germany) headquarters presence. What is not known from reporting figures is the extent to which women and gender field responsibilities have been added onto other tasks.[22]

Decentralization looks good on paper. The United States probably has the most decentralized bilateral institution in staffing (rather than in funding decision) terms. Yet central policy controls generally weaken in decentralization, unless those in the field support those policies or have a stake in them. In the past, USAID's many field offices exhibited an enclave mentality, and its part-time WID officers felt beleaguered with many responsibilities, of which WID was but one. This has now changed somewhat, with shared authority between country national and U.S. personnel and with full-time WID advisers in some missions (not reflected in cryptic responses to OECD/DAC surveys, which also mask central office distinctions between direct hire, contract, and appointee staff).[23]

Staff presence does not automatically mean expertise through country programming. Despite extensive staff presence, only a third of CIDA's country programs have WID strategies, and of these, half had mechanisms to ensure women's participation.[24] For reasons such as this, CIDA and USAID have pursued gender training strategies. But gender training has yet to be coupled more effectively with field office responsiveness to women's demands in recipient countries, for in many countries, women lack political voice inside and outside their governments. Several Nordic countries and the Netherlands pursue a delicate balancing strategy to respond to women's voices.

Whether centralized or decentralized, bilateral institutions increasingly rely on other institutions to implement projects and programs, with all the uncertainty and limited control that that implies. These other institutions include recipient-country ministries, NGOs, and contractors. However strong their women/gender mainstreaming commitment, bilateral institutions cannot assume that other institutions will take that commitment seriously unless incentives are in place to encourage such seriousness. CIDA's "mandatory" training (strong language, since only half of its professionals have been trained) reaches just 20 percent of its partners (contractors). Besides, contractual responsibility is unenforceable, because no sanctions exist for nonperformance.[25]

Some bilateral institutions transfer resources selectively, to countries that have development missions that mesh with their mission. Sweden's concentrated assistance to select countries "funds partners, not projects."[26] (In my review of historical overviews of bilateral assistance, Sweden was the first to use "partnership" language.) Whereas once-socialist Nicaragua's (or

Tanzania's) agenda was consistent with Sweden's structural change mission, it was anathema to the 1980s emphasis in Britain (under Thatcher) and in the United States (under Reagan) on the "magic of the marketplace." Yet recipient-country partners, with development policy agendas to pursue structural and equitable change, do not always extend this logic to gender.

The institutional homes of the WID/gender mainstreaming effort have an important bearing on its conceptualization and content. Those bilateral institutions with ambitious foreign policy and commercial agendas will obviously part ways with those bilateral institutions more attuned to development missions with selected recipient countries, chosen for criteria that include poverty or democracy. Similarly, the larger the group of recipient countries, the larger the likelihood that the recipient pool includes countries for which foreign or commercial agendas exist—countries lacking democracy or poverty-alleviation agendas. A bilateral development mission that critiques traditional economic models that foster inequality (including gender inequality) resonates better with WID/gender mainstreaming. The Nordic countries have carved out a special role in making national equity commitments consistent with their international commitments in the United Nations and bilateral assistance policies.[27]

Rather than offering conclusions, I now move to Chapter 9 for the other side of institutional analyses. Institutions operate within contexts that are more or less amenable to women/gender mainstreaming.

Notes

1. Rounaq Jahan, *The Elusive Agenda: Mainstreaming Women in Development* (London: Zed, 1995), p. 1.
2. Judith Tendler, *Inside Foreign Aid* (Baltimore: Johns Hopkins University Press, 1975).
3. Jahan, *The Elusive Agenda*, pp. 46–7.
4. Tendler, *Inside Foreign Aid*; Wapenhans's critique of moving money is cited in U.S. General Accounting Office (GAO), *Multilateral Development: Status of World Bank Reforms* (Washington, D.C.: GAO, 1994); Janne Lenox and Desmond McNeill, *The Women's Grant: Desk Study Review* (Oslo: Royal Norwegian Ministry of Development Cooperation, 1989); Rideau Research Associates for Francoise Mailhot, CIDA/Evaluation, *Gender as a Cross-Cutting Theme in CIDA's Development Assistance—An Evaluation of CIDA's WID Policy and Activities, 1984–1992* (Ottawa: CIDA, 1993); Bruce Rich, *Mortgaging the Earth: The World Bank, Environmental Impoverishment, and the Crisis of Development* (Boston: Beacon Press, 1994).
5. UNDP, *Women's Participation in Development: An Inter-Organizational Assessment* (New York: UNDP, 1985), pp. 36–43.
6. Catherine Caufield, *Masters of Illusion: The World Bank and the Poverty of Nations* (New York: Henry Holt, 1996), pp. ix, 23, 24.
7. I thank UNRISD for this access. The term "women/gender advocates" is used

because agencies shift the discourses over time, for reasons that may or may not be related to mission and program. Like in Chapters 2 and 3, I view agency players as advocates, highlighting what sometimes becomes a politically charged role.

8. Caroline O. N. Moser, *Gender Planning and Development: Theory, Practice and Training* (London: Routledge, 1993).

9. Barbara Rogers, *The Domestication of Women: Discrimination in Developing Societies* (New York: St. Martin's Press, 1979); Maria Mies, *Patriarchy and Accumulation on a World Scale: Women in the International Division of Labour* (London: Zed, 1986).

10. Cecilia Anderson and Isa Baud, eds., *Women in Development Cooperation: Europe's Unfinished Business* (Antwerp, Belgium: UFSIA Centre for Development Studies, Technical University of Eindhoven, 1987).

11. Mary Tadesse and Margaret Snyder, *African Women and Development: A History* (London: Zed, 1994).

12. This paragraph and the preceding one are from Kathleen Staudt, *Women, Foreign Assistance and Advocacy Administration* (New York: Praeger, 1985).

13. Thanks to my student Olaf Bak, who provided me with updated and translated materials and interviews in Germany during fall 1994.

14. Lenox and McNeill, *The Women's Grant*.

15. Rita Brouwers et al., *Support to National Machinery for Women in Developing Countries: Efforts of OECD/DAC Members* (The Hague: Institute of Social Studies Advisory Service, 1992).

16. Aruna Rao et al., *Gender Training and Development Planning: Learning from Experience* (Bergen, Norway, and New York: Chr. Michelsen Institute and Population Council, 1991); Rideau Research Associates for Francoise Mailhot, CIDA/Evaluation, *WID Policies in Selected Development Agencies* (Ottawa: CIDA, 1992).

17. Robert D. Putnam, *Making Democracy Work* (Princeton, N.J.: Princeton University Press, 1993), p. 8.

18. Steven H. Arnold, *Implementing Development Assistance: European Approaches to Basic Needs* (Boulder, Colo.: Westview Press, 1982).

19. U.S. GAO, *A Profile for the Agency for International Development* (Washington, D.C.: GAO, 1992); also see Chapter 2 of this book.

20. Arnold, *Implementing Development Assistance*, p. 59.

21. K. van de Sand and R. Mohs, "Making German Aid More Credible," *Development and Cooperation* 1 (1992).

22. These numbers are from responses to reporting requirements in OECD/DAC, *Third Monitoring Report on the Implementation of the DAC Revised Guiding Principles on Women in Development (1989)* (Paris: OECD, 1992), and Rounaq Jahan, "Assessment of Policies and Organizational Measures in Women in Development Adopted by DAC Member Countries" (draft, 1994). Field presence ranges, for example, from all field mission offices of the bilateral donor, including full-timers (Sweden), to zero (Germany). Heavy headquarters presence is found in Canada, with scores of full- and part-timers who supply some technical assistance; light presence is found in Germany's BMZ and Norway, with one full-timer plus two part-timers and three full-timers, respectively (early 1990s figures).

23. Staudt, *Women, Foreign Assistance*, chap. 5. Mari Clark, USAID/WID, interview and written communication, 1995.

24. Rideau, *Gender as a Cross-Cutting Theme*, p. 6.

25. Rideau, *Gender as a Cross-Cutting Theme*, pp. 28, 31–32.

26. Arnold, *Implementing Development Assistance*, p. 105.

27. Hilkka Pietila and Ingride Eide, *The Role of the Nordic Countries in the Advancement of Women within the United Nations System* (Stockholm: Nordic UN Project, 1990).

9 Institutional Strategies
Analyzing Political Contexts

In the last chapter, we examined bilateral assistance institutions, their missions, and the diverse discourses they have used to justify action on women/gender. Clearly, some institutions offer more hospitable climates for mainstreaming women/gender than others. The analysis would be incomplete without also connecting political contexts and constituencies to internal strategies for change. This I do here, focusing particularly on the extent to which political institutions provide space to alternative voices and ideologies.

National Contexts: Political Democracies?

Bilateral assistance institutions are creatures of their political environments. These environments consist of political structures and cultures, the latter of which express values, norms, and ideologies around which the public coheres.

Structures: Political Space for Women/Gender?

The bilateral institutions analyzed here are embedded in diverse national political structures. Those structures range from single-member (SM) constituency parliamentary (Canada) and presidential (United States) systems to proportional-representation (PR) parliamentary systems (Netherlands, Nordic countries), the latter of which provide incentives for multiple parties of different ideological stripes to compete for positions proportional to votes received. (Germany mixes SM and PR.)

PR parliamentary systems provide a more representative voice for women *inside* of multiple political parties, legislative bodies, and government bodies. Ironically, though, this insider influence does not necessarily coexist with flourishing and autonomous women's lobbies and movement groups that engage with government.[1] Germany's conservative government (along with political women within it) parts ways with more radical women's groups. Engagement is tantamount to co-optation.

In the U.S. presidential system, interests are more often expressed through lobby groups or nongovernmental organizations (NGOs) than political parties. In parliamentary systems, in contrast, parties bear major responsibilities for expressing ideologically distinctive policy agendas. Whether in SM, PR, presidential, or parliamentary systems, NGOs are not monolithic. Their diversity was discussed earlier, via David Korten's distinction between autonomous and dependent groups. Funders include bilateral assistance institutions, and the dangers of co-optation are obvious.

The U.S. Agency for International Development (USAID), renamed and reorganized numerous times since its birth in the 1940s, is a chronically vulnerable and unpopular mission. To increase its popularity—even ensure its survival—USAID courts Congress and public opinion with figures that demonstrate its healthy effects on the U.S. economy. These strategies reinforce its image as an export-promotion operation, even when it goes through stages that emphasize poverty alleviation or growth with equity (the nearest U.S. language that approaches structural change).

USAID is more heavily scrutinized through congressional oversight and evaluation in this separate-branched presidential system than are bilateral institutions in parliamentary systems.[2] Each year, the U.S. General Accounting Office (GAO) (a congressional evaluation operation) publishes studies about USAID. Accountability leverage is possible through mechanisms like this.

Besides the long-standing work of the GAO, a government-wide reform effort has been in place since 1992 that aims to streamline operations, to evaluate programs based on "outputs" (performance and results) rather than "inputs" (budgets), and to make institutions responsive to their "customers" (users, clients, citizens, and/or constituencies). In 1993, Vice President Gore produced a far-reaching "Reinventing Government" plan that reaches into all parts of government, including USAID. Such action bodes well for accountability mechanisms.

USAID operates within a weak-party presidential system with levels of female political representation that chronically fall below global norms (10 percent at national levels).[3] Outside of a Women's Bureau within the Department of Labor, the U.S. government has no cabinet or subunit charged with gender equality. Although the proportion of female representation at local and regional (state) level now averages 20 percent in this decentralized federal system, non-national governments are not responsible for bilateral assistance.

USAID depends heavily on NGOs, with various material and ideological stakes in its policies and spending, to carry it through the annual funding trauma in Congress. Budget appropriation is a tense and uncertain process for USAID, given its public unpopularity. Many of these NGOs increasingly lean toward the contractor rather than the independent mode. Traditionally, women's lobbies have concentrated primarily on domestic policy, though after the 1973 congressional WID mandate, internationally oriented constituencies emerged, such as the Association for Women in Development, the Coalition for Women in Development, and women's public-service contractors. Universities acquire extensive contracts for development work, although women are weakly organized in university bureaucracies.[4]

European bilateral institutions operate in strong multiparty parliamentary systems. In the Nordic countries, center-left ideologies framed the policy, foreign policy, and development assistance agendas for considerable periods in the postwar era. For two decades, women's political representation has surpassed global norms in the Nordic countries (and now in the Netherlands, as well), reaching 30 percent or more at national levels—higher than in Germany, where the conservatives have long governed.[5] Outside of Germany, social democratic ideologies drive bilateral policy agendas that are more oriented toward the alleviation of poverty and of structural inequalities between rich and poor countries.

Despite low U.S. female representation, women representatives caucus across partisan lines to support issues such as women in development. The 1994 elections, with less than 40 percent voter turnout, produced conservative majorities in both houses that drew sharp ideological lines opposed to equality agendas.

European countries have women's movements and organizations, apart from political parties, some of which traditionally view the state as suspect. Autonomous women's groups increasingly see the importance of working with the state, although radical feminists keep a further distance from the state in Germany. The German Green Party incorporates feminism into its Left-libertarian ideological agenda (as well as gender parity in representation) but rarely gains more than 5 percent of parliamentary seats. Among all European countries considered, Sweden has the weakest autonomous women's movement, ostensibly because women's interests have long been mainstreamed in national equity policies (called state feminism by some).[6] Equality discourse is pervasive in U.S. public opinion polls, perhaps compensating for low female representation levels,[7] but its strength is being put to the test in the aftermath of the 1994 elections.

Canada's female representation levels are higher than those in the United States, and its women's movements flourish. Unlike what Joyce Gelb calls the interest group, ideological, and state feminism models (of the United States, United Kingdom, and Sweden, respectively), Canada combines interest group, ideological, and state commitment inside various government bodies that address equality agendas and on which representatives of women's groups sit.[8] Through workshops conducted as early as the mid-1970s, women's organizations and CIDA recommended an advisory committee to increase project benefits to women.[9]

Political structures provide more or less space for women, politicizing gender to greater or lesser degrees, with ideological parties that are more or less hospitable to women's and feminist groups. Also relevant is the political culture.

Political Cultures

Enormous diversity exists in the North, leading to a feminist characterization of European countries as conservative, progressive (Nordic), and creative traditional (Netherlands), with the latter two reflecting policy conceptions of women as citizens or individuals rather than as mothers and wives.[10]

Of the European countries considered in this chapter, Germany in the past fell in the "conservative" category. Germany's policy discourse addressed women as dependents within nuclear families longer than had the other countries under analysis. Robert Moeller traces the basis for this orientation to postwar reconstruction, as Germany recovered from the devastation of war and distanced itself from the German Democratic Republic's socialist discourse on women. The Ministry for Family Affairs embodied conservative political Catholicism.[11]

Germany's government bureaucracies and parties are heavily centralized and hierarchical, characteristics that the autonomous feminist movements set themselves apart from. Such distance reduces the ability of those movements to alter policy discourse. West German women participated in the labor force and establishment politics at lower levels than did their northern European neighbors. In the *Women and Men of Europe*'s 1983 survey, 42 percent of German women believed that "politics was men's business," compared with 19 percent of women in the Netherlands and 20 percent in Denmark. In that same survey, just 34 percent of German women expressed confidence in women doctors, compared with 78 percent in a Nordic country (Denmark).[12] Such thinking may be changing, for 1990–91 attitudinal data from a smaller number of countries show that 63 percent of German women say that they have a fair amount of political interest (versus 40 percent of Swedish women, the other overlapping country in this study).[13]

Political culture encompasses values about gender, which influence officials' views of program action in their own and other countries. Germany's conservatism is reflected in the discourse surrounding the government institutionalization of women's interests in domestic terms: a family ministry.[14] That discourse meshes with the BMZ discourse.

European democracies, particularly those in Nordic countries and the Netherlands, establish consultative bodies in which nonelected representatives of organized interests dialogue with civil servants (known as "neo-corporatist" political structures). Historically, female appointments lagged behind their elected parliamentary representation and population parity,[15] but appointive representation has increased through measures such as Norway's 1978 Equal Status Act, which includes political representation under its charge.

The Nordic countries have established several tiers of advisory bodies that work toward gender equality. Each country charges a minister with equality affairs, a discourse that departs from that of Germany.

Cultural Hospitability to Mainstreaming

Besides the political receptiveness to women as citizens, several bilateral assistance institutions have established advisory bodies on women/gender. The Council of Swedish Women for Development, consisting of eleven organizations, serves as an advisory body. Norway developed a Women's Contact Group as far back as 1973. Norway's Foreign Ministry has a WID committee, on which representatives sit to advise on ways to support women in development (Rs).[16] External political pressure to support women in development preceded mainstreaming strategies.

The Netherlands Directorate General for International Cooperation has elaborate mechanisms for public consultation, besides those that occur through democratic elections and representation. The directorate has a large National Advisory Council. Development assistance enjoys public support, enhanced through international emphases on educational curricula at all levels. The directorate traditionally works with internationally minded NGOs. It helps support a national lobby network, Vrouwenberaad, which works to promote more women-responsive policies (Rs). Whether such support continues with diminished public subsidies is questionable, for recent cutbacks have occurred.

Universities contain strong academic programs with expertise on development assistance and women, such as Leiden University's Women and Autonomy group and the Institute for Social Studies (ISS) at the Hague. Faculty do action-oriented research, of value to their institutions and with support from the government. ISS hosts the largest master's-level Women and Development Program in the world, begun in 1979. More than 6,000 participants from 120 countries have participated in all ISS programs.[17] Alumnae of the program work with official and NGO assistance activities. The conceptualization of women and development

in the Netherlands values women's empowerment and political autonomy, as discussed earlier.

If bilateral institutions consult with women about programs and projects
outside their democratic boundaries and fund women-friendly NGOs
and women's organizations, the potential for empowerment exists at the
recipient-country level. Women's projects had near-pariah status a decade
ago, but they now enjoy renewed legitimacy, *if* they are linked strategically
to the mainstream. Support for women can also have an empowerment
dimension, thus strengthening prospects for political accountability in recipient countries. In a U.S. example, funding supported seminars to "put
women on the political agenda" in Malawi. But are these people's organizations or contractors, whose efforts may die when funding ends?

The OECD/DAC collects data on what it calls "consultation" (linked to
participation?). Several bilateral institutions put money behind their intentions to consult with women's organizations, such as Canada, Norway, and
the Netherlands. The cryptic questionnaire responses, condensed in
OECD/DAC survey reports, exclude USAID's actual support for women's
NGO partnerships in planning and coalition building.[18] Steady financial
support could strengthen those organizations, but if an organization relies
solely on a funder, it runs into the danger of disappearance and ideological
dependence in the ways that Korten outlined.

From interviews and documents, we have no way to determine the extent
to which women's organizations coalesce with other NGOs that have (or
should have) a stake in gender equity and fairness. Group coalition partners
potentially include environmentalists and human rights activists, among
many others. We do know, however, that women's organizations often make
overtures to potentially like-minded groups, but such groups respond belat-
edly or not at all. For example, it took UNIFEM's funding of an environmental expert to attend the 1992 UN environmental meeting to remind
environmentalists of the gender connection and ensure that documents contained relevant resolutions, as discussed earlier. Political coalitions that
include women among many other partners would strengthen the prospects
for democratically accountable development programs.

The national political structures and cultures in which bilateral institutions are situated have profound effects on their overall conception of
development in their national foreign policy, on the broad ideological orienta-
tions that officials (male and female alike) use in their work, and on the
ability of women to share a voice in establishment politics, whether from
inside legislatures or from outside pressure. This section shows the especially friendly context that the Netherlands and Nordic countries provide
for mainstreaming women in official political bodies.

Internal Coalition Building

The birth of women/gender policies was a rhetorical event, not necessarily followed up with plans, actions, and implementation. Typically, a single woman (with a few more professionals, as years passed) sought to change large bureaucracies, sometimes with the limited leverage of a policy document (amid many others). In her insightful comparison of two bilateral and two multilateral organizations, Rounaq Jahan concludes that the WID unit "structures made very little difference," with their "near impossible task of criticizing and reforming the very organizations they serve."[19]

Bureaucratic transformation cannot occur from an enclave office with a few staff and limited resources. Coalitions must be built that ultimately change the incentives to which staff respond. A cross-unit committee—alternatively named "steering committee" (Netherlands, Canada), or "advisory committee" (Norway)—is a necessary but insufficient step to build a coalition with meaning in between committee meetings. Accountability mechanisms must also be in place that give this internal representation stake and meaning in mainstreaming.

Bilateral institutions historically consisted of male-majority professionals. Initially, most WID advocates were female. Women professionals who work in male-majority workplaces encounter special obstacles, as discussed in Chapter 3. A lone woman is burdened by prejudice and caricatures.

We would expect obstacles to vary according to the degree to which gender equality has been mainstreamed in political culture. Thus, male prejudice should be less in the Nordic countries, a finding borne out in comparative cultural studies.[20] Several agencies, among them CIDA and USAID, have made it a point not only to appoint men in WID/gender offices but also to appoint male directors, as Canada has done on several occasions.[21]

Women also face separate career tracks. Women's tracks tend to have short ladders, stranding them in fields of lower priority, such as personnel. Women/gender is one of the fields in which one can get stuck,[22] unless other offices have a stake in mainstreaming, as demonstrated through their recruitment of staff with gender expertise.

USAID's WID program offers the only baseline from which to assess the challenges of coalition building within large bureaucracies. To extend Chapter 3's summary, congressional mandates to integrate women in development relied on presidential-appointee USAID executives to turn official policy into practice. Initial responsibility was lodged in the USAID executive's office, but its mesh with equal employment opportunity (EEO) confused the purpose in the minds of mainstream staff. Ultimately, the Policy Bureau reluctantly accepted WID in its bureaucratic home.

WID remained in Policy until a 1991 move to the newly reorganized Research and Development Bureau. Subsequently, significant reorganization after the 1992 election made its home the Bureau for Global Programs, Field Support, and Research. High-level internal appointments were made in pioneering positions for women, true also in other parts of government.

WID/gender unit location is highly idiosyncratic to the institution in which it is housed, and bilateral institutions have their own peculiar organizational charts and reorganizations. Yet analyzed from within, WID/gender location can facilitate (or discourage) coalition-building activities.

In early years of the 1970s, USAID executives were unenthusiastic about WID and its administrative complications. U.S. political appointees rotate frequently (every two years, on average), and the agency's policy agenda is crowded. Appointees generally reflect partisan ideology and loyalty to the president and, ultimately, electoral majority vote. Thus, they cast an ideological shadow on bureaucratic programs. For reasons like this, WID's technical credibility and legitimacy sustain it through difficult electoral times, although supportive political coalitions are the larger umbrella under which this operates.

By the late 1970s, the WID Office was headed by a subexecutive political appointee and staffed with several professionals. Its budget was less than a million dollars in a multi-billion-dollar agency. With few budgetary resources to leverage project action in the regional and sectoral bureaus, and authority only to comment on rather than to veto projects in the complicated and lengthy project-approval process, advocates relied on research and persuasion with part-time WID officers in other bureaus and recipient-country field offices. As Chapter 2 discusses, the WID Office used expertise, alliances, and procedural reform, always grappling with paper promises and the substitute of studies for action. USAID's evaluation office had a limited "people" focus.

USAID's early separatist approach to mainstreaming was comprehensive and thorough. Ironically, though, it helped perpetuate a sideline operation, from which its advocates have learned mainstreaming strategies, as discussed later. Among the more significant lessons of this learning have been "matching funds" for increased budgets and more personnel spread deeper throughout the agency. WID survived, even thrived, throughout the 1980s through technical institutionalization combined with pointed political support from interest groups and the congressional women's caucus.

In a perceptive essay on SIDA, Karen Himmelstrand traces WID advocates' strategies in what then and now is perceived to be a progressive bilateral institution.[23] Like other institutions, Sweden established a WID office, provided special funds, appointed a wider oversight group, adopted action- and country-specific plans, appointed officers in recipient countries, and established a regional WID office in the field. The country focus moved Sweden into greater action, but following Sara Longwe's lead on the meaning of empowerment, Himmelstrand argues that grassroots women's groups must participate in and control projects. Speaking to a global audience, she warns that institutional WID efforts will otherwise be mired in a co-optation phase, wherein it fits its own established structures rather than takes its cues from women in recipient countries.

For all the bilateral institutions, external sources of leverage strengthened internal coalition-building activities. The most eventful involved preparations for international meetings during the women's decade. However, regular meetings and reporting to a permanent organization sustained such action among bilateral institutions. In 1977, Canada hosted a meeting in which WID advocates dialogued with their institutional counterparts. Eventually this led to the creation of an official Correspondents' Group in OECD/DAC.[24]

In 1983, OECD/DAC adopted Guiding Principles to Aid Agencies for Supporting the Role of Women in Development, subsequently revised and strengthened in 1989. The bureaucratic recipe contained guidelines in four areas: administration, implementation, coordination, and consultation. Surveys solicit information from members and monitor change, so that advocates can make comparative assessments and use outside knowledge to leverage change. However, these approaches treat institutions and their national contexts as monolithic.

Bureaucratic strategies carry with them the potential dangers of top-down, hierarchical, and fragmented change, which perpetuates bureaucracy. As Kathy Ferguson argues, bureaucracy spawns more bureaucracy.[25] It is quite true that plans, checklists, guidelines, and considerable numbers of WID staff have multiplied. Yet to the extent that bureaucratic strategies build coalitions with and spread responsibility to other parts of the institution, they further the mainstreaming agenda, particularly its integrationist approach. The dividing line between just enough and too much regulation is a fine one, however.

In different degrees, advocates use accountability-focused strategies that spread interest, expertise, and responsibility throughout their institutions. Primary among these are gender training, funding targets and evaluations, and veto power.

Gender Training

During the 1980s, gender training strategies were vigorously pursued in some agencies. At a 1991 gender training conference, Canada and Sweden were featured as prominent "success stories" in establishing agencywide awareness, but all the bilateral institutions analyzed in this chapter have experimented with gender training.[26]

With gender training comes recognition of the need to change officials' attitudes and skills. In other words, men's attitudes (the dominant force in most institutions) are problematized, and attitudinal change is part of the solution. As the minister of development cooperation in the Netherlands presented to Parliament through a 1990 white paper: "a change is needed in attitudes to women, including those prevalent among the staff involved in the whole decision-making process on development cooperation. Instead of regarding women as passive objects, we must see them as actors who themselves determine their own situation." The directorate makes twice-yearly training compulsory for staff, a task contracted out to research institutes and universities with expertise and experience. The Royal Tropical Institute in Amsterdam offers a Women and Development Training Program, itself showcasing model programs in Southern countries at a 1993 conference.[27]

Training is more sporadic elsewhere. For German bilateral staff, it is voluntary and irregular. Jahan's comparative study, including Norway and Canada, found that trainees were primarily female junior staff.[28] USAID grounds its voluntary training in the complex technical procedures of its lengthy project-approval process. It boasts a male-majority trainee pool.[29] More recently, USAID has moved toward training in substantive issues, such as the environment, HIV/AIDS, and economic growth, that includes cooperating agency staff and those in the field, including NGOs. Once funded solely by the WID unit, USAID's other units now share costs. Besides streamlining its lengthy project-approval process, USAID now emphasizes program-level as opposed to project language.[30] Contributions toward training provide other offices with a stake in the usefulness of training and a likely commitment to use that training.

Training developed only recently in Norway. The Training Centre for Development Cooperation opened in 1991, and NORAD staff underwent training from 1992 onward. Two courses are offered: one is informative, and the other is "methodologically integrated," as it focuses on operational reviews of project and program proposals from gender, environmental, economic, and institution perspectives (Rs).

In 1988–89, SIDA's WID Office was renamed the Gender Office, and its strategy aimed to incorporate gender dimensions into all areas using existing routines and procedures. According to SIDA gender advocate Carolyn Hannan-Andersson, "the objective is not to develop gender specialists but to ensure that all personnel and consultants . . . recognize their responsibility and develop the necessary awareness and capacity to include a gender perspective as relevant in their normal work."[31] This occurs through training and through gender profiles developed at the country level in this decentralized agency.

With directives from senior staff, CIDA required training for its staff, part of a comprehensive management strategy to mainstream women in its work. It used the technical, project approach first developed at Harvard University.[32] Subsequent evaluations showed that CIDA's "mandatory" training was never really mandatory: only half of its staff received the training.[33] Yet CIDA makes a greater effort to reach staff than do most institutions. One cannot help but wonder about the "mandatory" and "requirement" language of other bilateral institutions.

Evaluations of gender training rarely document behavioral change in any institution, beyond the attitudinal component evaluated at the completion of the training program. CIDA has gone furthest to evaluate these matters and make results publicly transparent. Although training increased sensitivity for most, only a fifth of staff have used a formal framework for gender analysis.[34]

Training is presumably related to job performance and evaluation. Among bilateral institutions, CIDA is the only agency to include WID work in its performance appraisal. Ultimately, such a review was judged to be too vague and diffuse. With its noncorporate, flatter hierarchy, NORAD opted against this sort of accountability strategy.[35] Ironically, a less bureaucratic hierarchical style (unusual in government) reduces the incentives and tools available to mainstream new initiatives.

Evaluations and Funding Targets

As analyzed in the introduction, the ability to evaluate programs has been a belated and relatively underdeveloped function in development bureaucracies. Performance is rarely connected with funding decisions. Rather, institutional incentives focus attention on proposal design and approval, not on quality implementation.

Development projects are implemented in highly uncertain environments, dependent on outside contractors and recipient-country institutions that lie beyond the control of bilateral institutions. These are the sorts of conditions that bureaucrats dread, particularly if they assume responsibility for evaluations that document poor performance. Consequently, the evaluation units suffer a lack of autonomy and frequently treat their analyses guardedly. After all, public information about mistakes, inefficiencies, and ineffectiveness may undermine prospects for maintaining and augmenting next year's budget.

Given the chronic institutional problems associated with evaluation, it is remarkable when strong evaluation units report outcomes publicly or when institutional executives set financial targets against which their performance will be judged. Several bilateral institutions are beginning to produce evaluations, outcome documentation, and financial targets and achievements on women/gender. Others recognize the deficiencies of evaluations that document nothing of substance on gender. When institutions do this, the foundations are laid for responsibility to spread to the whole agency, not just the women/gender unit, to prove specific and particular levels of performance. The move toward evaluative and financial accountability is a recent one, usually emerging a decade or more after a WID policy has been adopted.

In 1991, the Netherlands raised women and development, along with environment and poverty alleviation, to mandatory stature. As a spearhead program, it increased funding from 17 million to 35 million guilders in 1995. Other policy priorities incorporate a women's dimension, as in the identification of "political poverty" for women. The Netherlands has also adopted measurable objectives against which performance can be judged. For example, one goal states that 25 percent of all funding should result in increased autonomy for women, to rise to 50 percent several years thereafter. Criteria like these are a standard against which project proposals are judged as well. A "women's impact assessment" was developed to operationalize these criteria in the institutional cycle. At the country level, profiles contain baseline data on women, and impact studies document change (Rs).[36]

In Norway, WID commitment is institutionalized through accountability measures. Goals are set within sectors, such as 20 percent direct assistance in agriculture by 1990, earmarked funds for credit, and 50 percent of fellowship funds for women in education.[37] These targets are not always achieved without outside political pressure and internal commitment. Jahan reports mixed achievements in assistance programming goals but dramatic improvement in goals to increase women professional and management staff with "gender-responsive career development policies."[38]

As accountants would term it, though, the "bottom line" constitutes women's share of development funding. Using the OECD/DAC statistical reporting system for "WID-specific" and "WID-integrated" projects, both CIDA and NORAD spent a fifth of total aid on women in 1991, minute fractions of which were for women-specific projects (about 1 percent). Women were the sole agents and beneficiaries in WID-specific projects, whereas WID-integrated projects "covered the full value of each project in which women were identified,"[39] suggesting exaggerated amounts. Norway added a category called "WID-relevant," to denote projects in which one to three of the four OECD/DAC criteria for WID-integrated projects were present. For Norway, overall WID figures improved from 18.2 percent in 1988 to 21.1 percent in 1991, but the largest category was WID-relevant.[40]

USAID continues to report its spending on WID in public and transparent ways, although it does not set targets. Pie charts show spending, by sector, and how that changes over fiscal years. In the early 1990s, women represented two-fifths of trainees from recipient countries. Microenterprise lending, a priority in which gender is also central, is easily amenable to gender documentation by loan recipients and loan amounts.[41]

The U.S. Congress earmarked funds in 1989, and increased the amount in 1993, to serve as matching funds for WID activities. These positive incentives are used as leverage to stimulate financial commitments elsewhere in the agency. Over the years, the WID Office has contributed a declining proportion of total funding,[42] a positive indicator that other units see value in using more of their own funds.

The OECD/DAC WID guidelines say that "all evaluations concerned with effects on target groups should describe and analyze possible gender differences. This will require WID-competence on the teams." Although wary of the cryptic terms by which institutions respond through questionnaires, which are then condensed, we do learn from OECD/DAC charts that evaluations have WID in terms of reference (Germany). Other bilateral institutions opt to place at least one woman on evaluation teams. Such is the practice in Norway, backed up with measurable goals.[43] In preparations for the 1995 Beijing meeting, OECD/DAC members were assessing WID policies and programs in three ways, one of which was evaluation. Evaluation's thematic importance, providing a stake for DAC member evaluation units, suggests that more changes may be forthcoming.

The U.S. GAO serves the branch of government controlling the budget. In 1993, GAO conducted its first-ever evaluation of USAID's WID program, entitled "U.S. Had Made Slow Progress in Involving Women in Development." It took the agency to task for lack of accountability:

> [US]AID has not centrally monitored the implementation of these policies and cannot verify compliance with them. Accountability for program design and results are hampered by [US]AID's failure to routinely collect gender data and develop useful program indicators. . . . [US]AID has no mechanisms for rewarding accomplishments in women-in-development.[44]

USAID has a working committee, including the evaluation office, that is responding to these concerns, as directed by USAID's chief executive. His directive reiterates the shared responsibility of all bureaus for mainstreaming the tracking and operating system (into which gender indicators have been built) and the WID Office's monitoring role.

Coinciding with governmentwide reform efforts toward performance assessment, USAID has instituted a program performance information for strategic management (PRISM) system. Gender performance indicators are being developed alongside other people-oriented outcome measures.

USAID has looked seriously and critically at its shortcomings in documenting gender performance. This was part of the OECD/DAC thematic effort. In a study of 532 evaluations, 45 percent had no gender information, and another 17 percent had inadequate gender information. Further analysis of evaluations attentive to gender revealed some conditions under which substantive analysis was more likely: women on evaluation teams and in hospitable sectors, such as those in human development.

Canada has evaluated its overall WID effort in remarkably reflective terms. Neither "top secret" nor for "limited distribution," efforts like these demonstrate commitment to transparency and public accountability.

CIDA evaluators said that it was impossible to calculate how much was spent on WID, except for the money spent for headquarters administration and one of three categories of WID expenditures in which reasonable confidence existed that women benefited. When evaluators surveyed staff to obtain their estimates of the percentage of resources devoted to WID, 60 percent estimated less than 15 percent of country programs.[45] This figure bears uncanny resemblance to the 20 percent figure cited earlier (a fifth of total spending), inflated by the inclusion of benefits to men in the WID-integrated projects.

In the review of CIDA evaluations, few were found to have a methodology for measuring the extent to which WID objectives were achieved. A 1991 CIDA study found that 60 percent of evaluations addressed WID, about half of them in a token fashion.[46] The much-vaunted personnel evaluation system, which ostensibly rewards good WID performance, played a minor role for 27 percent of staff. All in all, the language of WID objectives was too vague ("encourage, promote, support, increase, collaborate") to fix accountability (useful language consists of "targets, deadlines, requirements, must or will achieve").[47]

From the outset, CIDA strategy departed from others in trying to establish line management responsibility for WID. Deliberately taking a backseat role, its advocates, according to its 1986 action plan, promoted "a corporate responsibility approach to WID [wherein] the WID Directorate acts primarily to ensure that the systems are in place for senior management to govern its WID strategy." In evaluative hindsight, this quickly installed managerial approach allowed regular CIDA staff too much discretion to declare efforts integrated, before real incentives were really in motion to change their behavior.[48]

Veto Power

Germany's countersignature authority is unique. Its questionnaire response to OECD/DAC surveys states that all projects must be counter-signed by the WID-equivalent office. It offers the promise of ensuring that all institutional projects include attention to women and the threat of delay or rejection to all those staff who seek to move projects and money. This BMZ regulation became effective on January 1, 1993. Only the undersecretary of state can overrule the veto.

Based on 1994 interviews, this authority provides the opportunity for dialogue (to avoid delay) and for compromise should conflict exist. The undersecretary has never yet been involved, for proposals have been revised to resolve issues and respond to questions.[49]

The task of reviewing more than a thousand projects yearly is a challenging one for four staff members. Initially, half of project proposals were refused (that is, delayed), but this decreased to a quarter by the end of 1993. General staff presumably responded to the incentive (or delay penalty) and changed their proposal-writing behavior. For advocates in BMZ, this procedure has been far more effective in encouraging cross-sector project attention to women than any other used.

The true test of countersignature authority will come if and when evaluations document the gender outcomes of cross-sector projects that promised to take women into account. Veto powers have their drawbacks. First, as earlier sections of this chapter analyze, paper promises can be ritualistic recycling, conforming to "requirements"—a strong word for rules that may or may not be enforced. Staff may insert just enough language to pass the process, as did USAID staff in the "woman-impact statement" required for projects in early years. Second, veto power is a rules-oriented rather than a voluntaristic approach that could backfire in institutions with a different character. As the preceding chapter's discussion of BMZ made clear, however, the countersignature authority is consistent with its mode of operation. Finally, countersignature review responsibilities are extremely time-consuming, potentially burdening the few WID advocates with virtually the sole task of proposal review.

To summarize this section, internal coalition building is essential to spread responsibility throughout the institution. With multiple methods to establish accountability, coalition prospects are maximized, although methods must be tailored to the institutional setting. Successful bilateral institutions have used training in conjunction with project review and precise goal setting (including financial reports and goals) to produce outcomes that benefit women. Effective training strategies move increasingly toward substance, but nowhere do donors report their linkage to personnel evaluation. Claims about mainstreaming will be supported when bilateral agencies report figures, set targets, and make honest evaluations of people indicators openly available. Veto-power regulations seem suited to Germany's institutional home but represent the kind of bureaucratic regulation that would incur resistance or sabotage in other agencies.

Coalition-building strategies imply that bargains and compromises get struck, but with whom? Once again, we return to the modest ambitions of the integrationist approaches to mainstreaming. Internal coalition building to foster accountability is a strategy that speaks to bureaucrats in the funding or the recipient country. Political forces in which women are a part can provide transformative potential to pitiful funding or evaluative achievements.

Implications

The comparison of six bilateral institutions shows the importance of both technical and political approaches in development strategies to mainstream women. Political strategies provoked the very establishment of WID/gender policies and sustained them when sufficient accountability data are available to judge agency results. With results-oriented data, integrationist approaches to mainstreaming can be put into place. More is necessary, however. Accurate and honest results permit public assessment of development paradigms. With women's voices in both funder and recipient country, paradigms can be critiqued and transformed.

These six bilateral institutions have taken diverse strategies toward mainstreaming, contingent on their peculiar development missions and political contexts. Although bureaucratic procedural recipes provide ideas, they are rarely tailored to the institutional and political contexts, which are, inevitably, complex and varied. Policy analysis is as much an art as a science for understanding that political complexity.

This chapter supports the contention that mainstreaming as transformation is enhanced and developed in those institutions already undergoing a transformation of old development paradigms. The Netherlands and the

Nordic countries pioneered in forward-looking approaches to development that reduced North-South inequalities and emphasized human development and empowerment. They surpass other donors in percentage commitment of gross national product development. They were among the earliest to dialogue about partnership. The bureaucratic structure they reinvented for development focuses on country levels and alternatives to centralized hierarchical forms.

Not coincidentally, these bilateral development efforts pursue WID/ gender mainstreaming in vigorous, albeit distinctive ways. They have no reticence about female empowerment as a theme. WID-specific funding is legitimate and consistent with hospitable empowerment themes. These agencies demonstrate the synergy possible when drawing together mutually supportive agendas: transformative development paradigms with WID as transformative mainstreaming.

For the Netherlands, Norway, and Sweden, the political context in which development assistance is situated is one in which women's political representation is moving toward balance, as measured by parliamentary and cabinet seats. These are not merely democracies for men, but democracies for men and women. Norway, the most gender-balanced political system in the world, is just ahead of other Nordic countries and the Netherlands. Other structures exist to transform policies into gender-equitable practice through government bodies and networks with women's organizations and researchers. Not coincidentally, these countries are also attentive to female empowerment in recipient countries through institutional decentralization and women's programming.

Bilateral institutions that offer genuine public accountability must be accountable not only to their own citizens but also to the users of projects and programs in recipient countries. Country-level accountability occurs in democracies or in countries in transition toward democracy with critical masses of women who share power. Women-specific empowerment strategies can facilitate mainstreaming in recipient countries by providing women with political voice and shared authority.

The move away from project funding toward program and policy funding makes the centrality of female empowerment all the more imperative. Bureaucratic and technical controls with an inside-agency focus work best with top-down project designs of limited funding duration. For program and policy funding to move beyond the small clique of likely beneficiaries in partially democratic countries, broad-based women-inclusive coalitions must be in place.

Also remarkable about this comparative study, however, is the move toward mainstreaming that has taken place in bilateral agencies that are less hospitable to the transformation of development paradigms. The United States, Germany, and Canada pursue development through more traditional bureaucratic hierarchies in countries with a women's political agency that is centered in society more than inside government. These bilateral institutions have pursued effective internal coalition-building strategies that have spread responsibility partially throughout the institutions. With support from management, Canada has gone far toward using training, personnel, and evaluation with corporate consistency. In the United States and Germany, technical strategies have protected WID from prevailing conservative political winds in agencies with multiple goals, the most important of which promote commercial and foreign policy interests. This integrationist mainstreaming built internal coalitions that spread responsibility for women/gender in ways unique to their own contexts.

Although this analysis has many positive things to say about diverse, contextually specific mainstreaming strategies, there is a downside as well. Responsibility involves more than paper promises; it is documented through results. Bureaucratic agencies seem to mystify their work as much as clarify it through transparent results.

Readers and analysts must wade through lots of rhetoric and anecdotes before deriving the essence of documentable action. Of course, some might ask: What's new about that? Isn't this bureaucracy? Yet it must surely be discouraging for feminists seeking to demystify and simplify public spending for critiques and transformative action. The bottom lines on funding are, first, that agencies do not report such essential information, and second, that those that do (probably among the most mainstreamed) report about 20 percent. A fifth of spending is not enough for half the population—a half that is burdened with decades of preferential spending toward men. To evoke themes from the previous chapter, but especially from Chapter 1, these masters' institutional houses keep their resources carefully locked. Are they worth the sustained political struggle necessary to unlock those budgets and spread the resources to those who deserve them?

Until we have fuller and more transparent information from agencies about their spending and internal and external politics, we will constantly struggle for information that ought to be our own, as members of the public and as global citizens. In the Orwellian world of bureaucracies, will data, courage, and frankness be forthcoming?

If bell hooks's "teaching to transgress" has meaning for us here, it signifies the need to think strategically about research for action. It also means crossing the line from outside (conventional) to inside politics, in the bureaucracies in which many of us are housed. It finally means getting our own political houses in order, whether their structures, cultures, or funding priorities. Global poverty is driven by political decisions all over the world, including Northern countries where many readers of this text reside.

Transformative mainstreaming will occur in decentralized bilateral institutions that are attentive to women's voices in their own national politics. Technical approaches ground accountability to women with logical rationale, until such time as the male monopolization of politics and of bureaucratic authority ends. Ultimately, though, bureaucracies must become responsive to popular will, a will that represents both female and male voices.

Notes

1. Gisela Kaplan, *Contemporary Western European Feminism* (New York: New York University Press, 1992); Mary Fainsod Katzenstein and Carol McClurg Mueller, eds., *The Women's Movements of the United States and Western Europe* (Philadelphia: Temple University Press, 1987); Barbara Nelson and Najma Chowdhury, eds., *Women and Politics Worldwide* (New Haven, Conn.: Yale University Press, 1994), frame their forty-three-chapter collection in "engagement" terms; selected chapters are cited later.
2. Ronald Levin, "In-Country Presence: The Experience of Other Donors," *AID Evaluation News* 4, no. 4 (1992): 5–8.
3. Barbara Nelson and Kathryn Carver, "Many Voices, but Few Vehicles: The Consequences for Women of Weak Political Infrastructure in the United States," in Nelson and Chowdhury, *Women and Politics Worldwide*, pp. 737–57. See Kathleen Staudt, "Political Representation: Engendering Democracy," in *Background Papers: Human Development Report 1995* (New York: UNDP, 1996), pp. 21–70, on figures for different kinds of representation. The UNDP's *Human Development Report 1995* (New York: Oxford University Press, 1995) was devoted to gender, including political decision-making positions.
4. Katherine Jensen, "Getting to the Third World: Agencies as Gatekeepers," in *Women, International Development and Politics: The Bureaucratic Mire, 2d ed.*, edited by Kathleen Staudt (Philadelphia: Temple University Press, 1997).
5. Even the Conservative Democratic Union adopted 30 percent quotas to woo women voters.
6. Kaplan, *Contemporary Western European Feminism*; Russell J. Dalton and Manfred Kuechler, eds., *Challenging the Political Order: New Social and Political Movements in Western Democracies* (New York: Oxford University Press, 1990); Joni Lovenduski and Pippa Norris, eds., *Gender and Party Politics* (London: Sage, 1993); Christiane Lempke, "Women and Politics: The New Federal Republic of Germany," and Monique Leijenaar and Kees Niemöller, "Political Participation of Women: The Netherlands," in Nelson and Chowdhury, *Women and Politics Worldwide*, pp. 261–84, 496–511; Katzenstein and Mueller, *Women's Movements*; Joyce Gelb makes a three-way distinction, including state feminism, in *Feminism and Politics: A Comparative Perspective* (Berkeley: University of California Press, 1989); Staudt, "Political Representation."
7. Gelb, *Feminism and Politics*.
8. Gelb, *Feminism and Politics*; Jill Vickers et al., *Politics as if Women Mattered: A*

Political Analysis of the National Action Committee on the Status of Women (Toronto: University of Toronto Press, 1993).

9. Rounaq Jahan, *The Elusive Agenda: Mainstreaming Women in Development* (London: Zed, 1995), p. 32.

10. See Kaplan, *Contemporary Western European Feminism*, on the labels and categories, with conservative including Switzerland, Liechtenstein, and Austria (chap. 4).

11. Robert G. Moeller, *Protecting Motherhood: Women and the Family in the Politics of Postwar West Germany* (Berkeley: University of California Press, 1993).

12. Cited in Kaplan, *Contemporary Western European Feminism*, pp. 116, 45, 56.

13. Ronald Inglehart, *A World View of Women: Social, Political and Economic Attitudes* (Washington, D.C: U.S. Information Agency, 1994).

14. Kaplan, *Contemporary Western European Feminism*.

15. Leijenaar and Niemöller, "Political Participation of Women,"; Helga Maria Hernes, "The Welfare State Citizenship of Scandinavian Women," in *The Political Interests of Gender*, edited by Kathleen B. Jones and Anna G. Jonasdottir (London: Sage, 1988), pp. 187–213, slightly revised from her *Welfare State and Woman Power* (Oslo: Norwegian University Press, 1987); Gelb, *Feminism and Politics*.

16. Jahan, *The Elusive Agenda*, p. 31.

17. Aruna Rao, *Women's Studies International: Nairobi and Beyond* (New York: Feminist Press, 1991), p. 216.

18. Mari Clark, USAID/WID, oral and written communication, 1995. OECD/DAC, *Third Monitoring Report on the Inplementation of DAC Revised Guiding Principles on Women in Development (1989)* (Paris: OECD, 1992).

19. Jahan, *The Elusive Agenda*, pp. 42, 119.

20. Dutch organizational theorist Geert Hofstede, with probably the largest sample (116,000 in forty countries), ranks Nordic countries and the Netherlands as "low masculinity" in *Culture's Consequences* (Beverly Hills, Calif.: Sage, 1984); but see questions in Staudt, "Political Representation," about his conceptualization.

21. Rideau Research Associates for Francoise Mailhot, CIDA/Evaluation, *Gender as a Cross-Cutting Theme in CIDA's Development Assistance—An Evaluation of CIDA's WID Policy and Activities, 1984–1992* (Ottawa: CIDA, 1993).

22. Things may be changing, considering women leaders at the helm of UNICEF, UNFPA, UNHCR, and others; a feminist economist vice president at the Inter-American Development Bank; and Alexis Herman, who rose from the Women's Bureau position in the U.S. Department of Labor up through other career pathways and is now at the helm of the Labor Department.

23. Karen Himmelstrand, "Can an Aid Bureaucracy Empower Women?" in Staudt, *Women, International Development and Politics*, p. 111; Jahan, *The Elusive Agenda*, p. 41.

24. Marilyn Richards, *Approaches to Women in Development by Donor Countries Other than the U.S.* (Washington, D.C.: Equity Policy Center, 1983).

25. Kathy Ferguson, *The Feminist Case against Bureaucracy* (Philadelphia: Temple University Press, 1984), pp. 40–41.

26. Aruna Rao et al., *Gender Training and Development Planning: Learning from Experience* (Bergen, Norway, and New York: Chr. Michelsen Institute and Population Council, 1991); Rs; OECD/DAC, *Third Monitoring Report on the Implementation of the DAC Revised Guiding Principles on Women in Development (1989)* (Paris: OECD, 1992).

27. D. Platenga, *VENA* (Leiden: Leiden University, 1991); Aruna Rao et al.,

Reflections and Learnings: Gender Trainers Workshop Report (Amsterdam and New York: Royal Tropical Institute and Population Council, 1993).

28. Jahan, *The Elusive Agenda*, p. 63.

29. Rao et al., *Gender Training*; Rs.

30. Clark, oral and written communication, 1995; Ellen Fenoglio, "Case Study of the Institutionalization of the DAC Women in Development Guiding Principles by the United States Government" (manuscript, November 1993).

31. Carolyn Hannan-Andersson, "Experiences with Gender Training—How Did it Work and How Was It Used? Some Experiences from the Swedish International Development Authority 1988–1991," paper presented at the Gender Training and Development Planning Conference, Chr. Michelsen Institute, Norway, May 13–15, 1991.

32. Catherine Overholt et al., *Gender Roles in Development Projects: A Case Book* (West Hartford, Conn.: Kumarian Press, 1985).

33. Rideau, *Gender as a Cross-Cutting Theme*, p. 31.

34. Rideau Research Associates for Francoise Mailhot, CIDA/Evaluation, *WID Policies in Selected Development Agencies* (Ottawa: CIDA, 1992), p. 31.

35. Jahan, *The Elusive Agenda*, p. 45.

36. Jahan cites the year 1998, p. 115, for the 50 percent goal in fellowship funds.

37. Rideau reviews other bilateral agencies in Europe in *WID Policies*, p. 4.

38. Jahan, *The Elusive Agenda*, pp. 53, 60, 82.

39. Jahan, *The Elusive Agenda*, p. 30.

40. Jahan, *The Elusive Agenda*, pp. 87–91.

41. U.S. Agency for International Development, *Women in Development Report FYs 1991 and 1992* (Washington, D.C.: USAID, n.d.).

42. Fenoglio, "Case Study," pp. 10–11.

43. OECD, *Third Monitoring Report*; Rounaq Jahan, "Mainstreaming Women in Development in Different Settings," paper presented at OECD/DAC WID Expert Group Seminar, Paris, May 19–20, 1992. Many thanks to Mari Clark, social scientist at USAID/WID, for a lengthy 1995 phone interview, numerous published and unpublished materials, and written feedback to a draft of this material.

44. U.S. GAO, *U.S. Had Made Slow Progress in Involving Women in Development* (Washington, D.C.: GAO, 1993), p. 17

45. Rideau, *WID Policies*, pp. 24–25.

46. Rideau, *Gender as a Cross-Cutting Theme*, pp. 28, 40.

47. Rideau, *Gender as a Cross-Cutting Theme,* pp. 34, 6.

48. Rideau, *Gender as a Cross-Cutting Theme*, p. 14.

49. Rounaq Jahan, "Assessment of Policies and Organizational Measures in Women in Development Adopted by DAC Member Countries" (draft, 1994). For research assistance, again, I appreciate the work of Olaf Bak.

10 Engaging and Changing the Political Mainstream

In this book, we have analyzed mainstream policies and so-called women's policies, only to discover that women and gender are at the heart of transformation toward sustainable global change that enhances human capabilities. We have examined the national and international institutions that currently manage what is now known as "development," and we find them lacking. At their core, most institutions reflect a mind-set that prizes accumulation, overproduction and overconsumption, aggression, and tolerance of obscene inequalities, based on gender, class, cultural group, and nation.

Those who "man" these institutions have not taken seriously the budgetary commitments and enforcement processes necessary to increase human capacity and to provide safety to the broader public, of which women are a large part, in both peacetime and war. Threaded throughout this book was an emphasis on political analyses, strategies, and actions. Readers encountered many questions and cases that encouraged them to consider strategic thinking for engagement in the political process, broadly defined. Political engagement takes many forms, ranging from civil service employment to conventional elections, from lobby groups and legislatures to nongovernmental organizations (NGOs), feminist groups, and resistance to complicity with corrupt governments and markets.

Let me make a few statements about "avoidances." The text encouraged readers to avoid making commitments to "development" definitions and ideologies until they had time to reflect and consider implications for action. Now is the time to make some decisions and commitments. Although I have avoided imposing any definitions of development or feminism, I do have a bias: encouraging diverse analysis and action. This book is meant to avoid instilling political paralysis. This final chapter summarizes chapters and lays out implications for action.

Chapter Summaries

In Chapter 1, we examined the discourse that is commonly used in analyzing policies from global to local. We housed that discourse in the mainstream (the master's house?) and saw that the terminology was problematic for those who take women and gender seriously. Definitions of democracy, or categorizations of countries on democratic terms, are turned on their heads if we include women's voice and accountability to women. The chapter also engaged discourses of feminisms and celebrated the diverse frameworks they provide in thinking politically about policy analysis and solutions. Subsequent chapters revisited that language, only to find intriguing contestations and coalitions. No matter what the discourse and practice, ethical dilemmas surround the theory and practice of the field.

Chapter 2 looked at the historical emergence of development thinking since World War II. It showed how women/gender thinking sought connection with development, perhaps tainting that marginal movement. Despite the rhetoric of development institutions at national and international levels, we laid the foundations in this chapter for an "industry" obsessed with technical issues that mask political and budgetary realities that devalue human development.

Chapter 3 emphasized how institutions matter, whether national political systems, representative of women and men, or bureaucratic agencies. Bureaucracies are invariably nonrepresentative machinery, but some are more or less amenable to constituency interaction and political direction through appointee leaders. The chapter analyzed the obstacles and strategies that women/gender offices face in national and international machinery. Readers at that point might have wondered about engagement with their own political and bureaucratic institutions to address "development," for that global process *always* has national and local connections.

Beginning with Chapter 4 and closing with Chapter 7, we began to examine substantive policies in which gender is central. We first looked at mainstream policies related to education and work. Each chapter contained hypothetical and real case material appended for readers, as individuals or in groups, to reflect on the ethical and political issues associated with action.

Chapter 4 allowed questions to be raised about the devaluation of broadly based education, a devaluation with a probable connection to its key constituency (children) and the mostly feminized occupational groups that work with children (teachers). In this chapter, special attention was provided to budgets and comparative performance.

In Chapter 5, we examined a wide variety of women's labor activities, ranging from paid to unpaid work, and the measurement and counting problems therein. Wage work is on the rise, just as global forces benefit from that rise. Agriculture continues to be a women's mainstay in some world regions. Although their work is increasingly recognized (even augmented), it is not necessarily rewarded in the form of new income or landownership. Microenterprise, formalizing what is often informal or self-employment, has increasingly captured the imagination of NGOs, governments, and international agencies. The chapter illustrated some major differences among types of microenterprise programs, from narrow to comprehensive, and from market to empowerment, all with consequences for meeting women's practical and strategic interests.

The next two chapters took on issues that have usually been deemed "women's interests" to show their connection to the mainstream of population and public safety. Chapter 6 focused on the connections between population, overconsumption, and reproductive health. It highlighted, especially, the changing international dialogues in United Nations–sponsored meetings wherein women and gender, especially the users of health programs, have become central. Budgetary resources for people's ability to live securely in good health were contrasted with financial support for security in its more commonly understood sense—the military. This chapter, like the one before, provided insights on the kinds of data collection and evaluation efforts that are alternatively associated with different approaches to reproductive health.

In Chapter 7, we examined women's heretofore nonenforced human rights to be secure from murder, rape, and beatings in their own homes and in times of civil conflict and war. The moral bankruptcy of gender subordination reveals its ugly side in the problems of and the possible solutions to decreasing violence against women.

In these four substantive policy chapters, readers probably discerned both the distinctiveness of some feminisms and the convergence of multiple feminisms. Socialist feminism prioritizes certain issues, especially relating to work in the global economy, whereas expanded liberal feminism and practical radical feminism join priorities in areas relating to body and human rights. As for state feminism, these and the next two chapters made it clear that it needs vigilance and monitoring in democratic contexts wherein diverse women have voices.

In the last section, we brought Parts I and II together, joining contextual and institutional analysis with the mainstream and so-called women's policies. We examined six bilateral technical assistance institutions, with more or less progressive agendas and abilities to mainstream gender in transformative ways. Chapter 8 laid out the institutions and their missions, with varying hospitality to gender, human development, and inequality. Readers might imagine comparative work on their own national agencies. Many obstacles would be identical, requiring considerable political struggle and talent to overcome.

Chapter 9 compared the institutions in their political contexts, and the (supposed) democracies in which they are housed nationally, along with the insider politics. We saw compatibility between progressive gender politics nationally and gendered development institutionally. Political accountability is an important part of the equation, but not all. Several technical procedures nudged institutions toward progressive mainstreaming. They include financial and evaluative accountability, training to deal with what Marysia Zalewski and Jane Parpart call the "man problem,"[1] and coalition-building strategies. Ultimately, power sharing with users across national boundaries, especially gender-balanced users, is critical to transformation.

Lessons Learned

This text, including its hypothetical and real cases about political strategy and action, might leave readers with several lessons for reflection.

1. Analysts and activists must focus not just on conventional politics and NGOs but also on institutions, along with their insider and constituency politics.

2. Enforcement and implementation are as important as policy.

3. Coalition building, among activists and academics and across those lines, is necessary to build the critical mass base to promote change. Alliances among diverse feminisms already exist and can be strengthened.

4. Ethics is at the heart of many strategic decisions, from conventional politics to bureaucratic action and protest movements.

5. All mainstream policies are women/gender policies; all women/gender policies are mainstream policies. Analysts and academics must engage the mainstream even as they criticize and challenge that mainstream.

6. Global economies affect the region, nation, and local communities. Strategies must take into account the concentrated hegemony along with grassroots response and resistance.

7. We must all get our own houses in order, from household to community and higher levels. Inaction perpetuates injustice.

Note

1. Marysia Zalewski and Jane Parpart, eds., *The Man Question in International Relations* (Boulder, Colo.: Westview Press, 1997).

Appendix: The United Nations Convention on the Elimination of All Forms of Discrimination against Women

The UN Convention on the Elimination of All Forms of Discrimination against Women (CEDAW) is the culmination of thirty years of effort by the UN Commission on the Status of Women. Since its establishment in 1946, the work of the commission has resulted in several UN declarations and conventions on women's rights, of which this convention is the latest and by far the most comprehensive. A full version of this convention is available from the United Nations (in six languages) and from IWRAW (International Women's Rights Action Watch) at the University of Minnesota.

Article 1   Defines Discrimination
- Any distinction, exclusion, or restriction made on the basis of sex.

Article 2   Policy Measures to Eliminate Discrimination
- Embody principle of equality in national constitutions, civil codes, or other laws.
- Legal protection against discrimination by the establishment of tribunals.
- Ensure that public authorities and institutions refrain from discrimination.
- Abolish all existing law, customs, and regulations that discriminate against women.

Article 3   Guarantees Basic Human Rights and Fundamental Freedoms

Article 4   Temporary Special Measures to Accelerate Women's Equity
- These affirmative actions, including maternity protection, shall not be considered discriminatory.

Article 5   Sex Roles and Stereotyping
- Practices based on the inferiority or superiority of either sex shall be eliminated.
- Ensure that family education teaches that both men and women share a common role in raising children.

Article 6   Prostitution
- Measures shall be taken to suppress all forms of traffic in women and exploitation of women through prostitution.

Article 7   Political and Public Life
- Right to vote in all elections and be eligible for election to all elected bodies.
- To participate in formulation of government policy and hold office at all levels of government.
- To participate in nongovernmental organizations.

Article 8   Representation and Participation at International Levels Guaranteed

Article 9   Nationality
- Equal rights to acquire, change, or retain their nationality and that of their children.

Article 10   Equal Rights in Education
- Career and vocational guidance.
- Curricula, examinations, teaching staff, standards, and equipment.
- Scholarships and study grants.
- Continuing education, including literacy programs.
- Reduction of female dropout rates.
- Coeducation; elimination of stereotyping in texts.
- Participation in sports and physical education.
- Access to health and family planning information.

Article 11   Employment Rights
- Same employment rights as men.
- Free choice of profession and employment; training.
- Equal remuneration, benefits, evaluation.
- Social security.
- Health protection and safety.
- Prohibition against dismissal for pregnancy or marital status.
- Maternity leave.
- Social services provision encouraged.
- Special protection during pregnancy against harmful work.

Article 12   Health Care and Family Planning
- Equal access to; appropriate pregnancy services.

Article 13   Economic and Social Benefits
- Equal access to family benefits; loans and credit.
- Right to participate in recreational activities, sports, cultural life.

Article 14   Rural Women
- Recognition of particular problems of rural women, of the special roles they play in economic survival of families, and of their unpaid work.
- Right to participate in development planning and implementation.
- Right to health care and family planning.

- Right to benefit directly from social security.
- Right to training and education.
- Right to organize self-help groups and cooperatives.
- Right to participate in all community activities.
- Right to access to credit, loans, marketing facilities, and appropriate technology and equal treatment in land and agrarian reform and resettlement.
- Right to adequate living conditions—housing, sanitation, electricity, water, transport, and communications.

Article 15 Equality before the Law

- Same legal capacity as men—to contract, administer property, appear in court or before tribunals.
- Contractual and other private restrictions on legal capacity of women should be declared null and void.
- Freedom of movement; right to choose residence and domicile.

Article 16 Marriage and Family Law

- Equal rights and responsibilities with men in marriage and family relations.
- Right to freely enter into marriage; choose spouse.
- Equal during marriage and at its dissolution.
- Right to choose freely number and spacing of children; access to information, education, and means to make that choice.
- Equal rights to guardianship and adoption of children.
- Same personal rights as husband; right to choose family name, profession or occupation.
- Equal rights and responsibilities regarding ownership, management, disposition of property.
- Minimum age and registration of marriage.

Article 17 CEDAW Election

- Establishes committee; service in individual capacity.
- Election by secret ballot; nominations by states parties.
- Notification by secretary-general of election; soliciting nominations.
- Election by majority vote of states parties present at meeting.
- Terms of CEDAW members.
- Vacancies filled by appointment by state party whose expert leaves.
- Emoluments; staff and facilities to be provided by UN.

Article 18 Reporting

- Ratifying and acceding countries to report on measures adopted to give effect to convention and progress made.
- Include factors and difficulties affecting fulfillment.

Article 19 CEDAW Procedure

- Adopts its own rules of procedure.
- Officers elected for two-year terms.

Article 20   CEDAW Meetings
- Normally for no more than two weeks annually; at UN Headquarters or other place as designated.

Article 21   Reports of CEDAW
- CEDAW shall report to the General Assembly through the Economic and Social Council; Commission on the Status of Women to receive report.
- CEDAW may make suggestions and general recommendations to the General Assembly.

Article 22   Specialized Agency Participation
- Specialized agencies may be represented at consideration of reports.
- Committee may invite specialized agencies to submit reports on pertinent subjects.

Articles 23–30   Administration of the Convention

Bibliography

Abwunza, Judith M. *Women's Voices, Women's Power: Dialogues of Resistance from East Africa*. Peterborough, Ontario, Canada: Broadview Press, 1997.

Agarwal, Bina. "Environmental Action, Gender Equity and Women's Participation." *Development and Change* 28 (1997): 1–44.

Alba, Francisco, and Joseph Potter. "Population and Development in Mexico since 1940." *Population and Development Review* 12, no. 1 (1986): 47–75.

Allison, Graham, and Morton Halperin. "Bureaucratic Politics: A Paradigm and Some Policy Implications." *World Politics* 24 (1972): 40–79.

Alvarez, Sonia. "Contradictions of a 'Women's Space' in a Male-Dominant State: The Political Role of the Commissions on the Status of Women in Postauthoritarian Brazil." In *Women, International Development and Politics*, 2d ed., edited by Kathleen Staudt. Philadelphia: Temple University Press, 1997.

Anderson, Cecilia, and Isa Baud, eds. *Women in Development Cooperation: Europe's Unfinished Business*. EADI Series no. 6. Antwerp, Belgium: UFSIA, Centre for Development Studies, Technical University of Eindhoven, 1987.

Anderson, Mary. *Focusing on Women: UNIFEM's Experience in Mainstreaming*. New York: UNIFEM, 1993.

Anderson, Mary. *Women on the Agenda: UNIFEM's Experience in Mainstreaming with Women 1985–1990*. New York: UNIFEM, 1990.

Apthorpe, Raymond. "Development Policy Discourse." *Public Administration and Development* 6 (1986): 377–89.

Arnold, Steven H. *Implementing Development Assistance: European Approaches to Basic Needs*. Boulder, Colo.: Westview Press, 1982.

Ashworth, Georgina, ed. *A Diplomacy of the Oppressed: New Directions in International Feminism*. London: Zed, 1995.

Assad, Marie, and Judith Bruce. *Empowering the Next Generation: Girls of the Maqattam Garbage Settlement*. New York: Seeds #19, 1997.

Baden, Sally, and Anne Marie Goetz, "Who Needs [Sex] When You Can Have [Gender]? Conflicting Discourses on Gender at Beijing." In *Women, International Development and Politics*, 2d ed., edited by Kathleen Staudt. Philadelphia: Temple University Press, 1997.

Bandarage, Asoka. "Women in Development: Liberalism, Marxism and Marxist-Feminism." *Development and Change* 15 (1984): 495–515.

Bardach, Eugene. *The Implementation Game*. Cambridge, Mass.: MIT Press, 1977.

Barkes, Barbara, et al. *American Government and Politics Today: The Essentials 1996–1997*. St. Paul, Minn.: West, 1996.

Basu, Amrita, ed. *The Challenge of Local Feminisms*. Boulder, Colo.: Westview Press, 1995.

Bazitti, Susan, ed. *Putting Women on the Agenda*. Johannesburg: Raven Press, 1991.

Bellah, Robert, et al. *The Good Society*. New York: Vintage, 1991.

Bellick, Pam. "A Woman's Killer Is Likely to Be Her Partner." *New York Times*, March 31, 1997.

Benería, Lourdes. "Accounting for Women's Work: The Progress of Two Decades." *World Development* 20, no. 11 (1992): 1547–60.

Benería, Lourdes, and Shelley Feldman, eds. *Unequal Burden: Economic Crises, Persistent Poverty, and Women's Work*. Boulder, Colo.: Westview Press, 1992.

Benería, Lourdes, and Martha Roldán. *The Crossroads of Class and Gender: Industrial Homework, Subcontracting and Household Dynamics in Mexico City*. Chicago: University of Chicago Press, 1987.

Benería, Lourdes, and Gita Sen. "Class and Gender Inequalities and Women's Role in Economic Development—Theoretical and Practical Implications." *Feminist Studies* 1 (1982): 157–76.

Bennett, Vivienne. "Gender, Class, and Water: Women and the Politics of Water Service in Monterrey, Mexico." *Latin American Perspectives* 22, no. 2 (1995): 76–99.

Berger, Marguerite, and Mayra Buvinić, eds. *Women's Ventures: Assistance to the Informal Sector in Latin America*. West Hartford, Conn.: Kumarian Press, 1989.

Biron, Rebecca. "Feminist Periodicals and Political Crisis in Mexico: *fem, Debate Feminista*, and *La Correa Feminista* in the 1990s." *Feminist Studies* 22, no. 1 (1996): 151–69.

Blumberg, Rae. "Gender, Micro-enterprise, Performance, and Power: Case Studies from the Dominican Republic, Ecuador, Guatemala, and Swaziland." In *Women in the Latin American Development Process*, edited by Christine E. Bose and Edna Acosta-Belén. Philadelphia: Temple University Press, 1995.

Bonder, Gloria. "Altering Sexual Stereotypes through Teacher Training." In *Women and Education in Latin America*, edited by Nelly Stromquist. Boulder, Colo.: Lynne Rienner, 1992.

Bose, Christine E., and Edna Acosta-Belén, eds. *Women in the Latin American Development Process*. Philadelphia: Temple University Press, 1995.

Boserup, Ester. *Woman's Role in Economic Development*. New York: St. Martin's Press, 1970.

Bradley, Christine. "Why Male Violence against Women Is a Development Issue: Reflections from Papua New Guinea." In *Women and Violence*, edited by Miranda Davies. London: Zed, 1994.

Braslavsky, Cecilia. "Educational Legitimation of Women's Economic Subordination in Argentina." In *Women and Education in Latin America*, edited by Nelly Stromquist. Boulder, Colo.: Lynne Rienner, 1992.

Bratton, Michael. "Peasant-State Relations in Postcolonial Africa: Patterns of Engagement and Disengagement." In *State Power and Social Forces*, edited by Joel Migdal et al. New York: Cambridge University Press, 1994.

Brouwers, Rita, et al. *Support to National Machinery for Women in Developing Countries: Efforts of OECD/DAC Members*. The Hague: Institute of Social Studies Advisory Service, 1992.

Bruce, Judith. "Users' Perspectives on Contraceptive Technology and Delivery Systems." *Technology in Society* 9 (1987): 350–83.

Brydon, Lynn, and Sylvia Chant. *Women in the Third World: Gender Issues in Rural and Urban Areas*. New Brunswick, N.J.: Rutgers University Press, 1989.

Bunch, Charlotte, in Heidi Hartmann et al. "Bringing Together Feminist Theory and

Practice: A Collective Interview." *Signs: Journal of Women in Culture and Society* 21, no. 4 (1996): 942–43.

Burnham, Margaret. "The New South African Constitution and Customary Law." *P*A*S* [Program of African Studies] News and Events* 7, no. 2 (1997): 2, 5.

Butt, Tariq. "Interrogate Lovingly." *Populi: The UNFPA Magazine* 21, no. 6 (June 1994): 5.

Buvinić, Mayra. "Projects for Women in the Third World: Explaining Their Misbehavior." *World Development* 14, no. 5 (1986): 653–64.

Buvinić, Mayra. *Women and Poverty in the Third World*. Baltimore: Johns Hopkins University Press, 1983.

Buvinić, Mayra, and Nadia Youssef. *Women-Headed Households: The Ignored Factor in Development Planning*. Washington, D.C.: USAID, 1978.

Bystydzienski, Jill. "Norway: Achieving World-Record Women's Representation in Government." In *Electoral Systems in Comparative Perspective*, edited by Wilma Rule and William Zimmerman. Westport, Conn.: Greenwood Press, 1994.

Camp, Sharon. "Global Population Stabilization: A 'No Regrets' Strategy." *Conscience: Women, Population and the Environment* 14, no. 3 (1993): 7–8, 10–11.

Carloni, Alice. *Women in Development: A.I.D.'s Experience, 1973–1985*. Vol. 1. Washington, D.C.: USAID, 1987.

Cartaya, Vanessa. "Informality and Poverty: Causal Relationship or Coincidence?" In *Contrapunto*, edited by Cathy Rakowski. Albany, N.Y.: SUNY Albany Press, 1994.

Caufield, Catherine. *Masters of Illusion: The World Bank and the Poverty of Nations*. New York: Henry Holt, 1996.

Center for the Investigation and Study of Agrarian Reform (CIERA), Rural Women's Research Team. "Tough Row to Hoe: Women in Nicaragua's Agricultural Cooperatives." In *Women, International Development and Politics*, 2d ed., edited by Kathleen Staudt. Philadelphia: Temple University Press, 1997.

Chaney, Elsa. *Supermadre: Women in Politics in Latin America*. Austin: University of Texas Press, 1979.

Chaney, Elsa, and Mary García Castro, eds. *Muchachas No More: Household Workers in Latin America and the Caribbean*. Philadelphia: Temple University Press, 1989.

Chanock, Martin. *Law, Custom and Social Order: The Colonial Experience in Malawi and Zambia*. Cambridge: Cambridge University Press, 1985.

Charlesworth, Hilary. "Women as Sherpas: Are Global Summits Useful for Women?" *Feminist Studies* 22, no. 3 (1996): 537–47.

Charlton, Sue Ellen. *Women in Third World Development*. Boulder, Colo.: Westview Press, 1984.

Charlton, Sue Ellen, et al., eds. *Women, the State and Development*. Albany, N.Y.: SUNY Albany Press, 1989.

Chazan, Naomi. "Engaging the State: Associational Life in Sub-Saharan Africa." In *State Power and Social Forces*, edited by Joel Migdal et al. New York: Cambridge University Press, 1994.

Chen, Martha. "A Matter of Survival: Women's Right to Employment in India and Bangladesh." In *Women, Culture and Development: A Study of Human Capabilities*, edited by Martha Nussbaum and Jonathan Glover. New York: Clarendon/Oxford, 1995.

Chuchryk, Patricia. "Subversive Mothers: The Women's Opposition to the Military Regime in Chile." In *Women, the State and Development*, edited by Sue Ellen

Charlton et al. Albany, N.Y.: SUNY Albany Press, 1989.

Cohn, Carol. "Sex and Death in the Rational World of Defense Intellectuals." *Signs: Journal of Women in Culture and Society* 12, no. 4 (1987): 687–718.

Collins, Patricia. "The Social Construction of Black Feminist Thought." *Signs: Journal of Women in Culture and Society* 14, no. 4 (1989): 745–73.

Conly, Shanti. "The Missing Billions." In *People and the Planet* (1996). Reprinted on the UNFPA Web site (www.unfpa.org).

Connolly, Priscilla. "The Politics of the Informal Sector: A Critique." In *Beyond Employment: Household, Gender and Subsistence*, edited by N. Redcliff and E. Mingione. London: Basil Blackwell, 1986.

Connors, Jane. "Government Measures to Confront Violence against Women." In *Women and Violence*, edited by Miranda Davies. London: Zed, 1994.

Cornia, Giovanni Andrew, Richard Jolly, and Frances Stewart, eds. *Adjustment with a Human Face*. 2 vols. Oxford: Clarendon Press, 1987.

Correa, Sonia, with Rebecca Reichmann. *Population and Reproductive Rights: Feminist Perspectives from the South*. London: Zed, with DAWN, 1994.

Cowen, M. P. and R. W. Shenton. *Doctrines of Development*. London: Routledge, 1996.

Cox, Elizabeth Shrader. "Gender Violence and Women's Health in Central America." In *Women and Violence*, edited by Miranda Davies. London: Zed, 1994.

Crane, Barbara B., and Jason L. Finkle. "The United States, China, and the United Nations Population Fund: Dynamics of U.S. Policymaking." *Population and Development Review* 15 (1989): 23–59.

Dalton, Russell J., and Manfred Kuechler, eds. *Challenging the Political Order: New Social and Political Movements in Western Democracies*. New York: Oxford University Press, 1990.

Dangarembga, Tsitsi. *Nervous Conditions*. Seattle: Seal Press, 1988.

Dasgupta, Shamita. "Feminist Consciousness in Woman-Centered Hindi Films." *Journal of Popular Culture* 30, no. 1 (1996): 173–90.

Davies, Miranda, ed. *Women and Violence: Realities and Responses Worldwide*. London: Zed, 1994.

de Barbieri, M. Teresita. "Gender and Population Policy." *Conscience* 14, no. 3 (1993): 30–35.

Deere, Carmen Diana, and Magdalena León de Leal, eds. *Rural Women and State Policy: Feminist Perspectives on Latin American Agricultural Development*. Boulder, Colo.: Westview Press, 1987.

Di Stefano, Christine. *Configurations of Masculinity: A Feminist Perspective*. Ithaca, N.Y.: Cornell University Press, 1991.

Dixon-Mueller, Ruth. *Women in Third World Agriculture*. Geneva: ILO, 1985.

Dorkenoo, Erua, and Scilla Elworthy. "Female Genital Mutilation." In *Women and Violence*, edited by Miranda Davies. London: Zed, 1994.

Doss, Cheryl R. *African Professional Women in Agriculture: An Analysis of Two Roundtable Discussions*. Morrilton, Alaska: Winrock International Institute for Agricultural Development, 1991.

Downs, Anthony. *Inside Bureaucracy*. Boston: Little, Brown, 1966.

Dwyer, Daisy, and Judith Bruce, eds. *A Home Divided: Women and Income in the Third World*. Stanford, Calif.: Stanford University Press, 1988.

Ebdon, Rosamund. "NGO Expansion and the Fight to Reach the Poor: Gender Implications of NGO Scaling-up in Bangladesh." In "Getting Institutions Right for Women in Development," edited by Anne Marie Goetz. *IDS Bulletin* 26, no. 3 (1995).

Edelman, Murray. *The Symbolic Uses of Politics*. Champaign and Urbana: University of Illinois Press, 1964.

Einhorn, Barbara. *Cinderella Goes to Market: Citizenship, Gender, and Women's Movements in East and Central Europe*. London: Verso, 1993.

el Saadawi, Nawal. *The Hidden Face of Eve*. London: Zed, 1980.

Elson, Diane. "From Survival Strategies to Transformation Strategies: Women's Needs and Structural Adjustment." In *Unequal Burden*, edited by Lourdes Benería and Shelley Feldman. Boulder, Colo.: Westview Press, 1992.

Elson, Diane. "Male Bias in Macro-Economics: The Case of Structural Adjustment." In *Male Bias in the Development Process*, edited by Diane Elson. Manchester: Manchester University Press, 1991.

Enloe, Cynthia. *Bananas, Beaches, and Bases*. Berkeley: University of California Press, 1989.

Enloe, Cynthia. *The Morning After*. Berkeley: University of California Press, 1993.

Esteva, Gustavo. "Development: Metaphor, Myth, Threat." *Development: Seeds of Change* 3 (1985).

Evans, Peter, et al., eds. *Bringing the State Back In*. Cambridge: Cambridge University Press, 1985.

Evans, Sara. *Personal Politics*. New York: Vintage, 1980.

Eviota, Elizabeth. *The Political Economy of Gender: Women and the Sexual Division of Labour in the Philippines*. London: Zed, 1992.

Fenoglio, Ellen. "Case Study of the Institutionalization of the DAC Women in Development Guiding Principles by the United States Government." Manuscript, November 1993.

Ferguson, James. *The Anti-Politics Machine: "Development," Depoliticization and Bureaucratic Power in Lesotho*. New York: Cambridge University Press, 1990.

Ferguson, Kathy. *The Feminist Case against Bureaucracy*. Philadelphia: Temple University Press, 1984.

Ferguson, Kathy. "Women, Feminism, and Development." In *Women, International Development and Politics*, 1st ed., edited by Kathleen Staudt. Philadelphia: Temple University Press, 1990.

Fernández-Kelly, María Patricia, and Anna M. García. "Informalization at the Core: Hispanic Women, Homework, and the Advanced Capitalist State." In *The Informal Economy: Studies in Advanced and Less Developed Countries*, edited by Alejandro Portes et al. Baltimore: Johns Hopkins University Press, 1989.

Fink, Mary. "Women and Popular Education in Latin America." In *Women and Education in Latin America*, edited by Nelly Stromquist. Boulder, Colo.: Lynne Rienner, 1992.

Finkle, Jason L., and Barbara B. Crane. "Ideology and Politics at Mexico City: The United States at the 1984 International Conference on Population." *Population and Development Review* 11 (1985): 1–28.

Finkle, Jason L., and Barbara B. Crane. "The Politics of Bucharest: Population, Development, and the New International Economic Order." *Population and Development Review* 1 (1975): 87–114.

Fisher, Elizabeth, and Linda Gray McKay. *Gender Justice: Women's Rights Are Human Rights*. New York: Unitarian Universalist Service Committee, 1996.

Ford Foundation. *Violence against Women: Addressing a Global Problem*. New York: Ford Foundation, 1992.

Freeman, Donald B. *A City of Farmers: Informal Urban Agriculture in the Open Spaces of Nairobi, Kenya*. Montreal: McGill-Queen's University Press, 1991.

Freeman, Jo. *The Politics of Women's Liberation*. New York: David McKay, 1975.

Freire, Paulo. *Pedagogy of the Oppressed*. New York: Continuum, 1970.

Frohmann, Alicia, and Teresa Veldés. "Democracy in the Country and in the Home: The Women's Movement in Chile." In *The Challenge of Local Feminisms*, edited by Amrita Basu. Boulder, Colo.: Westview Press, 1995.

García-Moreno, Claudia, and Amparo Claro. "Challenges from the Women's Health Movement: Women's Rights versus Population Control." In *Population Policies Reconsidered*, edited by Gita Sen et al. Cambridge, Mass.: Harvard University Press, 1994.

Gelb, Joyce. *Feminism and Politics: A Comparative Perspective*. Berkeley: University of California Press, 1989.

Germain, Adrienne, Sia Nowrojee, and Hnin Hnin Pyne. "Setting a New Agenda: Sexual and Reproductive Health and Rights." In *Population Policies Reconsidered*, edited by Gita Sen et al. Cambridge, Mass.: Harvard University Press, 1994.

Germain, Adrienne, and Jane Ordway. *Population Control and Women's Health: Balancing the Scales*. New York: International Women's Health Coalition, 1989.

Gilligan, Carol. *In a Different Voice*. Boston: Harvard University Press, 1981.

Gladwin, Christina H., ed. *Structural Adjustment and African Women Farmers*. Gainesville: University of Florida Press, 1991.

Goetz, Anne Marie. "From Feminist Knowledge to Data for Development: The Bureaucratic Management of Information on Women and Development." *IDS Bulletin* 25, no. 2 (1994): 27–36.

Goetz, Anne Marie. "Local Heroes: Patterns of Field Worker Discretion in Implementing GAD Policy in Bangladesh." Discussion Paper no. 358. Sussex: IDS, 1996.

Goetz, Anne Marie, ed. "Getting Institutions Right for Women in Development." *IDS Bulletin* 26, no. 3 (1995).

Goetz, Anne Marie, and R. Sen Gupta. "Who Takes the Credit? Gender, Power and Control over Loan Use in Rural Credit Programmes in Bangladesh." *World Development* 24, no. 1 (1996): 45–64.

Goldberg, Gertrude, and Eleanor Kremen. "The Feminization of Poverty: Not Only in America." In *Different Roles, Different Voices: Women and Politics in the United States and Europe*, edited by Marianne Githens, Pippa Norris, and Joni Lovenduski. New York: HarperCollins, 1994.

Goldsworthy, David. "Thinking Politically about Development." *Development and Change* 19 (1988): 505–30.

Greer, Germaine. *Sex and Destiny*. New York: Harper & Row, 1984.

Guyer, Jane I., ed. *Feeding African Cities: Studies in Regional Social History*. Bloomington: Indiana University Press, 1987.

Hannan-Andersson, Carolyn. "Experiences with Gender Training—How Did It Work and How Was It Used? Some Experiences from the Swedish International Development Authority 1988–1991." Paper presented at the Gender Training and Development Planning Conference, Chr. Michelsen Institute, Norway, May 13–15, 1991.

Hansen, Karen Tranberg, and Leslie Ashbaugh. "Women on the Front Line: Development Issues in Southern Africa." In *WID Annual*, vol. 2, edited by Rita Gallin and Anne Ferguson. Boulder, Colo.: Westview Press, 1991.

Harmon, Amy. "The Internet: For Parents, a New and Vexing Burden." *New York Times*, June 27, 1997.

Hashemi, Syed M., Sidney Ruth Schuler, and Ann P. Riley. "Rural Credit Programs and Women's Empowerment in Bangladesh." *World Development* 24, no. 4 (1996): 635–54.

Heilbroner, Robert. "Reflections: The Triumph of Capitalism," *The New Yorker*, January 23, 1989.

Henderson, Hazel. *Building a Win-Win World: Life beyond Global Economic Warfare*. San Francisco: Berrett-Koehler, 1996.

Henderson, Helen, ed. *Gender and Agricultural Development: Surveying the Field*. Tucson: University of Arizona Press, 1993.

Hernes, Helga Maria. "The Welfare State Citizenship of Scandinavian Women." In *The Political Interests of Gender*, edited by Kathleen B. Jones and Anna G. Jonasdottir. London: Sage, 1988. (This is a slightly revised article from her *Welfare State and Woman Power*. Oslo: Norwegian University Press, 1987.)

Himmelstrand, Karen. "Can an Aid Bureaucracy Empower Women?" In *Women, International Development and Politics*, 2d ed., edited by Kathleen Staudt. Philadelphia: Temple University Press, 1997.

Hirschman, Albert O. *Exit, Voice and Loyalty: Responses to Decline in Firms*. Cambridge, Mass.: Harvard University Press, 1970.

Hobsbawn, E., and Terence O. Ranger, eds. *The Invention of Tradition*. Cambridge: Cambridge University Press, 1983.

Hofstede, Geert. *Culture's Consequences*. Beverly Hills, Calif.: Sage, 1984.

Holcombe, Susan. *Managing to Empower: The Grameen Bank's Experience at Poverty Alleviation*. London: Zed, 1995.

Honig, Emily, and Gail Hershatter. *Personal Voices: Chinese Women in the 1980s*. Stanford, Calif.: Stanford University Press, 1988.

hooks, bell. *Teaching to Transgress: Education as the Practice of Freedom*. London: Routledge, 1994.

Horn, Nancy E. *Cultivating Customers: Market Women in Harare, Zimbabwe*. Boulder, Colo.: Lynne Rienner, 1994.

Illo, Jeanne Frances I., and Cynthia C. Veneración. *Women and Men in Rainfed Farming Systems: Case Studies of Households in the Bicol Region*. Manila: Institute of Philippine Culture, Ateneo de Manila University, 1988.

Inglehart, Ronald. *A World View of Women: Social, Political and Economic Attitudes*. Washington, D.C.: U.S. Information Agency, 1994.

Inkeles, Alex. *Becoming Modern*. Cambridge, Mass.: Harvard University Press, 1974.

Inter-American Development Bank (IDB). *Women in the Americas: Bridging the Gender Gap*. Washington, D.C.: IDB, 1995.

International Labour Organization (ILO). *Child Labor: Targeting the Intolerable*. Geneva: ILO, 1996.

International Planned Parenthood Federation (IPPF). *IPPF Charter on Sexual and Reproductive Rights*. London: IPPF, 1995.

Jahan, Rounaq. "Assessment of Policies and Organizational Measures in Women in Development Adopted by DAC Member Countries." Draft, 1994.

Jahan, Rounaq. *The Elusive Agenda: Mainstreaming Women in Development*. London: Zed, 1995.

Jain, Anrudh, and Judith Bruce. "A Reproductive Health Approach to the Objectives and Assessment of Family Planning Programs." In *Population Policies Reconsidered*, edited by Gita Sen et al. Cambridge, Mass.: Harvard University Press, 1994.

Jain, Devaki, and Nirmala Banerjee, eds. *Tyranny of the Household: Investigative Essays on Women's Work*. New Delhi: Shakti Books, 1985.

Jain, Pankaj S. "Managing Credit for the Rural Poor: Lessons from the Grameen Bank." *World Development* 24, no. 1 (1996): 79–90.

James, Stanlie, and Abena Busia. *Theorizing Black Feminisms*. London: Routledge, 1993.

Jaquette, Jane. "Gender and Justice in Economic Development." In *Persistent Inequalities*, edited by Irene Tinker. New York: Oxford University Press, 1990.

Jaquette, Jane. "Women and Modernization Theory: A Decade of Feminist Criticism." *World Politics* 34, no. 2 (1982): 276–84.

Jaquette, Jane, ed. *The Women's Movement in Latin America*. 2d ed. Boulder, Colo.: Westview Press, 1994.

Jaquette, Jane, and Kathleen Staudt. "Women as 'At Risk' Reproducers: Biology, Science and Population in U.S. Foreign Policy." In *Women, Biology and Public Policy*, edited by Virginia Sapiro. Beverly Hills, Calif.: Sage, 1985.

Jensen, Katherine. "Getting to the Third World: Agencies as Gatekeepers." In *Women, International Development and Politics*, 2d ed., edited by Kathleen Staudt. Philadelphia: Temple University Press, 1997.

Jethmalani, Rani. "India." In *Empowerment and the Law: Strategies of Third World Women*, edited by Margaret Schuler. Washington, D.C.: Overseas Education Fund, 1986.

Jiggins, Janice, with Paul Maimbo and Mary Masona. "Breaking New Ground: Reaching Out to Women Farmers in Western Zambia." In *Seeds 2*, edited by Ann Leonard. New York: Feminist Press, 1995.

Joekes, Susan. *Women in the World Economy: An INSTRAW Study*. New York: Oxford University Press, 1987.

Joekes, Susan, and Ann Weston. *Women and the New Trade Agenda*. New York: UNIFEM, 1995.

Johnson-Odim, Cheryl. "Common Themes, Different Contexts: Third World Women and Feminism." In *Third World Women and the Politics of Feminism*, edited by Chandra Talpade Mohanty et al. Bloomington: Indiana University Press, 1991.

Jones, Mark. "Increasing Women's Representation via Gender Quotas: The Argentine Ley de Cupos." *Women & Politics* 16, no. 4 (1996): 75–98.

Kabeer, Naila. *Reversed Realities: Gender Hierarchies in Development Thought*. London: Verso, 1994.

Kanter, Rosabeth. *Men and Women of the Corporation*. 2d ed. New York: Basic Books, 1993.

Kaplan, Gisela. *Contemporary Western European Feminism*. New York: New York University Press, 1992.

Kardam, Nüket. "The Adaptability of International Development Agencies: The Response of the World Bank to Women in Development." In *Women, International*

Development and Politics, 2d ed., edited by Kathleen Staudt. Philadelphia: Temple University Press, 1997.

Kardam, Nüket. *Bringing Women In: Women's Issues in International Development Programs*. Boulder, Colo.: Lynne Rienner, 1991.

Katzenstein, Mary Fainsod, and Carol McClurg Mueller, eds. *The Women's Movements of the United States and Western Europe*. Philadelphia: Temple University Press, 1987.

Kay, Bonnie J., Adrienne Germain, and Maggie Bangser. *The Bangladesh Women's Health Coalition*. Quality/Calidad/Qualite series, no. 3, edited by Anne Leonard. New York: Population Council, 1991.

Kishwar, Madhu, and Ruth Vanita, eds. *In Search of Answers: Indian Women's Voices from Manushi*. London: Zed, 1984.

Korten, David C. *Getting to the 21st Century: Voluntary Action and the Global Agenda*. West Hartford, Conn.: Kumarian Press, 1990.

Kumar, Radha. "From Chipko to Sati: The Contemporary Indian Women's Movement." In *The Challenge of Local Feminisms*, edited by Amrita Basu. Boulder, Colo.: Westview Press, 1995.

Lakhova, Ekaterina. "Women Should Participate in the Construction of Civil Society at All Levels." Paper presented at Prospects for Equal Democracy in Russia, April 22–23, 1997. Distributed by Human Rights Information Network (HURINet).

Lamas, Marta, Alicia Martínez, María Luisa Tárres, and Esperanza Tuñon. "Building Bridges: The Growth of Popular Feminism in Mexico." In *The Challenge of Local Feminisms*, edited by Amrita Basu. Boulder, Colo.: Westview Press, 1995.

Lamphere, Louise. "Introduction: The Shaping of Diversity." In *Structuring Diversity: Ethnographic Perspectives on the New Immigration*. Chicago: University of Chicago Press, 1991.

Lapham, Robert L., and W. Parker Mauldin. "Contraceptive Prevalence: The Influence of Organized Family Planning Programs." *Studies in Family Planning* 16, no. 3 (1985): 117–37.

Leijenaar, Monique. "Positive Action and Quota Policies in Europe: Empower Women in Politics." Paper prepared for the American Political Science Association annual meeting, New York, September 1–4, 1994.

Leijenaar, Monique, and Kees Niemöller. "Political Participation of Women: The Netherlands." In *Women and Politics Worldwide*, edited by Barbara Nelson and Najma Chowdhury. New Haven, Conn.: Yale University Press, 1994.

Lele, Uma. "Women and Structural Transformation." *Economic Development and Cultural Change* 34, no. 2 (1986): 195–221.

Lemke, Christiane. "Women and Politics: The New Federal Republic of Germany." In *Women and Politics Worldwide*, edited by Barbara Nelson and Najma Chowdhury. New Haven, Conn.: Yale University Press, 1994.

Lenox, Janne, and Desmond McNeill. *The Women's Grant: Desk Study Review*. Evaluation Report 2.89. Oslo: Royal Norwegian Ministry of Development Cooperation, 1989.

Leonard, Ann, ed. *Seeds: Supporting Women's Work in the Third World*. New York: Feminist Press, 1989.

Leonard, Ann, ed. *Seeds 2: Supporting Women's Work around the World*. New York: Feminist Press, 1995.

Leonard, David. *Reaching the Peasant Farmer: Organization Theory and Practice in Kenya*. Chicago: University of Chicago Press, 1977.

LePrestre, Philippe. *The World Bank and the Environmental Challenge*. Toronto: Associated University Presses, 1989.

Levin, Ronald. "In-Country Presence: The Experience of Other Donors." *AID Evaluation News* 4, no. 4 (1992): 5–8.

Lewis, Barbara. "Farming Women, Public Policy, and the Women's Ministry: A Case Study from Cameroon." In *Women, International Development and Politics*, 2d ed., edited by Kathleen Staudt. Philadelphia: Temple University Press, 1997.

Lim, Linda. *More and Better Jobs for Women: An Action Guide*. Geneva: ILO, 1996.

Lim, Linda. "Women's Work in Export Factories: The Politics of a Cause." In *Persistent Inequalities*, edited by Irene Tinker. New York: Oxford University Press, 1990.

Lorde, Audre. "The Master's Tools Will Never Dismantle the Master's House." In *Sister Outsider*. Freedom, Calif.: Crossing Press, 1984.

Lotherington, Ann Therese. *Implementation of Women-in-Development (WID) Policy*. Oslo: University of Oslo, Centre for Development and the Environment, 1991.

Lovenduski, Joni, and Pippa Norris, eds. *Gender and Party Politics*. London: Sage, 1993.

Lowi, Theodore. *The End of Liberalism*. New York: W. W. Norton, 1979.

Lyon, Evelyn Folch, Luis de Lamacorra, and S. Bruce Schearer. "Focus Group Survey Research on Family Planning in Mexico." *Studies in Family Planning* 12 (1981): 413–15.

Marchand, Marianne H., and Jane L. Parpart, eds. *Feminism/Postmodernism/Development*. London: Routledge, 1995.

Massell, Gregory. *The Surrogate Proletariat: Moslem Women and Revolutionary Strategies in Soviet Central Asia, 1919–1929*. Princeton, N.J.: Princeton University Press, 1974.

Mayoux, Linda. *From Vicious to Virtuous Circles? Gender and Micro-enterprise Development*. Occasional Paper no. 3. Geneva: UNRISD, 1995.

Mazumdar, Vina. "Seeds for a New Model of Development: A Political Commentary." In *Seeds: Supporting Women's Work in the Third World*, edited by Ann Leonard. New York: Feminist Press, 1989.

Mbeo, Mary Adhiambo, and Oki Ooko-Ombaka, eds. *Women and Law in Kenya: Perspectives and Emerging Issues*. Nairobi: Public Law Institute, 1989.

McGrath, Patricia L. *The Unfinished Assignment: Equal Education for Women*. Washington, D.C.: Worldwatch, 1976.

McKean, Cressida S. "Training and Technical Assistance for Small and Micro-enterprise: A Discussion of Their Effectiveness." In *Contrapunto*, edited by Cathy Rakowski. Albany, N.Y.: SUNY Albany Press, 1994.

Mies, Maria. *Patriarchy and Accumulation on a World Scale: Women in the International Division of Labour*. London: Zed, 1986.

Migdal, Joel, Atul Kohli, and Vivienne Shue, eds. *State Power and Social Forces: Domination and Transformation in the Third World*. New York: Cambridge University Press, 1994.

Moeller, Robert G. *Protecting Motherhood: Women and the Family in the Politics of Postwar West Germany*. Berkeley: University of California Press, 1993.

Moghadam, Valentine M. "Economic Reforms and Women's Employment in the Middle East and North Africa." *WIDER Angle* 1 (1995): 8–9.

Mohanty, Chandra, Ann Russo, and Lourdes Torres, eds. *Third World Women and the Politics of Feminism*. 2d ed. Bloomington: Indiana University Press, 1991.

Molyneux, Maxine. "Mobilization without Emancipation? Women's Interests, the State, and Revolution in Nicaragua." *Feminist Studies* 11, no. 2 (1985): 377–89.

Momsen, Janet. *Women and Development in the Third World*. London: Routledge, 1991.

Moser, Caroline O. N. *Gender Planning and Development: Theory, Practice and Training*. London: Routledge, 1993.

Moser, Caroline O. N. "Gender Planning in the Third World: Meeting Practical and Strategic Needs." *World Development* 17, no. 11 (1989).

Naihua Zhang, with Wu Xu. "Discovering the Positive within the Negative: The Women's Movement in a Changing China." In *The Challenge of Local Feminisms*, edited by Amrita Basu. Boulder, Colo.: Westview Press, 1995.

Narasimham, Sakuntala. "India: From Sati to Sex Determination Tests." In *Women and Violence*, edited by Miranda Davies. London: Zed, 1994.

Nash, June, and María Patricia Fernández-Kelly, eds. *Women, Men, and the International Division of Labor*. Albany, N.Y.: SUNY Albany Press, 1983.

Nelson, Barbara, and Kathryn Carver. "Many Voices, but Few Vehicles: The Consequences for Women of Weak Political Infrastructure in the United States." In *Women and Politics Worldwide*, edited by Barbara Nelson and Najma Chowdhury. New Haven, Conn.: Yale University Press, 1994.

Nelson, Barbara, and Najma Chowdhury, eds. *Women and Politics Worldwide*. New Haven, Conn.: Yale University Press, 1994.

Nelson, Sara. "Constructing and Negotiating Gender in Women's Police Stations in Brazil." *Latin American Perspectives* 23, no. 1 (1996): 131–48.

Norway, Government of. *The Norwegian Equal Status Act: With Comments*. Oslo: 1985.

Nuita, Yoko, et al. "The U.N. Convention on Eliminating Discrimination against Women and the Status of Women in Japan." In *Women and Politics Worldwide*, edited by Barbara Nelson and Najma Chowdhury. New Haven, Conn.: Yale University Press, 1994.

Nzomo, Maria, and Kathleen Staudt. "Man-Made Political Machinery in Kenya: Political Space for Women?" In *Women and Politics Worldwide*, edited by Barbara Nelson and Najma Chowdhury. New Haven, Conn.: Yale University Press, 1994.

Okonjo, Kamene. "The Dual Sex Political System in Operation: Igbo Women and Community Politics in Midwestern Nigeria." In *Women in Africa: Studies in Social and Economic Change*, edited by Nancy Hafkin and Edna Bay. Stanford, Calif.: Stanford University Press, 1976.

Ong, Aihwa. "Spirits of Resistance." In *Situated Lives: Gender and Culture in Everyday Life*, edited by Louise Lamphere, Helena Ragone, and Patricia Zavella. New York: Routledge, 1997.

Ooko-Ombaka, Oki. "An Assessment of National Machinery for Women." *Assignment Children* 49, 50 (1980): 45–61.

Organization for Economic Cooperation and Development/Development Assistance Committee (OECD/DAC). "Financial Flows to Developing Countries in 1995: Sharp Declines in Official Aid; Private Flows Rise." Press release. Paris: June 1996.

Organization for Economic Cooperation and Development/Development Assistance Committee (OECD/DAC). *Third Monitoring Report on the Implementation of the*

DAC Revised Guiding Principles on Women in Development (1989). Paris: OECD, 1992.

Overholt, Catherine, et al. *Gender Roles in Development Projects: A Case Book*. West Hartford, Conn.: Kumarian Press, 1985.

Oxaal, Zoe. "Changing Institutions in Women's Interests." In *Development and Gender in Brief*, 5 (1997).

Palmer, Ingrid. *Gender and Population in the Adjustment of African Economies: Planning for Change*. Geneva: ILO, 1991.

Palmer, Ingrid. *The Nemow Case*. West Hartford, Conn.: Kumarian Press, 1985.

Parpart, Jane, and Kathleen Staudt, eds. *Women and the State in Africa*. Boulder, Colo.: Lynne Rienner, 1989.

Peña, Devon. *The Terror of the Machine: Technology, Work, Gender and Ecology on the U.S.-Mexico Border*. Austin: Center for Mexican American Studies, University of Texas at Austin, 1997.

Peterson, V. Spike, and Anne Runyan. *Global Gender Issues*. Boulder, Colo.: Westview Press, 1993.

Pettman, Jan Jindy. *Worlding Women: A Feminist International Politics*. London: Routledge, 1996.

Pietila, Hilkka, and Ingride Eide. *The Role of the Nordic Countries in the Advancement of Women within the United Nations System*. Report no. 16. Stockholm: Nordic UN Project, 1990.

Plantenga, D. *VENA*. Leiden: Leiden University, 1991.

Potts, Malcolm. "Family Planning: The Male Point of View." IPPF Web site (www.ippf.org), 1996.

Preston, Julia. "Woman's Shooting of Attacker Rivets Mexico." *New York Times*, February 5, 1997.

Putnam, Robert D. *Making Democracy Work*. Princeton, N.J.: Princeton University Press, 1993.

Rakowski, Cathy, ed. *Contrapunto: The Informal Sector Debate in Latin America*. Albany, N.Y.: SUNY Albany Press, 1994.

Ramphele, Mamphela. *Crossing Boundaries*. New York: Feminist Press, 1997.

Rao, Aruna. *Women's Studies International: Nairobi and Beyond*. New York: Feminist Press, 1991.

Rao, Aruna, Hilary Feldstein, Kathleen Cloud, and Kathleen Staudt. *Gender Training and Development Planning: Learning from Experience*. Bergen, Norway, and New York: Chr. Michelsen Institute and Population Council, 1991.

Rao, Aruna, and David Kelleher. "Engendering Organizational Change: The BRAC Case." In "Getting Institutions Right for Women in Development," edited by Anne Marie Goetz. *IDS Bulletin* 26, no. 3 (1995).

Rao, Aruna, et al. *Reflections and Learnings: Gender Trainers Workskhop Report*. Amsterdam and New York: Royal Tropical Institute and Population Council, 1993.

Rathgeber, Eva. "WID, WAD, GAD: Trends in Research and Practice." *Journal of Developing Areas* 24 (1990): 489–502.

Rau, Bill. *From Feast to Famine: Official Cures and Grassroots Remedies to Africa's Food Crisis*. London: Zed, 1991.

Razavi, Shahrashoub, and Carol Miller. *From WID to GAD: Conceptual Shifts in the Women and Development Discourse*. Occasional Paper no. 1. Geneva: UNRISD, 1995.

Reich, Robert. *The Wealth of Nations.* New York: Vintage, 1991.

Remick, Helen, ed. *Comparable Worth and Wage Discrimination: Technical Possibilities and Political Realities.* Philadelphia: Temple University Press, 1984.

Rich, Bruce. *Mortgaging the Earth: The World Bank, Environmental Impoverishment, and the Crisis of Development.* Boston: Beacon Press, 1994.

Richards, Marilyn. *Approaches to Women in Development by Donor Countries Other than the U.S.* Washington, D.C.: Equity Policy Center, 1983.

Rideau Research Associates for Francoise Mailhot, CIDA/Evaluation. *Gender as a Cross-Cutting Theme in CIDA's Development Assistance—An Evaluation of CIDA's WID Policy and Activities, 1984–1992.* Ottawa: CIDA, 1993.

Rideau Research Associates for Francoise Mailhot, CIDA/Evaluation. *WID Policies in Selected Development Agencies.* Working Paper no. 3. Ottawa: CIDA, 1992.

Roberts, Bryan. "Enterprise and Labor Markets: The Border and the Metropolitan Areas." *Frontera Norte* 5, no. 9 (1993): 33–66.

Rogers, Barbara. *The Domestication of Women: Discrimination in Developing Societies.* New York: St. Martin's Press, 1979.

Rose, Laurel. "A Woman Is Like a Field: Women's Strategies for Land Access in Swaziland." In *Agriculture, Women, and Land: The African Experience*, edited by Jean Davison. Boulder, Colo.: Westview Press, 1988.

Rossiter, Bernard D. *The Global Struggle for More: Third World Conflicts with Rich Nations.* New York: Harper & Row, 1987.

Rubin, Gayle. "The Traffic in Women: Notes on the 'Political Economy' of Sex." In *Toward an Anthropology of Women*, edited by Rayna Reiter. New York: Monthly Review Press, 1975.

Ruiz, Vicki L., and Susan Tiano, eds. *Women on the U.S.-Mexico Border: Responses to Change.* Boston: Allyn & Unwin, 1987.

Rule, Wilma, and William Zimmerman, eds. *Electoral Systems in Comparative Perspective: Their Impact on Women and Minorities.* Westport, Conn.: Greenwood Press, 1994.

Sadker, Myra, and David Sadker. *Failing at Fairness: How Our Schools Cheat Girls.* New York: Simon & Schuster, 1995.

Saito, Katrine A., and C. Jean Weidemann. *Agricultural Extension for Women Farmers in Africa.* Washington, D.C.: World Bank, 1990.

Sanday, Peggy. *Female Power and Male Dominance.* New York: Cambridge University Press, 1981.

Sara-Lafosse, Violeta. "Coeducational Settings and Educational and Social Outcomes in Peru." In *Women and Education in Latin America*, edited by Nelly Stromquist. Boulder, Colo.: Lynne Rienner, 1992.

Sassen, Saskia. *Cities in a World Economy.* Thousand Oaks, Calif.: Pine Forge Press of Sage, 1995.

Scott, Alison MacEwen. "Informal Sector or Female Sector? Gender Bias in Urban Labour Market Models." In *Male Bias in the Development Process*, edited by Diane Elson. Manchester: Manchester University Press, 1991.

Scott, Catherine. *Gender and Development: Rethinking Modernization and Dependency Theory.* Boulder, Colo.: Lynne Rienner, 1995.

Scott, James. *Everyday Weapons of the Weak.* New Haven, Conn.: Yale University Press, 1985.

Seager, Joni. *The State of Women in the World Atlas.* New York: Penguin, 1997.

Selby, Henry, et al. *The Mexican Urban Household: Organizing for Self-Defense*. Austin: University of Texas Press, 1990.

Sen, Amartya. "Gender and Cooperative Conflicts." In *Persistent Inequalities*, edited by Irene Tinker. New York: Oxford University Press, 1990.

Sen, Amartya. "More Than 100 Million Women Are Missing." *New York Review of Books*, December 20, 1990.

Sen, Gita, Adrienne Germain, and Lincoln C. Chen, eds. *Population Policies Reconsidered: Health, Empowerment, and Rights*. Cambridge, Mass.: Harvard University Press, 1994.

Sen, Gita, and Caren Grown. *Development, Crises, and Alternative Visions: Third World Women's Perspectives*. New York: Monthly Review Press, 1987.

Sharpe, Gilian. "Yugo War Crimes." Distributed by the Human Rights Information Network (HURINet), April 22, 1997.

Shiva, Vandana. *Staying Alive: Women, Ecology and Development*. London and New Delhi: Zed and Kali for Women, 1988.

Sims, Calvin. "Justice in Peru." *New York Times*, March 12, 1997.

Sims, Holly. "Malthusian Nightmare or Richest in Human Resources?" In *India Briefing, 1992*, edited by Leonard Gordon and Philip Oldenburg. Boulder, Colo.: Westview Press, 1992.

Skjeie, Hege. "Ending the Male Political Hegemony: The Norwegian Experience." In *Gender and Party Politics*, edited by Joni Lovenduski and Pippa Norris. London: Sage, 1993.

Skjønsberg, Else. *Change in an African Village: Kefa Speaks*. West Hartford, Conn.: Kumarian Press, 1989.

Slayter-Thomas, Barbara, et al. *Tools of Gender Analysis*. Worcester, Mass.: Clark University, ECOGEN, 1993.

Smith, Peter. *Labyrinths of Power: Political Recruitment in Twentieth Century Mexico*. Princeton, N.J.: Princeton University Press, 1970.

Snyder, Margaret. *Transforming Development: Women, Poverty and Politics*. London: Intermediate Technology Publications, 1995.

Spener, David, and Kathleen Staudt, eds. *The U.S.-Mexico Border: Transcending Divisions, Contesting Identities*. Boulder, Colo.: Lynne Rienner, 1998.

Standing, Guy. "Global Feminization through Flexible Labor." *World Development* 17, no. 7 (1989): 1077–95.

Staudt, Kathleen. *Agricultural Policy Implementation: A Case Study from Western Kenya*. West Hartford, Conn.: Kumarian Press, 1985.

Staudt, Kathleen. *Free Trade? Informal Economies at the U.S.-Mexico Border*. Philadelphia: Temple University Press, 1998.

Staudt, Kathleen. "Gender Politics in Bureaucracy: Theoretical Issues in Comparative Perspective." In *Women, International Development and Politics*, 2d ed., edited by Kathleen Staudt. Philadelphia: Temple University Press, 1997.

Staudt, Kathleen. "The Impact of Development Policies on Women." In *African Women South of the Sahara*, 2d ed., edited by Margaret Jean Hay and Sharon Stichter. New York: Longman, 1995.

Staudt, Kathleen. "Integrating Women into Development Studies." In *Women, Development and Population: Revising Theories and Approaches*. Working Paper no. 24. Tucson: University of Arizona, Southwest Institute for Research on Women, 1986.

Staudt, Kathleen. *Managing Development: State, Society and International Contexts*. Newbury Park, Calif.: Sage, 1991.

Staudt, Kathleen. "Political Representation: Engendering Democracy." In *Background Papers for the Human Development Report 1995*. New York: UNDP, 1996.

Staudt, Kathleen. "Planting Seeds in the Classroom." In *Seeds* and *Seeds 2*, edited by Ann Leonard. New York: Feminist Press, 1989, 1995.

Staudt, Kathleen. "Programming Women's Empowerment? A Case from Northern Mexico." In *Women on the U.S.-Mexico Border*, edited by Vicki L. Ruiz and Susan Tiano. Boston: Allyn & Unwin, 1987.

Staudt, Kathleen. "The State and Gender in Colonial Africa." In *Women, the State and Development*, edited by Sue Ellen Charlton et al. Albany, N.Y.: SUNY Albany Press, 1989.

Staudt, Kathleen. "Strategic Locations: Gender Issues in Business Management." In *Women at the Center: Development Issues and Practices for the 1990s*, edited by Gay Young, Vidyamali Samarasinghe, and Ken Kusterer. West Hartford, Conn.: Kumarian Press, 1993.

Staudt, Kathleen. "Uncaptured or Unmotivated? Women and the Food Crisis in Africa." *Rural Sociology* 52, no. 1 (1987): 37–55.

Staudt, Kathleen. "Women and High-Level Political Decision Making." Paper presented at the UN/DAW Conference, Vienna, September 1989.

Staudt, Kathleen. *Women, Foreign Assistance and Advocacy Administration*. New York: Praeger, 1985.

Staudt, Kathleen, ed. *Women, International Development and Politics: The Bureaucratic Mire*. 1st ed. Philadelphia: Temple University Press, 1990.

Staudt Kathleen, ed. *Women, International Development and Politics: The Bureaucratic Mire*. 2d ed. Philadelphia: Temple University Press, 1997.

Staudt, Kathleen, Irene Tinker, and Kathleen Cloud. *Teaching Women in Development Courses*. New York: U.S. Council for INSTRAW, 1988.

Staudt, Kathleen, and William Weaver. *Political Science and Feminisms: Integration or Transformation?* New York: Twayne/Macmillan, 1997.

Steeves, H. Leslie. *Gender Violence and the Press: The St. Kizito Story*. Athens: Ohio University Center for International Studies, 1997.

Stewart, Ann. "Should Women Give up on the State? The African Experience." In *Women and the State: International Perspectives*, edited by Shirin M. Rai and Geraldine Lievesley. London: Taylor & Francis, 1996.

Stichter, Sharon, and Jane Parpart, eds. *Women, Employment and the Family in the International Division of Labour*. Philadelphia: Temple University Press, 1994.

Stoddard, Ellwyn R. "Border Maquila Ownership and Mexican Economic Benefits: A Comparative Analysis of the 'Good,' the 'Bad,' and the 'Ugly.'" *Journal of Borderlands Studies* 6, no. 2 (1991): 23–50.

Stone, Deborah. *Policy Paradox: The Art of Political Decision Making*. 2d ed. New York: W. W. Norton, 1997.

Stromquist, Nelly. "Feminist Reflections on the Politics of the Peruvian University." In *Women and Education in Latin America*, edited by Nelly Stromquist. Boulder, Colo.: Lynne Rienner, 1992.

Stromquist, Nelly. "Women and Literacy in Latin America." In *Women and Education in Latin America*, edited by Nelly Stromquist. Boulder, Colo.: Lynne Rienner, 1992.

Stromquist, Nelly, ed. *Women and Education in Latin America: Knowledge, Power, and Change*. Boulder, Colo.: Lynne Rienner, 1992.

Sylvester, Christine. *Feminist Theory and International Relations in a Postmodern Era.* Cambridge: Cambridge University Press, 1994.

Tadesse, Mary, and Margaret Snyder. *African Women and Development: A History.* London: Zed, 1994.

Tadesse, Zen. "The Impact of Land Reform on Women: The Case of Ethiopia." In *Women, Land and Food Production.* Bulletin no. 11. Geneva: ISIS, 1979.

Tendler, Judith. *Inside Foreign Aid.* Baltimore: Johns Hopkins University Press, 1975.

Terborg-Penn, Rosalyn, et al., eds. *Women in Africa and the African Diaspora.* Washington, D.C.: Howard University Press, 1987.

Thomas, Dorothy Q. "In Search of Solutions: Women's Police Stations in Brazil." In *Women and Violence,* edited by Miranda Davies. London: Zed, 1994.

Timmer, C. Peter. *Getting Prices Right: The Scope and Limits of Agricultural Price Policy.* Ithaca, N.Y.: Cornell University Press, 1986.

Tinker, Irene. "The Adverse Impact of Development Policies on Women." In *Women and World Development,* edited by Irene Tinker and Michele Bo Bramsen. Washington, D.C.: Overseas Development Council; New York: Praeger, 1976.

Tinker, Irene, ed. *Persistent Inequalities: Women and World Development.* New York: Oxford University Press, 1990.

Todd, Helen. *Women at the Center: Grameen Bank Borrowers after One Decade.* Oxford: Westview Press, 1996.

Tong, Rosemarie. *Feminist Thought: A Comprehensive Introduction.* Boulder, Colo.: Westview Press, 1989.

United Nations. *Strategies for Confronting Domestic Violence.* New York: UN, 1993.

United Nations Children's Fund (UNICEF). *The State of the World's Children 1996.* New York: Oxford University Press, 1996.

United Nations Development Programme (UNDP). *Human Development Report.* New York: Oxford University Press, 1993, 1994, 1995, 1996.

United Nations Development Programme (UNDP). *Women's Participation in Development: An Inter-Organizational Assessment.* Evaluation Study 13. New York: UNDP, 1985.

United Nations Educational, Scientific, and Cultural Organization (UNESCO). *World Education Report 1995.* New York: Oxford University Press, 1995.

United Nations Fund for Population Activities (UNFPA). *Food for the Future: Women, Population, and Food Security.* New York: UNFPA, 1996.

United Nations High Commissioner for Refugees (UNHCR). *Working with Refugee Women: A Practical Guide.* Geneva: UNHCR, 1989.

United Nations Research Institute for Social Development (UNRISD). *States of Disarray.* Geneva: UNRISD, 1995.

U.S. Agency for International Development. *Women in Development Report, FYs 1991 and 1992.* Washington, D.C.: USAID, n.d.

U.S. General Accounting Office (GAO). *Multilateral Development: Status of World Bank Reforms.* GAO/NSIAD-94-190BR. Washington, D.C.: GAO, 1994.

U.S. General Accounting Office (GAO). *A Profile for the Agency for International Development.* GAO/NSIAD-92-148. Washington, D.C.: GAO, 1992.

U.S. General Accounting Office (GAO). *U.S. Had Made Slow Progress in Involving Women in Development.* GAO/NSIAD-94-16. Washington, D.C.: GAO, 1993.

van de Sand, K., and R. Mohs, "Making German Aid More Credible." *Development and Cooperation* 1 (1992).

Vickers, Jill, et al. *Politics as if Women Mattered: A Political Analysis of the National Action Committee on the Status of Women*. Toronto: University of Toronto Press, 1993.

Viveros, Elena. "Vocational Training and Job Opportunities for Women in Northeast Brazil." In *Women and Education in Latin America*, edited by Nelly Stromquist. Boulder, Colo.: Lynne Rienner, 1992.

Walker, Alice. *In Search of our Mothers' Gardens: Womanist Prose*. San Diego: Harcourt, Brace, Jovanovich, 1983.

Wallerstein, Immanuel. *The Modern World System*. New York: Academic Press, 1976.

Warwick, Donald. *Bitter Pills: Population Policies and Their Implementation in Eight Developing Countries*. Cambridge: Cambridge University Press, 1982.

West, Lois, ed. *Feminist Nationalism*. London: Routledge, 1997.

Wolchick, Sharon. "Women and the State in Eastern Europe and the Soviet Union." In *Women, the State and Development*, edited by Sue Ellen Charlton et al. Albany, N.Y.: SUNY Albany Press, 1989.

Women on Words and Images (WWI). *Dick and Jane as Victims*. Princeton, N.J.: WWI, 1975.

Women Working Worldwide (WWW). *World Trade Is a Women's Issue*. Manchester: WWW, n.d.

Women's Environment & Development Organization (WEDO). *Codes of Conduct for Transnational Corporations: Strategies toward Democratic Global Governance*. New York: WEDO, 1995.

World Bank. *World Development Report*. Washington, D.C.: World Bank, 1978, 1983, 1992.

Young, Gay. "Gender Identification and Working-Class Solidarity among Maquila Workers in Ciudad Juárez: Stereotypes and Realities." In *Women on the U.S.-Mexico Border*, edited by Vicki L. Ruiz and Susan Tiano. Boston: Allyn & Unwin, 1987.

Young, Kate. *Planning Development with Women: Making a World of Difference*. London: Macmillan, 1993.

Youniss, James, Jeffrey A. McLellan, and Miranda Yates. "What We Know about Engendering Civic Identity." *American Behavioral Scientist* 40, no. 5 (March/April 1997): 620–31.

Zalewski, Marysia, and Jane Parpart, eds. *The Man Question in International Relations*. Boulder, Colo.: Westview Press, 1997.

Zeitlin, Jennifer, Ramesh Govindaraj, and Lincoln D. Chen. "Financing Reproductive and Sexual Health Services." In *Population Policies Reconsidered*, edited by Gita Sen et al. Cambridge, Mass.: Harvard University Press, 1994.

Index

About the Author

LINDA TREJO

Kathleen Staudt is professor of political science at the University of Texas at El Paso. She has published fifty academic articles and ten books, the most recent of which is *Free Trade? Informal Economies at the U.S.-Mexico Border*. She has consulted with the Population Council and several UN agencies and provides service to several regional and community development efforts, including Seeds across the Border.

Books of related interest
from Kumarian Press

**Tools for the Field:
Methodologies Handbook for
Gender Analysis in
Agriculture**
Hilary Sims Feldstein,
Janice Jiggins, editors

Offers a practical set of tools for the
novice or experienced development
professional working on gender
analysis in agriculture.

US $18.95 Paper   0-56549-028-2

**All Her Paths Are Peace:
Women Pioneers in
Peacemaking**
Michael Henderson

Portrayals of sixteen maverick women
whose daring acts have made a difference. From Japan to Brazil, from
Northern Ireland to the United States,
the author relates their gripping stories and depicts the practical yet
often risky steps each woman took to
resolve the conflict facing her.

US $14.95 Paper   0-56549-034-7
US $42.00 Cloth   0-56549-035-5

**Gender Analysis in
Development Planning:
A Case Book**
Aruna Rao, Mary B. Anderson,
Catherine Overholt, editors

Provides useful learning tools to
help incorporate gender variables into
development projects. Designed for
gender training and easily self-
taught, the cases presented are
open-ended.

US $15.95 Paper   0-931816-61-0

**A Commitment to the World's
Women: Perspectives on
Development for Beijing and
Beyond**
Noeleen Heyzer with Skushma
Kapoor and Joanne Sandler

In anthology form, includes articles
by more than thirty thinkers, organizers, and leaders. The essays and
stories revisit the crucial issues and
processes that have affected women,
their families, and their societies.

US $14.95 Paper   0-912917-38-5

 Kumarian Press is dedicated to publishing and
distributing books and other media that will
have a positive social and economic impact
on the lives of peoples living in "Third World"
conditions no matter where they live.

**As well as books on Women and Gender,
Kumarian Press publishes books on the
Environment, Nongovernmental Organizations,
Government, International Development, and
Peace and Conflict Resolution.**

To receive a complimentary catalog or to request writer's
guidelines, call or write:

Kumarian Press, Inc.
14 Oakwood Avenue
West Hartford, CT 06119-2127 USA

Inquiries: 860-233-5895
Fax: 860-233-6072
Order toll free: 800-289-2664

e-mail: kpbooks@aol.com
internet: www.kpbooks.com